MW00810441

KEEP ON KEEPING ON

KEEP ON

CARTER G. WOODSON INSTITUTE SERIES

Deborah E. McDowell, Editor

KEEPING ON

The NAACP and the Implementation of
Brown v. Board of Education in Virginia

Brian J. Daugherity

University of Virginia Press | Charlottesville and London

University of Virginia Press

© 2016 by the Rector and Visitors of the University of Virginia

Printed in the United States of America on acid-free paper

First published 2016

ISBN 978-0-8139-3889-9 (cloth)
ISBN 978-0-8139-3890-5 (e-book)

9 8 7 6 5 4 3 2 1

Library of Congress Cataloging-in-Publication Data
is available from the Library of Congress

Cover art: Protest against school closings in Prince Edward County,
Virginia, ca. July 1963. (*Richmond Times-Dispatch*)

To my parents

CONTENTS

ACKNOWLEDGMENTS

This book is the result of a decade of work involving many people. First, I would like to thank the many archivists and librarians who have assisted me over the years. The Manuscript Division at the Library of Congress deserves special thanks for helping me navigate the massive Papers of the NAACP collection, especially Jeff Flannery, Adrienne Cannon, and the staff of the manuscript reading room. I'd also like to thank the staff at the Library of Congress Law Library. The staff at the Virginia Historical Society was extremely helpful during my visits, especially Frances Pollard, Toni Carter, and Gregory Stoner. At the same institution, I would like to thank Graham Dozier, Lauranett Lee, Bill Obrochta, and Lee Shepard for supporting my research and related projects. Brent Tarter and Gregg Kimball at the Library of Virginia deserve special thanks for help with research questions and for providing information on related aspects of Virginia history. Teresa Roane, formerly of the Valentine Richmond History Center (and now of the Museum of the Confederacy) assisted my search of the Valentine's tremendous collection of historic photographs, and regularly checked in on this project as it moved forward, which I always appreciated. Research trips to the University of Virginia were always a pleasure, due largely to the staff at Alderman Library and the Small Special Collections Library. The same holds true for the Special Collections staff at Virginia State University, where I'm especially grateful to Lucious Edwards and Francine Archer. Charles Bethea, former director of the Black History Museum and Cultural Center of Virginia, deserves special thanks for introducing me to research materials as well as to many individuals with firsthand knowledge of school desegregation in Virginia. At the University of Richmond, Jim Gwin was an indefatigable help as well as a cheerful and good-humored colleague. Jim obtained document collections related to my research and teaching, which aided in the development of this manuscript, as did Hope Yelich, formerly of Swem Library at the College of William & Mary.

I spent many years in school at William & Mary, and I would not have been able to write this book without the knowledge and support I found there. I'd like to thank professors Ed Crapol and Jim Whittenburg; both taught me as an undergraduate and later mentored me as a graduate student. They have shaped my outlook on history and education more than they know. Professor Richard Sherman provided advice and assistance when I decided to pursue graduate school in history, as did John Selby many years later. Carol Sheriff, former director of the graduate program in history, always provided helpful feedback on my work and my career. Civil rights expert Dave Douglas, dean of the William & Mary Law School, deserves special mention for supporting and encouraging this project from the beginning. And finally, I'd like to especially thank my doctoral advisor, Melvin Patrick Ely, for agreeing to oversee this project, and for the advice, knowledge, and editing skills that permeate the pages that follow. Mel's guidance and support have been irreplaceable.

Financial assistance helped me conduct research for this book. I thank the John Hope Franklin Research Center at Duke University for a Special Collections research grant, which allowed me to look through a number of relevant manuscript collections as well as an extensive collection of NAACP Papers microfilm. A Mellon Fellowship at the Virginia Historical Society helped me to clarify some of the larger questions related to this project, in addition to providing me the opportunity to review a number of manuscript collections related to school desegregation in Virginia. Financial support from the College of William & Mary History Department, the Office of the Dean of Arts and Sciences, and the Graduate Student Association made possible countless research trips to the Library of Congress, and funded presentations at a number of history conferences. The staff of the Virginia Foundation for the Humanities and Public Policy—especially David Bearinger and Rob Vaughan—deserve a special thank you. Over the years, the VFH has provided funding for a number of research projects related to school desegregation in Virginia that I have been involved in. Their commitment to telling Virginia history in an inclusive manner is unrivaled. Finally, I'd like to thank my current employer, Virginia

Commonwealth University, especially John Kneebone and Rob Tombes, for funding to conduct research and to include photographs in this book.

I've been fortunate to teach at a number of great institutions with wonderful colleagues during the writing of this book. I began my college teaching career at Richard Bland College in Petersburg, Virginia, which was like working with family. I am especially grateful to former president Jim McNeer, whose support and advice have been invaluable. At the University of Richmond, where I taught part-time while writing much of this book, I'd like to thank the entire History Department. Hugh West, Bob Kenzer, and Debbie Govoruhk deserve special thanks. At Virginia Commonwealth University, I'd like to thank former deans Bob Holsworth, Fred Hawkridge, and Jim Coleman for their support. The Department of African American Studies was my initial home at VCU, and I'd like to thank its faculty and staff, most especially the late Njeri Jackson. In VCU Special Collections, Ray Bonis has been a tremendous help as well as a great colleague. Ray's music compilations have fueled more than a few late night writing sessions. Also in VCU Libraries, John Ulmschneider, Jodi Koste, and Wesley Chenault deserve a special thanks. In the VCU History Department, where I currently teach, I'd like to thank all of my colleagues, the department staff, and years of terrific students for making VCU a truly great place to work.

Many friends, colleagues, students, and scholars have read portions, or all, of this work, or have supported the project in other ways. A number of them are cited in the pages that follow. Far from home, I'd like to thank my graduate advisor at the University of Montana, Mike Mayer, who has always served as a sounding board for my research and career ideas. Here in Virginia, Jim Hershman freely gave his time and knowledge while I completed my research and wrote the first iterations of this book. I can't thank him enough for encouraging me and for his assistance over the years. I'd also like to thank Jim Sweeney for many valuable research tips, and for being a model of teaching and writing about Virginia's civil rights era. Jim helped create the Desegregation of Virginia Education (DOVE) project, which seeks to locate and preserve primary source materials related to school desegregation in Virginia, and which seeks to publicize this history and its importance. I now serve as cochair of DOVE, and I'd like to thank Jim and Sonia Yaco for leading the way. I would also like to thank my cochair, Ann Jimerson, as well as DOVE's regional chairs and many supporters.

Peter Wallenstein's many publications on the civil rights era in Virginia have strongly informed my own writing, and his indefatigable energy has brought greater interest to this era among countless others. Charles Ford and Jeffrey Littlejohn's scholarship on Norfolk has also shaped my work, and I am excited to read their future work on school desegregation and civil rights in Virginia. A special thanks goes to Larissa Smith Fergeson, who has been a friend and supporter from the earliest days of this project, as well as a tremendous Virginia NAACP scholar. At the University of Richmond, I'd like to thank Melissa Ooten, a fellow graduate student and later fellow traveler on a series of highly successful civil rights "bus tours." I'd like to do that again. Chuck Bolton met with us on several of those bus tours, served as coeditor of my first book, read this entire book manuscript, and has always been an inspiration for his productivity, leadership, and humility. I can't thank him enough. Chuck also served as dissertation advisor to one of my former graduate students, Brian Lee, whose wherewithal and research skills have impressed us all. Brian graciously read most of this manuscript and has been a good partner on a number of related projects. Another Brian, Brian Grogan, provided feedback on this manuscript and is a coeditor on another book project. I think he deserves an honorary doctorate for the effort. Alyce Miller also graciously read the entire manuscript and still agreed to partner on a new research project. Her feedback helped me clarify a number of points for nonspecialists, for which I am very grateful. Another tremendous partner, for many years now, has been Jody L. Allen, who deserves a special thank you. Her research and teaching have strongly influenced my own, and her knowledge of African American and civil rights history in Virginia will greatly benefit future students and scholars. Finally, at VCU, I have subjected a number of undergraduate students to my work on civil rights and school desegregation, and they have been surprisingly receptive. Many have provided feedback, helpful ideas, and potential sources. Of the many, I would especially like to thank Arman Chowdhury, Manon Loustaunau, and Luke Murray.

I interviewed a number of individuals for this project, and their memories permeate the pages that follow. One of the most memorable was the late Oliver W. Hill Sr., who served as head of the Virginia NAACP legal staff during the decades before and after *Brown v. Board of Education*. Hill's intelligence, kindness, humility, and sense of humor strongly impacted me. Speaking with him was one of the great pleasures of this project. Thanks also to his son, Oliver W. Hill Jr., for permitting me to use material from meetings with his father. One of Hill's protégés, Henry L. Marsh III, also graciously shared recollections from decades of civil rights legal work with me on several occasions. For this I am extremely grateful. I would also like to commend Senator Marsh for his many years of distinguished public service. As an attorney, Marsh argued a number of cases before the late Judge Robert R. Merhige Jr., who also sat for an interview with me. Merhige's ability to clarify the finer points of civil rights law and his dedication to enforcing the law in the face of great public opposition fascinated me. A number of individuals related to a particularly important case that Merhige implemented, from New Kent County, shared their time with me as well. I know their memories will inform future work about this important but little-known story, including my own. Camilla Tramuel and LaVonne Allen of the New Kent Historical Society deserve special mention. I would especially like to thank the late Dr. Calvin C. Green, Mrs. Mary O. Green, and their sons. During the 1950s, the number of white Virginians who supported racial equality was small. One exception was Ed Peeples, who spoke out against discrimination during those hostile days and continues to do so now. Speaking and working with Ed since near the beginning of this project have been inspirational and invaluable, and I'd like to thank him also for his encouragement to see this project through to its conclusion.

The University of Virginia Press has been a tremendous partner from the beginning. I would especially like to thank Dick Holway, whose support and advice shepherded the manuscript through the peer review process. Dick's patience and willingness to answer all of my many questions earned my great appreciation. The press's anonymous readers provided comments and critiques that greatly improved the end result, and I'd like to thank them for their time, effort, and insights. For help with later stages of the publishing process, I'd especially like to thank Raennah Mitchell, Anna Kariel, and Morgan Myers.

Last and most important, I would like to thank my parents and my family. Without them, this book would not have been possible. I'm looking forward to spending more time with them now.

INTRODUCTION

Though not particularly well known, Virginia's role in the civil rights movement was substantial. This is particularly true with regards to school desegregation. One of the five cases that made up the historic *Brown v. Board of Education* decision began in the state in 1951, when representatives of the National Association for the Advancement of Colored People (NAACP) filed *Davis v. Prince Edward County*. Following the *Brown* decision, U.S. senator Harry F. Byrd Sr., Virginia's senior senator and head of the state's leading political organization, launched "massive resistance" to rally intense southern opposition to the decision. The "eyes of the world," as Byrd put it, focused on Virginia in 1958 after the public schools were closed in a number of localities rather than desegregated as ordered by federal judges. One county, Prince Edward, kept its schools closed for half a decade, resistance not replicated anywhere else. Virginia NAACP attorneys won another major Supreme Court victory in 1968. In *Green v. New Kent County*, the high court ordered school districts throughout the South to abandon any remaining vestiges of segregation and take the initiative to establish unitary school systems immediately. Though much of the scholarship on the civil rights movement deals with locations outside of Virginia, it is clear that Virginia's role in the struggle for racial equality was tremendous.[1]

The stories of massive resistance and the school closings in Prince Edward County received national media attention and have been written about by a number of scholars. A thorough telling of the story of "those who were on the other side," as Virginia scholar Jim Hershman has described Virginians who supported integration and opposed the massive resisters, is the purpose of this book. Its principal objective is to examine the Virginia State Conference of the NAACP and its efforts to implement the *Brown v. Board of Education* decision in Virginia from 1954 to roughly 1974.[2]

The Virginia State Conference of the NAACP was the state headquarters of the NAACP in Virginia. During the period covered by this book, its office was located in Richmond and included a small paid staff led by Executive Secretary W. Lester Banks. Annually elected officers located around the state held volunteer leadership positions, including president, vice president, and treasurer, and an elected board of directors provided input. A cadre of attorneys served as Virginia State Conference legal staff, and they were spread out around the state. The state conference and its leaders organized and oversaw Virginia's NAACP branches, which were located in local communities, and also served as their liaison to the national NAACP in New York City.

The NAACP was the largest and most important civil rights organization in Virginia during this era. NAACP branches existed in nearly every city and county in Virginia. Shortly after the *Brown* decision, the state conference counted thirty thousand dues-paying members, including much of Virginia's black religious, scholastic, civic, and commercial leadership. In fact, the number of members of the NAACP in Virginia surpassed that of every other southern state, and many states outside of the South. Moreover, the organization's commitment to racial equality enjoyed the broad support of Virginia's African American population—even those who never formally joined the organization.

The Virginia State Conference of the NAACP was well prepared to lead the struggle for equality in education in Virginia. Virginia's extensive network of NAACP branches facilitated its civil rights program, particularly the attempt to secure equality under the law. Lawsuits challenging inequities in education were sponsored by branches in all corners of the state. Virginia's proximity to the national NAACP's headquarters in New York City also increased the state conference's importance; the closeness facilitated communication, transportation, and cooperation.

Virginia's nearness to Howard University in Washington, D.C., the training ground for several generations of African American civil rights attorneys, also played an important role. Many of the Virginia NAACP's leading attorneys had ties to Howard, including Spottswood Robinson, S. W. Tucker, and Henry Marsh. In addition, it was at Howard University Law School that the Virginia NAACP's soon-to-be lead attorney met and befriended the man who would come to hold the same position in the organization's national office—Oliver W. Hill and Thurgood Marshall were the top two graduates of the class of 1933. By the late 1930s both worked for the NAACP, Hill in Virginia and Marshall in New York, and together they helped tear down the walls of segregation surrounding education in mid-twentieth-century America.

It is important to add the story of the NAACP's civil rights work to what we already know about this era in Virginia. Little is known about how the NAACP formulated and disseminated its program to implement *Brown v. Board of Education*, how this program was carried out in the state, and how the implementation program evolved over time. Discussing and analyzing the goals and activities of Virginia's African American population, including the state's leading civil rights organization, adds to our knowledge of Virginia during this important time period and, I hope, brings about a deeper understanding of the school desegregation struggle in the Commonwealth.[3]

Supplementing the history of resistance to school desegregation in Virginia with the story of the Virginia State Conference's pro-integration efforts sheds new light on aspects of the story. For example, it is increasingly clear that Virginia's segregationists and political figures were strongly affected by the NAACP's actions. This had been the case in Virginia long before the *Brown* decision, but its importance became that much clearer as the battle over school segregation heated up. The intersection of competing interests is most clear when the organization chose to file school desegregation lawsuits in early 1956, much to the dismay of Virginia's segregationists. That story is told below. In general, the addition of African American efforts to secure racial equality to the scholarship on the civil rights era in Virginia demonstrates the impact and influence African Americans had on the struggle over school desegregation in the state.

Although this manuscript focuses on the Virginia NAACP, it also discusses others who shaped the struggle over school desegregation in Virginia. The story includes state government officials, segregationist organizations, and others who—although not central to this story—influenced the process and, in some cases, the NAACP. A number of important scholarly works have already explored much of this information, and I am heavily indebted to their authors. I hope I have employed their insights suitably in the pages that follow. I have also drawn from scholarship on events outside of Virginia when relevant. The result—to the extent it is successful—blends African American, Virginian, southern, legal, and civil rights history in a way that allows the reader to obtain a broad understanding of the story of how school desegregation came about in Virginia.

Though this manuscript concentrates on the implementation of *Brown v. Board of Education* in Virginia, it also offers some insights into the civil rights movement in Virginia more generally. It discusses attempts to desegregate transportation, and public businesses and facilities, for example. A growing number of able historians are writing about this era, which is informative and encouraging. However, there is no overarching monograph on the civil rights era in Virginia, at least not yet. I hope this book contributes information that can be used by future scholars of the civil rights era in Virginia, as well as the enterprising individual who chooses to take on its first comprehensive text.[4]

My approach highlights the importance of the state as a unit in the school desegregation process. Individual states controlled their education policies, and state leaders, sometimes quite eagerly, assumed responsibility for responding to *Brown*. The NAACP, in planning its implementation efforts, assumed that each state would react differently, and that the association should vary its activities depending on the states' responses. After the association's 1954 annual convention, for example, lead attorney Thurgood Marshall stated that "the state level is the implementation level of national policy." And in 1955 he added, "We're going to actually adopt what we're going to do state by state, that's what I hope."[5] Organizing its implementation campaign in this way allowed the NAACP to respond to the individual policies of the southern states, while also allowing the national office of the organization to oversee the entire effort. The organization's state conferences served as vital and important links in the process.

This book is arranged chronologically in seven chapters. The manuscript begins with a description of the legal campaign that led to the *Brown v. Board of Education* decision in 1954, and then traces African American efforts to implement the ruling in the Commonwealth of Virginia for roughly the next two decades. Its afterword analyzes the results of this effort as well as how race and education have affected Virginia in recent decades.

My hope is that this book will appeal to historians and other academics as well as to the general public. The manuscript is based on many years of research, and I have tried diligently to convey the results of that research to scholars. However, I have also attempted to provide background information, sought to avoid overly academic language, and kept the story to a manageable length so that it can be easily understood and appreciated by a broader audience. I hope these same characteristics will increase its appeal to students—undergraduate, graduate, or other—of history and related subjects.

Understanding and explaining such a complex story requires a variety of sources of information. To study the NAACP, the best resource is the Papers of the NAACP collection at the Library of Congress, in Washington, D.C., and this book is based largely on this collection of records. The Papers of the NAACP manuscript collection includes records from the national office, state conferences, and local branches from throughout the nation, spanning much of the twentieth century and covering subjects including housing, voting, transportation, and education. The collection provides invaluable insights into the goals and actions of the organization and the African American community more broadly. A related source is the Papers of the NAACP microfilm collection, assembled by John Bracey and August Meier. This edited collection makes select portions of the original Library of Congress collection easily accessible to researchers outside of Washington, D.C. Other archival sources were important for comprehending specific aspects of the story in Virginia; a list of these can be found in the bibliography.

Newspapers are another essential source of information for understanding the story of school desegregation in Virginia. During the era of segregation, southern newspapers catered to racially defined audiences, so for this text I chose to consult both white and African American publications for insights into the thoughts and actions of the proponents and opponents of racial change. Interestingly, the more prominent white newspapers included detailed discussions of the NAACP, particularly its litigation. Fortunately, copies of the state's leading newspapers during this era are easily accessible and immeasurably helpful.

One periodical is worth discussing in some detail. In 1954, members of the American Society of Newspaper Editors created the Southern Education Reporting Service (SERS) to report on southern school desegregation in the wake of *Brown v. Board of Education*. Its staff was composed of southern and border state newsmen and newswomen who benefitted from their familiarity with the region but reported as objectively as possible. Between 1954 and 1965 SERS published *Southern School News*, a monthly periodical. When it was discontinued in 1965, SERS began publishing *Southern Education Report*, which ran until 1968. As part of its coverage, SERS collected data on school desegregation as it unfolded, and this data was included in *Southern School News* as well as its subsequent publications. For much of this era, its statistics served as a benchmark for reporting on the subject in the South. Many other southern newspapers relied on SERS's information, as did organizations including the United States Commission on Civil Rights. The Southern Education Reporting Service's publications and data offer an invaluable collection of insights on all aspects of the school desegregation story, particularly during the early stages of its development.

My research has also been complemented by interviews with individuals who were active in Virginia's school desegregation campaign during the 1950s and 1960s. This included of a few of Virginia's leading NAACP attorneys, whose memories validated much of what I uncovered in my research or explained matters I was unable to untangle using traditional sources. I was also able to speak with a small number of plaintiffs in NAACP cases, whose courage and commitment to the cause inspired me. In addition, a handful of white Virginians from this era offered their memories of its challenges and triumphs, including one of the federal judges who played a crucial role in the later stages of the school desegregation process. The memories of all of these interviewees served as an invaluable link to the records of the past and allowed me to see both how far we have come and how far we yet have to go to provide a quality education to all children regardless of their race or background.

In mid-1974, W. Lester Banks, the executive secretary of the Virginia NAACP, corresponded with Gloster B. Current, the organization's national director of branches.[6] Banks, who had been executive secretary for nearly thirty years by that point, had just returned from an extended medical leave of absence. Like many others at the heart of the civil rights struggle, Banks was feeling the effects of time. In their correspondence, Banks mentioned his desire to write a history of the civil rights movement in Virginia. By then, he had seen tremendous change and substantial progress in the direction of racial equality. Many scholars of Virginia would have loved to have read Banks's book. Instead, when he returned from medical leave, Banks returned to his position as the head of the state's largest civil rights organization and continued the fight for racial equality. I hope that in some small way, this book will do justice to what he would have written.

ONE

"A Source of Great Consternation"

The NAACP and *Brown v. Board of Education* in Virginia, 1902–1954

Racial segregation in Virginia's public school systems dated from their establishment just after the Civil War. Thirty years later, the state's 1902 constitution reiterated the requirement for segregated education; section 140 read: "White and colored children shall not be taught in the same school." During the debate over the constitution's adoption, Paul Barringer, chairman of the faculty at the University of Virginia and later president of Virginia Tech, argued that educational opportunities for African Americans should be limited to "Sunday-school training," because the principal function of black Virginians was as a "source of cheap labor for a warm climate." Barringer's words reflected the beliefs of many Virginia leaders.[1]

The results were devastating for black education. As elsewhere in the South, Virginia did not live up to the "separate but equal" doctrine, established by the U.S. Supreme Court in *Plessy v. Ferguson* in 1896. That principle required the state to provide equal public facilities, including schools, for blacks and whites. Instead, state and local governments in Virginia in 1925 spent an average of $40.27 per year on each white public school student, but only $10.47 on each black. Throughout Virginia, African American school facilities, teacher salaries, educational equipment, supplies, and course offerings suffered. In 1940, L. P. Whitten, a black citizen of Abingdon, wrote the NAACP: "If you will see that it is carried in the *Pittsburgh Courier*, I can secure pictures of all schools here so that the public may know of the deplorable conditions."[2]

Higher education for African Americans in Virginia suffered from similar disparities in state funding. In 1942, there were thirty-eight institutions of higher learning for whites in Virginia, but only six for blacks. None of the black schools offered courses in law, engineering, or medicine. As a result, in 1940 there was one white lawyer for every 636 white persons in Virginia, but only one black lawyer for every 13,780 blacks. Segregation restricted the educational opportunities of African Americans throughout the Commonwealth.[3]

In the 1930s, the National Association for the Advancement of Colored People (NAACP) in Virginia mounted legal attacks against these inequities as part of a school equalization campaign initiated by the national office of the NAACP in New York. The coordinated legal effort pressured Virginia and the South to provide equal educational opportunities to black students, relying on the "separate but equal" clause of the *Plessy* decision. As part of the process, state NAACP attorneys filed dozens of lawsuits to force Virginia's officials to appropriate additional money for black elementary and secondary schools, school transportation, and black teacher salaries. In addition to improving black educational opportunities, the campaign sought to highlight the financial cost of segregation in an attempt to undermine white support for its existence.[4] At the same time, the state NAACP filed lawsuits seeking the admission of qualified black students into white colleges and universities when those students wanted to enroll in programs not offered at black schools in Virginia. Throughout the 1930s and 1940s, NAACP attorneys in Virginia played a leading role in the equalization effort, gaining legal experience and strengthening the state NAACP's relationship with the national office of the NAACP.[5]

Located in New York City, the national office of the NAACP constituted the highest level of the traditionally hierarchical organization. Its staff made the major policy decisions for the NAACP and subsequently oversaw the implementation of those policies by lower levels of the organization. The executive secretary of the NAACP ran the office. Walter White served in that position from 1931 until 1955, and Roy Wilkins from 1955 to 1977. The executive secretary was guided by resolutions adopted at the organization's annual conventions and operated under the oversight of a forty-eight-person board of directors. Board members, who were elected by local NAACP members, served three-year terms on a voluntary basis. An elected chairman of the board oversaw their work and coordinated policy with the executive secretary. Channing Tobias held that position from 1953 to 1960, followed by Dr. Robert C. Weaver from 1960 to 1961, and then Bishop Stephen G. Spottswood from 1961 until 1975.[6]

The national office also housed a variety of NAACP departments and their staffs. One of the most important was the legal department, which included the NAACP's head counsel as well as the national legal staff. Other important departments for the school desegregation campaign were the branch and membership departments, which oversaw the local NAACP branches, numbering twelve hundred in 1955, and their members. Gloster B. Current served as director of branches from 1946 to 1976, while Lucille Black served as membership secretary from the mid-1940s until 1971. Both worked diligently to maintain NAACP vitality on the local level and to ensure that national NAACP policies were implemented correctly.[7]

Hierarchical control was a key concept for the NAACP. From its inception, the national office directed the organization and supervised the work of all of its branches. Branches operated under strict guidelines and policies, which were conveyed through correspondence as well as regular visits by national office staff. One NAACP mantra was that the association carried more weight when it was wielded collectively; it was not a collection of independent-minded branches. Throughout the era covered by this book, branches that violated national office protocol were regularly challenged, and occasionally disbanded.[8]

The national office also oversaw the NAACP Legal Defense and Educational Fund, Inc. (LDF), a separate but closely related organization created by the NAACP in 1939 to handle much of its legal work. Because the LDF avoided lobbying or political activities, financial contributions to the organization were tax deductible. This made it easier to raise money, which was then used for civil rights litigation. For almost twenty years after its creation, the LDF essentially served as the legal arm of the NAACP. The two organizations shared office space, staff members, and members of their boards of directors. The executive secretary of the NAACP technically led both organizations, though the LDF's special counsel (later titled the director-counsel) essentially ran the LDF. From its inception until 1961 that person was Thurgood Marshall.[9]

Within the NAACP, the level below the national office in the association's hierarchy was occupied by its state headquarters, known as state conferences. State conferences existed in every state by the time of the *Brown* decision, and they were charged with establishing and overseeing local NAACP branches within their jurisdiction. Equally as important, the state conferences were expected to publicize and help implement national office policies. Most state conferences also held annual gatherings of all the state's NAACP members, which is where the name "conference" originated.

The NAACP hierarchy also included an intermediate level—the regional office system—which was developed in the late 1940s to provide additional support for its state conferences and branches. The most important southern regional office for the NAACP's school desegregation campaign was the Southeast Regional Office, based in Birmingham. The Virginia NAACP, on the other hand, was located within Region 7, the Mid-Atlantic, which included Maryland and the District of Columbia. In theory, the regional offices were meant to coordinate multistate NAACP programs to advance the national office's initiatives. During the era covered by this book, however, the regional offices remained understaffed and fairly weak; a 1966 letter to the Virginia NAACP noted that Region 7 lacked a full-time director or field secretary. As a result, the Virginia NAACP worked more closely with the national office of the organization than its regional office.[10]

The Virginia State Conference of the NAACP had been created in 1935—the first in the nation. By the late 1940s, the state conference oversaw nearly one hundred branches located throughout the state, and it was regularly lauded by the national office as one of its most important state units. In fact, the state conference's successful implementation of national office policies and the rapid growth of its branches encouraged the national office to create other state conferences throughout the nation. These same factors allowed Virginia State Conference officials, based in Richmond, to develop a strong working relationship with the national office of the NAACP.[11]

The NAACP's state conferences also handled a significant amount of legal work for the association. Many state conferences, including Virginia's, maintained a network of attorneys, located throughout the state, who cooperated on civil rights litigation and executed the national office's legal strategies. Although generally paid for their NAACP work, these attorneys earned their livelihoods by handling non-NAACP litigation in private practices; their commitment to civil rights transcended monetary gain. Members of the legal team were elected at the state conference's annual convention each fall, for one-year terms. The group then chose a chairman and vice chairman; Oliver W. Hill of Richmond held the former position from the early 1940s until 1961. In this role, Hill recruited and cultivated a cadre of black attorneys from throughout Virginia, allowing the state conference to carry out an extensive legal campaign in state and federal courts. By expanding the number of cases that could be handled by the state conference, Hill's legal staff contributed significantly to the success of the NAACP's legal efforts in Virginia.[12]

Hill and the state conference legal staff worked in close coordination with the Legal Defense Fund. In fact, the relationship between state conference attorneys and national NAACP attorneys appears to have been exceptional. Thurgood Marshall and Oliver Hill graduated first and second, respectively, in the class of 1933 from Howard University Law School—while also becoming lifelong friends. Hill affectionately referred to Marshall as "Turkey"; he claimed the special counsel strutted like one. Marshall, in response, dubbed Hill "Peanut." Spottswood W. Robinson III, another key state conference attorney, also attended Howard Law, graduating a few years after Marshall and Hill. Trained, like Hill and Marshall, by Charles Hamilton Houston, "Spot" earned the highest grade point average ever from Howard Law and later served as its dean. Throughout the litigation leading to *Brown v. Board of Education* and its implementation, the close relationship between Marshall, Hill, and Robinson helped ensure that the Virginia State Conference of the NAACP would be crucial to the national NAACP's legal efforts.[13]

In 1940, for instance, Hill, Marshall, and fellow NAACP attorneys won a major equalization ruling from the U.S. Court of Appeals for the Fourth Circuit. Many Virginia localities paid white teachers more than African American educators, but in *Alston v. City School Board of Norfolk,* the federal appeals court held that racial discrimination in teacher salaries in Virginia violated the Fourteenth Amendment. The U.S. Supreme Court refused to hear the case on appeal, allowing a legal precedent to stand that the NAACP used in the 1940s to attack unequal teacher salaries, school facilities and transportation, and the like. The Virginia NAACP, and particularly Oliver Hill's legal expertise, had been crucial to obtaining the decision.[14]

In 1947, the national office allowed the Virginia State Conference to hire a full-time director to coordinate the organization's efforts. W. Lester Banks became the first full-time, paid state conference executive secretary in the nation. Banks's salary was paid by the national office, which increased the amount of money it collected from NAACP memberships in

Virginia to cover the additional expense. The state NAACP's close working relationship with the national NAACP—on equalization and civil rights issues more generally—strengthened in subsequent years.[15]

Banks, from Lunenburg County, had initially worked with Oliver Hill in the early 1940s. While serving as a high school principal in Charles City County, Banks invited Hill to visit in order to discuss the possibility of filing a teacher salary equalization lawsuit in the county. Shortly thereafter, both Banks and Hill were drafted into the military for the World War II effort; the lawsuit was abandoned, and the two saw each other next at Camp Claiborne, in Louisiana. Returning to Virginia after the war, Banks and Hill joined forces to lead the Virginia State Conference as executive secretary and lead attorney. By all accounts, the two got along famously. Banks remained in the position until 1976, and under his leadership, Oliver Hill later recalled, the Virginia NAACP was "the strongest and most active conference in the country and had the most extensive program challenging unlawful racial discrimination."[16] By 1955, the Virginia State Conference boasted a membership of more than thirty thousand in approximately one hundred branches, making it the largest in the South and one of the largest in the nation.[17]

As executive secretary, Banks worked closely with other leaders of the Virginia State Conference. A president, vice president, secretary, and treasurer were elected annually at the organization's fall convention, and an elected board of directors oversaw the work of this administrative staff. Dr. J. M. Tinsley, a Richmond dentist and one of the founders of the Virginia State Conference in the 1930s, served as president until 1955. At that point a term limit was placed on the position, and a host of individuals would occupy the presidency in later years.

Within the NAACP hierarchy, the state conferences served as the crucial link between the national office and the lowest level of the hierarchy, the NAACP's local branches. Branches, sometimes called chapters, were made up of a minimum of fifty dues-paying members. Each branch represented a particular locality, meaning a city or a county (in Virginia, cities and counties are separate entities). Branches were chartered by the national office and branches submitted their membership dues directly to the national office. However, branches were organized and overseen by the local state conference.

To increase the organization's financial resources and influence, the national office of the NAACP regularly pressed its state conference leaders and branch presidents to increase the number of memberships. The organization's branch and membership departments assigned annual membership goals to each branch and regularly dispatched officials to assist with membership drives. In addition, the national office notified state conference leaders when branches fell below the required membership minimum, and branches that did so were periodically disbanded by the national office.[18]

In Virginia, the NAACP was never a mass-based civil rights organization. Although the Virginia State Conference was the largest black civil rights organization in the state, its membership was limited to only a small percentage of the state's black population. While the state conference included more than thirty thousand dues-paying members at midcentury, Virginia's black population at the same time numbered just under 750,000. The relatively small number of members was largely due to the national NAACP's annual membership fee as well as the strictly enforced requirement that branches contain at least fifty dues-paying members.[19]

When recruiting members, NAACP branches often sought the support of the more economically independent, and wealthier, members of the local black community. Such individuals could afford the annual membership fee, which was an important consideration once the organization, in 1950, doubled the fee to two dollars, a considerable amount of money at the time. Wealthier members of the black community were also less susceptible to retribution for being associated with the NAACP, and could set aside time for NAACP activities. Professionals abounded within the association, particularly medical workers, educators, and attorneys, as did black business owners and religious leaders.[20]

Though most African Americans in Virginia never joined the NAACP, the state's black population largely supported the goals and activities of the organization. There were critics, of course, including black leaders and organizations who decried the NAACP's legalistic focus, its largely middle-class nature, or its hesitancy to use confrontational tactics. However, it is important not to overstate such criticisms. More important, the vast majority of African Americans in Virginia shared the NAACP's opposition to racial segregation and, sometimes for that reason alone, cheered the organization's victories as their own.

The NAACP welcomed white members and supporters, but in the South few whites regularly associated with the association. At the national level, whites had been integral to the founding of the group, and continued to serve in high-level positions into the 1960s. One example was Arthur Spingarn, who helped found the NAACP in 1909 and served as president of the organization from 1940 until 1966. In Virginia, however, the NAACP was a predominantly black organization. White members were primarily an urban or suburban phenomenon, and almost always represented the state's more liberal areas, which included the suburbs surrounding Washington, D.C., university towns, and the state's largest cities.[21]

In addition to its branches, the NAACP also included youth councils and college chapters. Youth councils were sponsored by adult branches and overseen by an advisor from the branch. Youth members paid a lower membership fee, and were essentially considered "apprentices" in the organization. To groom the next generation of activists, the Virginia State Conference encouraged each of its branches to establish and maintain a youth council. College chapters, as the name implies, existed on the campuses of black colleges and universities. In Virginia in 1958, the state conference counted four active college chapters, located at Virginia Union University, Virginia State College, the Norfolk Division of Virginia State College, and Hampton Institute.[22]

Founded in the 1910s, Virginia's earliest NAACP branches were among the first in the South. The organization grew slowly until the establishment of the state conference in 1935, when it had fewer than two dozen branches, and then expanded significantly during and after World War II. By 1949, the state conference consisted of ninety-seven branches. The largest branches were in Norfolk and Richmond, in each of which annual memberships reached five thousand in the late 1940s. Branches in other cities were also reliably active; county branches, particularly in rural areas, were less so. In terms of location, NAACP branches in Virginia extended throughout the state by the 1950s; only chapters in the extreme southwest portion of the state, and along the border with West Virginia, struggled to remain viable.[23]

Part of the challenge organizing NAACP branches in far western Virginia was the relatively small number of African Americans in that part of the state. In the mountains and valleys of western Virginia, a region Robbins Gates termed the "white belt," blacks made up less than 10 percent of the local population. In most cases, the figure was between 1 and 5 percent. To the east of this region, along the spine of the Blue Ridge Mountains, the number of African Americans was greater, but blacks still made up less than 40 percent of the local population.[24]

Instead, most African Americans in Virginia were concentrated in two large geographic regions—Southside and Tidewater. Roughly speaking, these two areas lie between Richmond and Lynchburg in the north, Martinsville in the west, North Carolina to the south, and the Chesapeake Bay and Atlantic Ocean to the east. Encompassing roughly thirty-five contiguous counties, this part of Virginia contains the state's most productive agricultural zone and is sometimes referred to as the Black Belt, for its dark soil. In the 1920s approximately 75 percent of Virginia's black population resided there. In 1950, blacks made up roughly 22 percent of the state's total population, but more than 40 percent of the population in each county in this area. The region also contained Virginia's only counties with majority-black populations.[25]

Throughout the South, white opposition to racial change was greatest in areas with large black populations, and this was true in Virginia as well. Southside and Tidewater were known as the most racially intransigent sections of the state, and here blacks faced extraordinary pressure to conform to the racial standards of the day. Blacks who lived in urban areas within the two regions were less directly affected than those in rural areas, but challenges to white supremacy or segregation were taken seriously throughout this area. The NAACP's principal opponent in the struggle to improve the status of African Americans in the Commonwealth was also based in Tidewater and (especially) Southside Virginia. This was the state's Democratic political machine, the Byrd Organization.

As governor in the 1920s, Harry Flood Byrd Sr. had used patronage to create a political oligarchy that governed Virginia during the mid-twentieth century. In positions of power throughout the state government, members of his organization implemented Byrd's plans and ideas with great effectiveness. Future governor J. Lindsay Almond Jr. explained the Byrd Organization this way: "It's like a club except it has no bylaws, constitutions, or dues. It's a loosely knit association, you might say, between men who share the philosophy of Senator Byrd." In 1949, in *Southern Politics in State and Nation*, V. O. Key wrote, "Of all the American states, Virginia can lay claim to the most thorough control by an oligarchy."[26] Jonathan Daniels, editor of the *Raleigh News and Observer*, smugly added, "Come with me to old Virginia, and see at one time and for one price the birthplace and grave of democracy."[27]

Byrd ran the organization from Washington, D.C., where he represented Virginia as a U.S. senator from 1933 to 1965. A southern Democrat known for his fiscal conservatism, Byrd regularly clashed with the national Democratic Party on spending issues and matters related to civil rights. The Byrd Organization's leadership strongly supported segregation, defining its stance as an effort to defend states' rights.[28]

One of the organization's concerns in the 1940s was the growing success of the NAACP's school equalization campaign. After the Fourth Circuit Court of Appeals ruled in favor of the NAACP in *Alston v. School Board of the City of Norfolk* in 1940, the NAACP expanded its school equalization campaign in Virginia, filing additional lawsuits statewide, particularly in the later 1940s. The Virginia State Conference legal staff handled the litigation, in close consultation with Thurgood Marshall and members of the national legal team, as part of its Schools Facilities and Opportunity Program. By the end of the decade the Virginia NAACP had filed teacher salary or facilities equalization lawsuits against more than a hundred school districts throughout the state, a time-consuming legal process that was required because each district was locally administered. The number of equalization lawsuits filed in Virginia was far greater than in any other southern state, reflecting the state NAACP's strength and vitality in the 1940s. The victories, which were recounted in the state's black newspapers, also helped the NAACP attract new members.[29] Moreover, court-ordered improvements to black educational facilities forced state officials to set aside substantial amounts of money for black education, particularly for the construction of new schools. In the early 1950s the *Washington Post* estimated that the NAACP's lawsuits had forced Virginia to spend more than fifty million dollars equalizing salaries and school facilities.[30]

World War II occurred in the middle of the NAACP's school equalization efforts, and the conflict had a mixed impact on the struggle for racial equality in Virginia. On the one hand, a number of civil rights leaders from Virginia entered the military, including Oliver W. Hill, W. Lester Banks, and attorney Samuel (S. W.) Tucker. Without a doubt, their absence slowed the push for racial equality—Hill even suspected that Harry Byrd purposefully had him drafted to hinder the equalization campaign. In their

NAACP representatives visit King George Training School in Edgehill, Virginia, in September 1948 as part of the NAACP's school equalization campaign. Shown (*left to right*) are Martin A. Martin, W. Lester Banks, executive secretary of the Virginia Teachers Association J. Rupert Picott, and Spottswood W. Robinson. (The man at the far left is unidentified.) (Courtesy of the *Richmond Times-Dispatch*)

absence, state conference president Dr. J. M. Tinsley, attorney Spottswood Robinson, and countless local leaders struggled to fill the void. At the same time, World War II clearly increased African American aspirations for better treatment, in part because the nation's stated war aims—including the defense and extension of basic human rights and civil liberties—seemed at odds with the realities of southern society. After the war, black veterans, including Hill, Banks, and Tucker, returned home more committed to racial change than ever before, and they were encouraged by growing signs of broader black discontent. In Virginia and elsewhere, the postwar era witnessed a growth in activism that propelled the struggle for civil rights to new levels.[31]

In the late 1940s, while its equalization campaign resumed, both the Virginia NAACP and the Legal Defense Fund focused attention on expanding higher education opportunities for African Americans. In 1948, a Legal Defense Fund case led the U.S. Supreme Court to order the admission of a black graduate student, Ada Sipuel, to the University of Oklahoma. The justices did so because the state did not offer a comparable educational opportunity to African Americans. In 1950, Virginia State Conference attorneys used the same logic to obtain the admittance of Gregory Swanson, a black citizen from Danville, into the University of Virginia Law School—the first African American to attend. In another Legal Defense Fund case, *Sweatt v. Painter,* the U.S. Supreme Court in 1950 ordered the admission of Heman Sweatt to the University of Texas Law School because "intangible factors," including the reputation of the newly created black law school and its networking connections for black graduates, were inferior to those of the white school. To the Legal Defense Fund's lead attorneys, the timing seemed right for a challenge of the legality of segregation itself.[32]

Both the shortcomings of the equalization strategy and the increasingly positive rulings emanating from the Supreme Court convinced the NAACP that the time was right for a change in strategy. The association's teacher salary and school facilities litigation had merely reaffirmed the "separate but equal" doctrine. Moreover, though the equalization campaign had noticeably improved the educational opportunities available to African Americans in the South, the cost to the NAACP, in terms of time and money, had been significant. Forced to file lawsuits against each individual school district, the organization's legal staff was spread thin as its equalization campaign continued in the late 1940s. When the U.S. Supreme Court's higher education rulings indicated growing wariness with segregated education, the NAACP's board of directors approved a policy change allowing its attorneys to directly challenge the constitutionality of southern segregation laws. Thurgood Marshall and his assistants had argued for this change and now put it into effect. By 1950, all new education cases filed by the NAACP challenged the legitimacy of southern segregation laws.[33]

The key to the NAACP's new legal strategy was the argument that segregation was harmful, and, therefore, discriminatory. The fact that southern schools were so disparately funded supported the NAACP's claim, but more important was psychological evidence gathered in the late 1940s by Dr. Kenneth Clark. Dr. Clark's "doll tests" involved showing black children dolls of different colors (i.e., races), and asking which dolls were more like them, and which dolls they preferred. Based on a statistical preference for the white dolls, Clark surmised that segregation was psychologically harming black students. In its new lawsuits, the NAACP used Dr. Clark's research, and related evidence, to argue that segregation harmed African Americans and was, therefore, a violation of the Fourteenth Amendment's equal protection clause.[34]

The Virginia State Conference welcomed the national office's decision to challenge the legality of segregation. State conference attorneys had worked closely with national NAACP attorneys throughout the equalization campaign, and had regularly traveled to New York City to discuss and debate legal strategies. By the late 1940s, Spottswood Robinson had joined the Legal Defense Fund's paid staff part-time, and Oliver Hill's close relationship with Thurgood Marshall continued to play an integral role in the national NAACP's legal proceedings within the state. Hill, Robinson, and the remainder of the state conference's legal staff quickly began to work on the association's new legal strategy.[35]

How African Americans in Virginia and elsewhere would react to the NAACP's new strategy was unclear. Spottswood Robinson reported to Thurgood Marshall in 1950 that he believed the association would have a difficult time finding plaintiffs in Virginia who were committed to attacking segregation outright. Challenging segregation was a substantial step beyond an equalization lawsuit, and doing so was likely to engender the animosity of the local white community and to invite retribution. Talking about the NAACP's new frontal attack on the constitutionality of segregation at midcentury, Hill noted, "It was a big lurch." Nonetheless, Robinson also reported that he knew of no instances in which black organizations had refused to go along with the NAACP's new policy.[36]

Soon enough, a group of Virginia high school students laid Robinson's fears to rest. Frustrated with the severely overcrowded and poorly appointed school they were consigned to in Prince Edward County, students at the all-black Robert Russa Moton High School, led by Barbara Johns, took matters into their own hands in the spring of 1951, boycotting the school in protest. Initially the students sought a new black high school, perhaps familiar with the NAACP's earlier equalization efforts, and they contacted the state NAACP seeking help. Oliver Hill and Spottswood Robinson explained that the association no longer filed equalization lawsuits, and that the NAACP would only file a lawsuit which sought to overturn segregation in the county's public schools and have the practice declared unconstitutional.[37]

Meetings with the students and their parents convinced Oliver Hill of their willingness to see the difficult litigation through to the end. State conference officials then suggested that the black community in Prince Edward convene to determine how to proceed. At two mass meetings held a week apart, state conference officials including W. Lester Banks and Spottswood Robinson explained the litigation process and what it entailed. At the second gathering, local blacks voted to support the NAACP's new legal strategy. Soon thereafter, the state conference legal staff submitted a petition to the local school board seeking desegregation. Signed by residents of the county with school-age children, the document represented a formal, legal request for admission. When this was rejected, Spottswood Robinson filed *Davis v. Prince Edward County* in federal district court in May 1951.[38]

Another World War II veteran, the Reverend L. Francis Griffin, guided Prince Edward County's black community during the school desegregation struggle that followed. Griffin, born in Norfolk but raised largely in Farmville, served in the army for four years during World War II and then attended Shaw University. After his father died in 1949, Griffin returned to Prince Edward County and took over as minister of his father's Baptist church. Recognizing the injustices of the county's educational system, Griffin and other black leaders pushed county officials to equalize the schools throughout the late 1940s, to no avail. After the student strike in 1951, Griffin served as a liaison between county residents and the NAACP, while the association's school desegregation lawsuit began its slow journey through the federal courts. He also served as president of the local NAACP branch, and later as president of the Virginia State Conference.[39]

To the great majority of white southerners, desegregating schools was an extremely troubling proposition — much scarier than equalizing black and white schools or even desegregating other areas of southern society, such as transportation. The fear of some, perhaps many, was that integrated classrooms might lead to integrated relationships, and possibly to biracial marriages and mixed race children — or "miscegenation." Many southern whites believed, moreover, that proximity to black children might promote disease among white youths, and that combining black and white schoolchildren would lower educational standards and reduce the effectiveness of Virginia's education system. As legal historian Michael Klarman explains, "Segregation of public grade schools lay near the top of the white supremacist hierarchy of racial preferences."[40]

As a result, white leaders in the South, including those in Virginia, vigorously resisted the NAACP's antisegregation litigation. Prince Edward County received extensive legal assistance from the Virginia state government to defend against the NAACP's legal attack. Future governor J. Lindsay Almond Jr., attorney general of Virginia at the time, played an integral role, coordinating efforts with county officials and some of the most prominent white attorneys in Virginia to defend the state's segregation statutes. The state government also increased its equalization efforts, hoping to forestall future attacks on segregation by convincing African Americans in Virginia to accept new, segregated schools. In September 1953, for instance, a new black high school opened in Farmville—the student strikers' original goal.[41]

In the meantime, *Davis v. Prince Edward County* worked its way through the federal court system. Because the case challenged Virginia's school segregation law, it was heard by a special three-judge panel in federal district court, which ruled against the NAACP in March 1952. As expected, state conference attorneys then appealed *Davis* to the U.S. Supreme Court, which agreed to hear the case in late 1952. The high court also bundled *Davis* with similar NAACP cases from Kansas, South Carolina, the District of Columbia, and Delaware. As Richard Kluger explains in *Simple Justice,* obtaining a decision from the Supreme Court took two years, during which Oliver Hill and Spottswood Robinson regularly traveled to New York to plan legal strategy and work on legal briefs and arguments for the Supreme Court with Thurgood Marshall and the Legal Defense Fund.[42]

In the spring of 1954, shortly before the Supreme Court announced its *Brown v. Board of Education* decision, Chief Justice Earl Warren traveled to Virginia. Warren had been stationed in the Commonwealth during World War I, at Camp Lee near Petersburg, and had a daughter named Virginia. On this particular trip, his goal was to visit Civil War monuments. After touring sites the first day, the chief justice checked into a hotel, leaving his African American driver to find another place to stay. The following morning, Warren realized the man had spent the night in the car. When the chief justice asked why, the man explained that he had been unable to find a hotel that would allow African American guests. Embarrassed and ashamed, the chief justice abandoned the trip immediately and returned home.[43]

TWO

"A New Day Is Being Born"
Brown and the Southern Backlash, 1954–1955

On Monday, May 17, 1954, the United States Supreme Court handed down its decision in *Brown v. Board of Education*. A unanimous ruling, *Brown* declared segregated schools inherently unequal and, therefore, unconstitutional, as the NAACP had argued. Chief Justice Earl Warren, author of the decision, wrote, "Does segregation of children in public schools solely on the basis of race, even though the physical facilities and other 'tangible' factors may be equal, deprive the children of the minority group of equal educational opportunities? We believe that it does."[1]

The decision overturned state-mandated school segregation in seventeen southern and border states, and locally based segregation policies in four others. In the seventeen requiring segregated education, including Virginia, the *Brown* decision affected more than eleven million black and white schoolchildren. Historian Richard Kluger later wrote, "Probably no case ever to come before the nation's highest tribunal affected more directly the minds, hearts, and daily lives of so many Americans."[2]

Reactions to the decision varied significantly. In the northern and western United States, responses were mostly favorable. An editorial in the *Pittsburgh Post-Gazette* proclaimed, "Every fair-minded American will, we believe, applaud the Supreme Court's unanimous decision," while the *San Francisco Chronicle* added, "This is the spirit, as well as the letter, of democracy speaking."[3] Southern states that bordered the former Confederacy also generally accepted the decision and pledged compliance. The governor of Maryland, for instance, called the idea of resistance "fantastic nonsense."[4] At least some districts in Delaware, West Virginia, Kentucky, Arkansas, Missouri, Kansas, Oklahoma, Texas, and the District of Columbia began school desegregation that academic year.[5]

In the remainder of the South, reactions were hostile. Officials from the eleven-state former Confederacy expressed near-total disagreement, with the strongest opposition coming from the Deep South. In Georgia, Governor Herman Talmadge said the decision had reduced the U.S. Constitution to a "mere scrap of paper." Senator James Eastland of Mississippi added that southerners "will not abide by nor obey this legislative decision by a political court." The Jackson, Mississippi, *Daily News* editorialized: "Human blood may stain southern soil in many places because of this decision, but the dark red stains of that blood will be on the marble of the United States Supreme Court Building."[6]

Virginia's political leaders reacted negatively to the *Brown* decision as well, but not uniformly. Governor Thomas B. Stanley initially said the decision called for "cool heads, calm study, and sound judgment." He added, "I shall call together as quickly as practicable representatives of both state and local governments to consider the matter and work toward a plan which will be acceptable to our citizens and in keeping with the edict of the court. Views of leaders of both races will be invited in the course of these studies."[7] When U.S. senator Harry Byrd, head of the state's political organization, learned of Stanley's statement, however, he was reportedly furious. Virginia attorney general J. Lindsay Almond Jr. later said, "I heard . . . that the top blew off the U.S. Capitol."[8] Instead, Senator Byrd denounced *Brown*, arguing that Virginia faced "a crisis of the first magnitude."[9] Then Byrd led Virginia's political leaders into a policy of resistance. By midsummer, the political elite had fallen into line. In mid-June, Governor Stanley declared, "I shall use every legal means at my command to continue segregated schools in Virginia."[10]

Southern opposition to the decision, including Virginia's, was based on a number of factors. Many southern whites criticized the decision's reliance on sociological evidence, including the studies and testimony of Dr. Kenneth Clark, the African American psychologist who argued that segregation harmed black students. Others pointed to Chief Justice Earl Warren's recent appointment to the court and his role in fashioning and drafting the decision; many denounced the "Warren Court." But these were secondary considerations. The underlying fears of many segregationists were that educating blacks and whites together would lower the quality of education, and that black and white children who were educated together might start relationships and have sexual relations, leading to the decline of the "superior" white race. This fear of miscegenation was widely used as a justification for resistance in Virginia.[11]

Worries about miscegenation haunted whites on the visceral level, but, in public discourse, probably the most widely accepted argument used to oppose the *Brown* decision in Virginia was the ideology of states' rights. Segregation had been accepted by the federal government since its codification after the Civil War (and even earlier in the northern states); mandating racial separation, therefore, was a recognized power of the states, the argument went. To take this right away was a disturbing expansion of federal power. In the years after *Brown v. Board of Education,* the states' rights argument reinforced other arguments for preserving segregation in Virginia and drew white Virginians who were not necessarily afraid of miscegenation into the camp of the segregationists.

Virginia's demography, meaning the size and distribution of its population, also influenced the response to *Brown.* Where African Americans made up a large percentage of the population—east of the Appalachian Mountains and south of the Rappahannock River, in Southside and Tidewater Virginia, resistance was greatest. Historian Mark Tushnet explains: "Southside politicians, an important force in Senator Harry Byrd's political organization, insisted that the state stand firm against desegregation anywhere. In contrast, white politicians and their constituents in the Virginia suburbs of Washington, D.C., did not welcome desegregation, but neither did they think that maintaining segregation was the state's highest priority; they could live with desegregation if they had to."[12]

Once Senator Byrd's position on the *Brown* decision became clear, state officials searched for means to preserve segregated education. On May 27, 1954, Superintendent of Public Instruction Dowell J. Howard announced the continuation of segregation statewide for the 1954–55 school year. In August, Governor Stanley appointed a thirty-two-man board, officially known as the Commission on Public Education but more commonly called the Gray Commission, to study the *Brown* decision and recommend a course of action. The committee was composed of state legislators, making it an all-white group. Virginia's Black Belt—including Southside and Tidewater Virginia—was disproportionately represented.[13] The group's chairman, Garland Gray, was a state senator from the Southside town of Waverly, in the heart of Virginia's peanut country, and a Byrd Organization stalwart. In October, Gray proclaimed, "I have nothing against the Negro race as such, and I have lived with them all my life, but I don't intend to have my grandchildren go to school with them."[14]

Governor Stanley also organized a meeting of southern governors in Richmond to rally resistance to *Brown*. Nine attended the June 1954 gathering, with three others sending representatives. After a daylong session, nine of the states resolved "not to comply voluntarily with the Supreme Court's decision against racial segregation in the public schools." The remaining states—Kentucky, Maryland, and West Virginia—decided their problems of adjustment were surmountable. That these three states bordered Virginia did not prevent the Old Dominion from aligning itself with states farther south.[15]

In fact, the meeting of southern governors suggested that Virginia was prepared to help lead the South in opposition to the Supreme Court's ruling. Supporters of this stance recalled the state's role in the founding of the nation and its leadership of the Confederacy during the Civil War. Many in the region also believed that the first post-*Brown* battles would be fought in the Upper South, meaning the northern portions of the region, including Virginia, where white resistance was thought to be less formidable than in the Deep South and where the NAACP would most likely concentrate its implementation efforts. Stalwart resistance in the Upper South would ensure the preservation of segregation farther south. As former state legislator Benjamin Muse put it in the *Washington Post*, "the South . . . looked to Virginia more than to any other state for leadership in this crisis. Virginia, with its glorious role in the early history of the republic and again in the struggle for the great Lost Cause—also with its genteel and honored political leadership of the day—was surely indicated to carry the banner of the South in this latest conflict."[16]

At the same time, the National Association for the Advancement of Colored People geared up to bring about the implementation of the historic decision. Largely responsible for *Brown v. Board of Education*, the organization's leadership was committed to playing a key role in the campaign for school desegregation thereafter. The association's implementation program, which was developed and directed by the national office in New York City, involved the coordination of thousands of representatives across the nation.

The task would occupy much of the NAACP's attention for the next twenty years.

Realizing that a favorable Supreme Court decision would require the NAACP to launch one of the most important projects in its history, the national office had begun formulating an implementation program early in 1954, and its leaders sponsored an NAACP meeting in Atlanta the weekend after *Brown* was handed down. Nearly one hundred NAACP representatives attended. At the gathering, staff from the national office outlined to the association's southern attorneys and state conference presidents a program for implementing *Brown* and bringing about school desegregation.[17] The southern representatives then adopted resolutions—proposed by the national office—mandating that local efforts to promote implementation of *Brown* be overseen by the national office and the state conferences.[18] The national office also requested that its southern state conferences call together representatives of their local branches and "instruct them on procedure to implement the [Atlanta] Declaration."[19] In a letter sent to all southern branches after the meeting, Executive Secretary Walter White and chairman of the NAACP board of directors Channing H. Tobias emphasized, "It is imperative that all of our units act in concert as directed to effectively implement this historic decision."[20]

The conference delegates also adopted the Atlanta Declaration, a ten-paragraph document that outlined the NAACP's implementation program for the immediate future. The program was remarkably moderate and conciliatory toward white southerners. As Channing Tobias counseled, "Let it not be said of us that we took advantage of a sweeping victory to drive a hard bargain or impose unnecessary hardships upon those responsible for working out the details of adjustment."[21] Branch leaders were encouraged to gather the support of black and white community organizations to help bring about desegregation. Rather than initiate widespread litigation to force desegregation, branches were ordered to negotiate and cooperate with their local school boards. Branches were told to collect signatures (on NAACP-developed petitions) from black parents who favored desegregation, an important step that portended possible legal action, but the threat of litigation was played down. Thurgood Marshall noted that the gathering of such petitions was to be accompanied by a request for a meeting with the school board to help develop desegregation plans. A follow-up letter from Walter White and Channing Tobias reiterated: "No legal action shall be undertaken without the express approval of the State Conference and the National Office."[22]

A month after the Atlanta Conference, the NAACP's annual convention in Dallas, Texas, endorsed the Atlanta Conference's implementation program and attempted to spur NAACP branches into action.[23] Daylong workshops, including one led by Spottswood Robinson, explained the national office program and the role of the branches. A key goal was building community support among whites as well as blacks to bring about desegregation. Local branches were encouraged to seek support for desegregation from churches, labor unions, educational organizations, and social and civic groups.[24] Court suits, potentially effective but abrasive, were to be avoided. Conference delegates resolved that "the enjoyment of many rights and opportunities of first class citizenship is not dependent on legal action but rather on the molding of public sentiment and the exertion of public pressure to make democracy work."[25]

Looking back, it is clear that NAACP leaders initially were overly optimistic about the implementation of *Brown.* Historian Alfred Kelly, who worked closely with Marshall and other leading NAACP attorneys, later noted, "In a sense, these men were profoundly naïve. They really felt that once the legal barriers fell, the whole black-white situation would change."[26] Marshall himself predicted that school segregation in the United States would be completely eliminated within three years.[27] Oliver Hill, head of the Virginia State Conference legal staff, later explained that his optimism was based on the belief that southern whites respected the law. When *Brown* declared segregation unconstitutional, however, Hill noted that "many Negroes experienced a rude awakening as white folks' reputed great respect for the law disappeared."[28]

African American optimism in 1954 was related to the *Brown* decision itself. The ruling did not address who would be responsible for the implementation of *Brown*, how the process would occur, or when desegregation would take place. Instead, the court instructed the parties involved in the case to submit supplementary briefs and prepare for additional arguments, after which the court would issue a follow-up ruling. This decision, commonly known as *Brown II*, was not handed down until May 1955. In the interim period, it was anyone's guess how school desegregation would proceed. As mentioned previously, a number of southern school districts began desegregation in the fall of 1954. This fact, in addition to the hope that the

Supreme Court's follow-up decision would mandate rapid and complete desegregation, as requested by the NAACP's attorneys, increased the optimism of African Americans throughout the nation.

The NAACP's 1954 annual convention and the association's original school desegregation plans emphasized the importance of the organization's southern state conferences in the implementation process. At the convention, meetings and workshops made sure the state units of the NAACP understood and followed the national implementation program. Keeping in close contact with its state conferences, the national NAACP could discern where to direct more, or less, attention—allowing it to respond more effectively to developments in the South as they unfolded. The importance of the state conferences continued throughout the desegregation process. As NAACP special counsel Thurgood Marshall noted after the 1954 annual convention, "the state level is the implementation level of national policy."[29]

The leaders of the Virginia State Conference, like the national office, welcomed the *Brown* decision. Spottswood Robinson, a teetotaler, said: "Don't try to reach me at the office tomorrow. I'm going out tonight and get drunk."[30] The weekend after the decision, nine members of the Virginia State Conference legal staff, as well as state conference president Dr. J. M. Tinsley and Executive Secretary W. Lester Banks, attended the Atlanta Conference. In June, Banks, Tinsley, Robinson, and Oliver W. Hill also represented the state conference at the NAACP's 1954 annual conference in Dallas. While the state NAACP's legal staff worked with national office lawyers on case briefs for the Supreme Court's implementation decision, the Virginia State Conference directed its branches to begin working toward school desegregation.[31]

The Virginia State Conference carefully followed the directives of the national office when working to implement *Brown*.[32] On May 26, 1954, Executive Secretary W. Lester Banks sent a letter to the officers of the state conference's eighty-eight branches announcing a "State-wide Emergency Meeting" to discuss carrying out the national office's implementation program in Virginia. The meeting took place in Richmond on June 6, and more than three hundred NAACP representatives from around the state attended. The delegates unanimously endorsed the recommendations of the Atlanta Conference. They decided that the state conference, in consultation with local branches, would develop a statewide program that would allow the Virginia NAACP to operate with both "uniformity and efficiency" while carefully following national office directives. In the meantime, the delegates asked Virginia's NAACP branches to refrain from desegregation activities, including the filing of petitions. Instead, the state conference would undertake a wait-and-see approach that summer. Shortly after the gathering, Executive Secretary Banks emphasized the organization's desire to help communities develop their school desegregation plans and said he hoped that "'friendly co-operation between school officials and the Virginia NAACP' would be possible."[33]

Also in May, Oliver Hill and four other African American leaders from Virginia were asked to meet with Governor Thomas B. Stanley. Hill's invitation highlighted the importance of the Virginia NAACP and its legal staff. Though Hill recommended that desegregation begin in some Virginia localities that September, he later recalled that the governor essentially asked them "to let things ride." During the closed-door session on May 24, the governor urged the black leaders to accept continued segregation in exchange for improvements to black schools throughout Virginia. The black leaders instead suggested the governor position Virginia to lead the South in compliance with the historic ruling.[34]

That summer, the state conference focused on organizing community support for the *Brown* decision and its implementation in Virginia. W. Lester Banks directed the organization's branches to reach out to civic, church, fraternal, labor, educational, business, and professional groups in an effort to build biracial support for school desegregation. Attorney Oliver Hill highlighted that the state NAACP would "try to work in a co-operative fashion" on school desegregation and that no legal action was being considered at the time.[35]

The national office, as expected, lent a hand to the state conference's efforts. In mid-June, in his first visit to the state since *Brown* was handed down, Thurgood Marshall addressed a Richmond branch membership drive. The NAACP's chief counsel and director of the Legal Defense Fund explained the *Brown* decision in detail before vowing to use the judgment to attack all remaining forms of segregation, including laws governing public assemblies and transportation. With regard to the schools, Marshall called for the decision's rapid and complete application and argued that decision making should be left to local school boards rather than to state governments; he may have recognized that some state officials were considering a policy requiring the maintenance of segregation statewide. Four months later, Marshall addressed the Virginia State Conference's annual meeting in Martinsville. Still optimistic about the progress and potential for southern school desegregation, Marshall said that "the NAACP never has been more encouraged nor more certain that the [country] is moving toward eventual desegregation."[36]

The following month, Oliver Hill and fellow NAACP legal staff member W. Hale Thompson attended a public hearing in Richmond sponsored by the Gray Commission. The hearing's purpose was to gather information about attitudes toward segregation and the *Brown* decision in Virginia, and the state conference rallied an impressive collection of biracial supporters to address the commission. Hill spoke at length, criticizing those who called for resistance to the decision and arguing for complete and immediate compliance instead. At the end of his remarks, Hill implored the commission, "Gentlemen, face the dawn and not the setting sun. A new day is being born."[37]

Most of those who addressed the commission, however, including a number of elected officials, demanded the continuation of segregation. In fact, the hearing underscored the substantial challenges facing the supporters of integration in Virginia. After Sarah Patton Boyle, a native white Virginian, spoke in favor of integration, an audience member accused her of supporting the mongrelization of the white race. One leading white newspaper, the Norfolk *Virginian-Pilot*, called the November 15 event a "field day for extremists."[38]

Extremists in this sense referred to the state's most committed segregationists, who were increasingly outspoken that fall. Virginia's leading pro-segregation organization, the Defenders of State Sovereignty and Individual Liberties, was established in October 1954 in Southside. At the time of its creation, the Defenders had approximately two thousand members located almost exclusively in the Black Belt. Within a year, it boasted five thousand members in twenty-eight chapters, and the organization continued to grow. The Defenders also established close ties to Virginia's political elite. State senator Garland Gray, head of the Gray Commission, for instance, was at the group's organizational meeting, and Byrd Organization regulars such as Congressman Watkins M. Abbitt Sr. and former governor William "Bill" Tuck often spoke at meetings. In the tradition of Virginia paternalism, the Defenders denounced violence, focusing instead on political persuasion and social and economic pressure to bring about its goals.

For nearly a decade, the group rallied white Virginians to oppose *Brown* on the basis of both white supremacy and states' rights.[39] Though only a small percentage of white Virginians joined the Defenders of State Sovereignty or other segregationist organizations, the vast majority did support the preservation of segregation.[40]

White Virginians who called for the abolishment of segregation and for racial equality more generally, on the other hand, constituted a small minority of the state's white population. They were referred to as white liberals. Many based their opposition to segregation on religious beliefs, personal relationships with blacks, or experiences outside the South. In the more racially tolerant regions of the state, which included northern Virginia and the largest cities, liberals were more numerous and more supportive of the NAACP. Some NAACP branches near Washington, D.C., in fact, contained substantial numbers of white members. During the tense years following *Brown*, however, segregationists regularly attacked white liberals who offered support for school desegregation, which made liberal support for the NAACP and its school desegregation efforts uncommon. In Virginia and elsewhere, even some white liberals asked the organization to slow its efforts to bring about school desegregation, fearing that pushing too hard, too quickly, would energize the segregationist camp.[41]

Another segment of Virginia's population—generally known as white moderates—strongly preferred segregation, but accepted compliance with *Brown* under certain circumstances. These Virginians especially condemned proposals to abandon the state's public school system in lieu of segregated private schools (presumably beyond the reach of the Supreme Court). Moderates' unwillingness to support complete and outright resistance, and their opposition to closing public schools in order to preserve segregation, distinguished them from those who supported outright defiance, who were known as massive resisters. In the years immediately following *Brown*, however, both moderates and massive resisters hoped to preserve segregation in the Commonwealth. During this era, segregationists of all persuasions dominated the debate over *Brown v. Board of Education* in Virginia, and they opposed white liberals, the NAACP, and the U.S. Supreme Court.[42]

In 1954, growing opposition to school desegregation was noticeable throughout the state. After the Gray Commission issued a statewide request for reactions to the *Brown* decision, county boards of supervisors and city councils around Virginia adopted resolutions calling for the maintenance of segregation. The trend began in the Southside, not surprisingly, and was strongest there. By the time of the commission's November 1954 public hearing, however, the governing bodies of more than half of Virginia's counties had expressed their disapproval of school desegregation.[43] African Americans opposed such resolutions—in Pittsylvania County an African American man was booed for speaking against a segregation resolution at a board of supervisors meeting. To Virginia's political leaders, though, the resolutions represented a clear statement of the white public's continued support for school segregation.[44]

Those who advocated resistance to *Brown*, however, were increasingly troubled by the willingness of some Virginia localities to comply with the high court. The chairwoman of the Arlington County school board, for instance, stated in May 1954 that the county would abide by the decision, something she reiterated at the November public hearing.[45] Also that fall, the Charlottesville school board unanimously supported the policy of "local option"; though they opposed the *Brown* decision in principle, they preferred that the decision of whether to comply, or not, be left to local officials. Shortly thereafter, the Charlottesville city council voted to comply with *Brown*.[46]

Meanwhile, state leaders in the fall of 1954 refined their arguments for the U.S. Supreme Court's upcoming hearings on the implementation of *Brown*. Virginia's legal brief called for time to implement the decision, saying the justices "must permit a now indeterminable period to elapse before requiring integration of the races in Virginia's public schools." The following April, in the oral arguments before the Supreme Court, Virginia's attorneys hinted at the supposed inferiority of blacks and the likelihood of southern defiance to reiterate the case for an indefinite delay in implementation of *Brown*. The state's legal team added that it considered integration in the public schools in Virginia "impossible at this time."[47]

The emergence of widespread, hard-core resistance and its promotion by the Byrd Organization ensured that implementation of the *Brown* decision in Virginia would be more difficult than previously imagined by the NAACP. Though school desegregation in the District of Columbia and a variety of border states began that fall, Virginia's state leaders appeared more intent on defiance. At its annual convention in 1954, the national NAACP had identified September 1955 as its target date for desegregation to begin in the South, and in April 1955 NAACP attorneys would ask the Supreme Court to adopt this date as well. Throughout 1954, Oliver W. Hill urged the state of Virginia to comply by this date as well. But in Virginia all signs were pointing toward growing white resistance. State NAACP officials—and those in the national office—recognized this. In early September 1954, after Governor Stanley reversed his pledge to appoint a biracial committee to plan for school desegregation in Virginia, W. Lester Banks told the *Richmond Afro-American* that the decision "comes as no surprise to me. It is plain that the governor is not seeking means of compliance, but rather means of circumventing the now law for the United States of America as it applies to public school education."[48]

Increasing denunciations of the NAACP by state officials, and segregationists more generally, troubled the association even more. Such attacks were not surprising, of course. In the 1930s and 1940s, the organization's success in equalizing Virginia's black and white teacher salaries and school facilities via legal action had forced the state to spend a reported fifty million dollars. During that time, as historian J. Douglas Smith has explained, the organization developed into "a source of great consternation to white Virginians." Subsequent NAACP legal victories in Virginia, including a U.S. Supreme Court decision outlawing segregation on interstate transportation in 1946 (*Morgan v. Virginia*), and its successful litigation to gain Gregory Swanson's admission into the University of Virginia Law School in 1950, heightened the concerns of state officials. Moreover, *Davis v. Prince Edward County*, filed in 1951 by state conference attorneys and later made part of the *Brown v. Board of Education* decision, meant the state had been battling the NAACP, unsuccessfully, in court since 1951 in an effort to preserve segregation. Some of the most vehement opposition to the NAACP in Virginia—not surprisingly—developed in Prince Edward County, the birthplace of the *Davis* lawsuit.[49]

With hostility toward the NAACP increasing after *Brown v. Board of Education*, state conference officials struggled to respond. In August 1954, attorney general J. Lindsay Almond Jr., one of the principal attorneys in the *Davis* litigation, declared that the "NAACP is not going to write the ticket in Virginia." The comment was reported in the *Richmond Times-Dispatch* and in response W. Lester Banks and David Longley of the Richmond branch penned a letter to the attorney general, condemning his "vicious

attacks." *Southern School News* later reported that the two NAACP officials also compared the attorney general's statements and thinking to those
of Adolf Hitler.[50]

In the fall of 1954, with state officials' opposition to school desegregation
increasingly obvious, the state conference of the NAACP intensified its
efforts to bring about the implementation of *Brown*. In September, Oliver
Hill explained that the organization now planned to proceed with a program of petitioning local school boards to integrate schools. The decision
marked a noteworthy change because legal petitions could be used as evidence in court and their development typically represented the first step
in a litigation program. Virginia's public officials understood this well; the
state NAACP had used petitions extensively in the 1940s during its statewide equalization effort.[51]

The state conference hosted its annual meeting in Martinsville the following month. A number of national office representatives attended, including lead counsel Thurgood Marshall and director of branches Gloster B.
Current. Dr. Kenneth Clark spoke about the desirability of rapid compliance with *Brown;* his research indicated that gradual desegregation was
less likely to succeed because it allowed for the development of greater segregationist opposition. Approximately fifteen hundred delegates attended
the gathering, including most of the leadership of the state conference.
In one stirring address, President Tinsley lashed out at Virginia attorney
general (and future governor) J. Lindsay Almond Jr. for encouraging the
rise of segregationist organizations and working to retain segregation in
Virginia. Tinsley stated: "These men and other officials like them, are our
enemies."[52]

The Supreme Court announced its ruling on the implementation of
Brown v. Board of Education, commonly referred to as *Brown II,* on May
31, 1955. The seven-paragraph decision gave some comfort to segregationists. Delays arising from issues such as school construction or changes in
pupil assignment practices were deemed acceptable, there was no set timetable under which the process was to unfold, and the lower federal courts —
presided over by white judges in the South — were ordered to oversee the
process. The decision required that local school authorities make "a prompt
and reasonable start" and that desegregation proceed "with all deliberate
speed," but clearly rejected the NAACP's argument that desegregation
should begin by the fall of 1955.[53]

Most white southerners celebrated the decision, and *Brown II* was widely viewed as a setback for the NAACP. Still, some in the NAACP saw a silver lining in the clouds. In a private conversation a few days after *Brown II* with Carl Murphy, owner of the *Baltimore Afro-American* newspaper and onetime member of the NAACP board of directors, Thurgood Marshall explained that "some people want most of the hog, other people insist on having the whole hog, and then there are some people who want the hog, the hair, and the rice on the hair. What the hell! The more I think about it, I think it's a damned good decision!" Outlining the NAACP's plan for the future, Marshall went on to say, "We're going to actually adopt what we're going to do state by state, that's what I hope. For example, we're going to treat Georgia one way, we're going to treat Maryland another way. But now if Maryland doesn't act right, then we treat Maryland like we treat Georgia. . . . Virginia we're going to bust wide open!"[54]

The weekend after *Brown II* was handed down, the national office of the NAACP sponsored another "Emergency" Southwide Conference on Desegregation in Atlanta. The gathering focused on the consequences of the latest ruling and on what course of action the association would take. The NAACP used the conference as a forum to downplay assertions that *Brown II* represented a setback for its cause. NAACP leaders highlighted that the ruling reaffirmed the original decision and ordered that desegregation take place as quickly as possible. Shortly after the conference, the national office reiterated this sentiment in a directive to its branches: "Make no mistake about it, this decision in no way cuts back on the May 17th [1954] pronouncement."[55]

In the spring and summer of 1955, the association reiterated its commitment to the national office's original implementation program established in 1954, which emphasized community organizing to bring about school desegregation. Reporting on the status of school integration in February 1955, Thurgood Marshall explained: "What needs to be done at this interim stage more than anything else is not legal action but social action which will stimulate a positive community acceptance of desegregation and prod local and state school authorities to emulate their counterparts who have already successful tackled desegregation."[56] That April, Roy Wilkins published a short essay, "The Role of the NAACP in the Desegregation Process," in the journal *Social Problems*. "Popular opinion to the contrary," Wilkins wrote, "the NAACP would prefer using legal action as a last resort in the many situations which will arise in hundreds of communities."[57] In early June, seemingly underestimating the additional hurdles posed by *Brown II*, the national office maintained that "in the overwhelming majority of instances it can be expected that compliance *without legal action* will be the rule, perhaps grudgingly and reluctantly in some areas, but compliance, nevertheless."[58] In late June, southern branches were requested to press local school boards and community organizations to implement desegregation that fall.[59]

At the same time, the NAACP also made alternative plans to bring about school desegregation should its community organizing approach fail to produce the desired results. Recognizing that *Brown II* had heartened southern segregationists and perhaps reduced the likelihood of voluntary compliance with *Brown*, delegates to the 1955 Atlanta Conference emphasized the association's willingness to revert to the courts to bring about school desegregation if needed. A memorandum from the national office, sent to all branches following the 1955 Atlanta Conference, directed branches to work with community organizations and their local school boards to help bring about school desegregation at the earliest practicable date. At the same time, branches were also instructed to submit petitions to their school boards to lay the groundwork for possible future legal action. Though the petitions were to be accompanied by an offer of cooperation toward the development of desegregation plans, the directive concluded: "If no plans are announced or no steps towards desegregation taken by the time school begins this fall, 1955, the time for a law suit has arrived."[60]

The Virginia State Conference dramatically increased its desegregation efforts following *Brown II*, again carefully following the dictates of the national office. On June 12, 1955, in Petersburg, the state conference sponsored another statewide meeting of members to explain how to carry out the NAACP program in Virginia. At the gathering, NAACP officials told branches in communities where authorities were acting in "good faith"—where school boards were making a "prompt and reasonable" start toward desegregation—to work with school officials and community organizations to bring about desegregation at the earliest practicable date.[61]

By mid-1955, however, the Virginia State Conference recognized that the national office's conciliatory implementation program was going to face significant challenges in the Commonwealth. It was clear by then that few school boards in Virginia were willing to consider voluntary school desegregation, as the national office had hoped. As a result, while the state conference encouraged its branches to press for voluntary compliance, it also ordered branches to formally petition their school boards for the admittance of black students into the white schools. The petitions, upon being ignored or rejected by white authorities, could be used in court as evidence of southern intransigence to comply with the law. The state conference would petition school boards for desegregation, wait a reasonable amount of time, and then file lawsuits if nothing was done to comply with the Supreme Court ruling.[62]

That summer, the Virginia State Conference provided instructions for the petitioning process to its local branches. Because school boards demonstrated discriminatory behavior most blatantly when they assigned students to black schools far from their homes, branches were asked to obtain signatures from individuals "living in mixed neighborhoods, or near . . . white schools." Branches were also advised to seek out parents who had an unwavering commitment to school desegregation. If the state conference decided to initiate litigation, it would need plaintiffs who were willing to "go all the way." Finally, the state conference instructed its branches to return the petitions directly to the state conference. Before filing the petitions with local school boards, the state conference would meet with the signatories to secure permission to represent them in court if necessary.[63]

Many NAACP branches in Virginia undertook the petitioning process in the summer of 1955. The Norfolk branch circulated its petition in June and submitted it to the school board in mid-July. The request included the signatures of more than 225 parents, and demanded an "immediate" end to segregation in the public schools. A week after it was delivered to school officials, branch leaders announced plans to take the school board to court "as soon as possible."[64] The Virginia State Conference later reported that fifty-five branches circulated petitions that summer; by the fall, the organization had submitted petitions to school boards in Alexandria, Arlington, Charlottesville, Isle of Wight County, Middlesex County, Newport News, Norfolk, and Princess Anne County. Others were in preparation. Still, each of these school boards refused to desegregate its schools that fall, as the NAACP had sought.[65]

In Virginia and throughout the South, observers recognized that the NAACP's petitions posed a grave threat to the status quo. In the Deep South, some NAACP petitioners were pressured to withdraw their names; those who refused sometimes lost their jobs or saw their children threatened. In

National and state NAACP lawyers prepare for a court hearing on the Prince Edward County case, July 1955. Pictured (*left to right*) are Robert L. Carter, Spottswood W. Robinson, and Oliver W. Hill. (Courtesy of the *Richmond Times-Dispatch*)

Virginia, the response to the petitions was also almost uniformly negative, and a growing number of white Virginians came to perceive the NAACP's efforts, as journalist Benjamin Muse later put it, as "something diabolical."[66] In mid-July, during a court hearing in which NAACP attorneys pressed for school desegregation in Prince Edward County, Attorney General Almond said the NAACP was "drunk with power" and "hell-bent in their orgy to produce chaos" in Virginia. The future governor recognized, better than most, the threat posed by the organization to the southern way of life.[67] Throughout the region, the NAACP's early efforts to bring about the implementation of *Brown v. Board of Education* stimulated white concern and resistance.[68]

Examples of defiance in Virginia were already evident, and they increased as the NAACP intensified its efforts to bring about school desegregation in the Commonwealth. In April 1955, the State Department of Education had adopted a policy allowing local school districts to fire teachers on thirty days' notice, a move aimed at intimidating African American educators and reducing black support for desegregation. At the oral arguments for the U.S. Supreme Court's follow-up decision to *Brown,* the same month, state officials had asked for an extended period of time to comply. Then in late June 1955, following *Brown II,* the State Board of Education mandated the preservation of segregation in all Virginia public schools during the 1955–56 school term.[69]

In November 1955, the Gray Commission issued its final report, outlining a number of ways the state could minimize the impact of *Brown.* The report made three principal suggestions. The first was to allow the adoption of locally administered pupil placement plans (meaning pupil assignment policies), which would enable school officials to maintain segregation, if that was their preference, without explicitly referring to race. Second, the commission suggested the state legislature amend its compulsory attendance law so that no child in Virginia would ever be forced to attend an integrated school. Finally, the commission urged the state to set up a publicly funded program that would award tuition "grants"—if requested—to any student assigned to a desegregated school. Technically available to both races, these funds would allow white students who were assigned to desegregated schools the option to attend private segregated schools at little to no cost instead.[70]

Although the Gray Commission called for resistance to school desegregation in Virginia, its suggestions were more moderate than many other proposals of the day. The commission, for instance, by suggesting local option in pupil placement, may have envisioned a time when small numbers of well-qualified black students might be willingly admitted to formerly white schools in the more liberal regions of the state. On the other hand, a growing number of political figures in Virginia supported the indefinite maintenance of school segregation statewide. The Defenders of State Sovereignty, for its part, suggested abandoning the state's public schools completely and setting up a system of publicly funded but private segregated academies should that prove the only way to avert desegregation. While most white Virginians favored the maintenance of segregation, they were divided on how to accomplish that end.[71]

The Gray Commission's tuition grant proposal required altering the state constitution, because section 141 of the constitution prohibited state appropriations to schools not owned or operated by the state. On November

30, 1955, a special session of the General Assembly, called by Governor Stanley, passed legislation establishing a referendum for Virginians to vote on whether or not to amend the constitution. Scheduled for January 9, 1956, the referendum would determine whether Virginia would call a constitutional convention as part of its antidesegregation efforts.[72]

The Virginia NAACP opposed the Gray Commission's proposals, especially the commission's recommendation to amend Virginia's constitution. Henry L. Marsh III—then president of the Student Government Association at Virginia Union University, later a member of the Virginia State Conference legal staff, and eventually Richmond's first black mayor—attended one lengthy General Assembly session in late 1955 during which legislators listened to public comments about whether or not to alter the state constitution. While Virginia's leading segregationists—including Garland Gray, chairman of the Gray Commission, and Collins Denny, attorney for the Defenders of State Sovereignty and Individual Liberties—offered vocal support for the change, a number of representatives of the Virginia NAACP also attended the hearing and made known their undivided disapproval. These included newly elected president of the state conference Dr. E. B. Henderson, state conference legal staff member W. Hale Thompson, and Oliver W. Hill.[73]

At the gathering, Henry Marsh watched in amazement as Hill spoke vigorously against altering the constitution and other attempts to avoid the implementation of *Brown* in Virginia. Marsh recalled, "I couldn't believe that a black man would stand up in front of the joint session of the General Assembly and shake his fist at them. I mean, I was looking around for the door. And when he said, if you do this, we will beat you, and he slammed his fist down, I ducked down. I said I'd better get out of here quick." It was the first time Marsh met the state NAACP's lead attorney, and Marsh later recalled it as "one of the great moments of my life."[74]

State officials, on the other hand, were increasingly influenced by the pen of James Jackson Kilpatrick, editor of the *Richmond News Leader,* in late 1955. Kilpatrick had stated his opposition to *Brown v. Board of Education* early on, and starting in 1955 he wrote a series of widely publicized editorials promoting the idea of "interposition" as a means of resisting the implementation of *Brown.* Rooted in antebellum southern political rhetoric, the theory of interposition asserted that the state government could "interpose its sovereignty" between the federal government and the state's localities in order to defend the interests of the latter and of the people. Despite the fact that many state leaders recognized the legal limitations of interposition, Kilpatrick's editorials nonetheless fueled support for resistance. Kilpatrick wrote, "In May of 1954, that inept fraternity of politicians and professors known as the United States Supreme Court chose to throw away the established law. These nine men repudiated the Constitution, sp[a]t upon the tenth amendment, and rewrote the fundamental law of this land to suit their own gauzy concepts of sociology."[75]

Segregationists in Virginia and elsewhere were also fortified by the lukewarm support for integration shown by President Dwight Eisenhower and by the actions of a strong axis of southern opposition in the U.S. Congress. The president publicly said he supported gradual change and compliance with the law, but Eisenhower declined to play a leading role in the school desegregation process. In part, this was due to the president's desire to increase white southern political support for the Republican Party.[76] Over time, Eisenhower's refusal to endorse *Brown* and his failure to demand southern compliance undermined his support among African Americans. NAACP executive secretary Roy Wilkins later commented: "President Eisenhower was a fine general and a good, decent man, but if he had fought World War II the way he fought for civil rights, we would all be speaking German today."[77]

In the midst of rising opposition to integration, the NAACP became increasingly skeptical about the prospects for voluntary compliance with *Brown*. Federal district court rulings in the summer of 1955—involving two of the locations that were part of the original *Brown* decision (Clarendon County, South Carolina, and Prince Edward County, Virginia)—fueled the association's concerns. In both cases, the courts failed to require school desegregation that fall, as the NAACP's attorneys had requested. In Richmond, after a two-and-a-half-hour hearing, the same three-judge district court panel that had rejected *Davis v. Prince Edward County* in 1952 explained that "it would not be practicable, because of the adjustments and rearrangements required for the purpose, to place the public school system of Prince Edward County upon a nondiscriminatory basis before the commencement of the regular school term in September, 1955."[78]

Commenting on the importance of the two cases before they were decided, Thurgood Marshall and NAACP assistant special counsel Robert Carter wrote, "Certainly the hearings in these cases will be of major significance because these courts may be the first to give definite and specific content to 'a prompt and reasonable start' and 'good faith compliance at the earliest practicable date.'"[79] The two attorneys had participated in the Richmond hearing with Oliver Hill and Spottswood Robinson, after weeks of plotting legal strategy.[80] In an NAACP press release after the rulings, Roy Wilkins hoped the decrees were "not necessarily 'typical of what will happen throughout the South.'"[81] Growing racial violence in the South, including the harassment of NAACP members and the murder of Emmett Till, a black adolescent from Chicago who had supposedly acted "fresh" toward a white woman while in Mississippi, also troubled NAACP leaders.[82]

By late 1955, a growing number of individuals within the NAACP's national office and the Legal Defense Fund came to believe that widespread litigation would be required to bring about southern compliance with *Brown*. Meetings that fall with southern NAACP attorneys and state conference presidents encouraged this assessment, because they reported vividly on growing resistance to school desegregation among southern officials and the general public. After a year and a half of virtual noncompliance with *Brown v. Board of Education*, particularly in the eleven states of the former Confederacy, the national office of the NAACP moved toward widespread litigation to bring about the implementation of *Brown*. In October, the NAACP national legal staff suggested to the NAACP's board of directors that "the only solution [to southern noncompliance] is to file law suits in every state."[83]

Virginia State Conference officials likewise recognized that legal action would be required to bring about compliance with *Brown*. By then the association had "waited and watched for some sign of good faith" for nearly two years, with little result. In October 1955, members of the state conference legal staff, including Oliver Hill and Spottswood Robinson, consulted with national office attorneys at the state conference's annual meeting in Charlottesville. Both NAACP executive secretary Roy Wilkins and special counsel Thurgood Marshall attended the meeting. Afterward, Wilkins noted that "no responsible official or body in Virginia has given any indication that it is willing to discuss plans for desegregation—any plan, slow or fast."[84] Shortly after the meeting, Virginia State Conference attorney

Spottswood Robinson approached representatives of the Arlington branch of the NAACP and informed them that the state conference was ready to prepare to file suit in that community. As Oliver Hill put it, "The reasonable time has passed." The NAACP had decided to return to the federal courts to attempt to force the white South to comply with *Brown v. Board of Education*.[85]

THREE

"Those Who Were on the Other Side"
The NAACP and the Rise of Massive Resistance, 1956

The national office of the NAACP shifted its strategy for securing implementation of *Brown v. Board of Education* in early 1956. During the previous year and a half, the association had instructed its southern branches
to cooperate with local school boards to bring about the implementation
of the Supreme Court's desegregation rulings. This approach worked only
in moderate areas of the South, however, and even there the policy failed
to bring about significant desegregation. In the more intransigent states,
including Virginia, the policy had failed to achieve any voluntary desegregation at all. Frustrated, the national office in 1956 began to file school
desegregation lawsuits in federal courts throughout the South. This change
in tactics resulted in a sharp rise in white southern resistance to desegregation, and pressure on the NAACP from both southern state governments
and from private groups reached new heights. The association weathered
the storm, but combating the attacks required a great deal of time, money,
and effort.

The national office announced its new implementation policy in a press
release dated January 3. In it, NAACP special counsel Thurgood Marshall
declared that the national office's legal staff would henceforth make itself
available to all branches requesting legal advice and assistance with desegregation litigation. Marshall emphasized that the association's commitment
to cooperation with local school boards would continue where progress was
being made, but the NAACP's shift in strategy highlighted the fact that
such cooperation was rarely forthcoming. Where the NAACP had earlier

filed lawsuits in federal courts only selectively to bring about desegregation in the South, Marshall explained that "the legal department is now ready to file suit in every community where such a suit is requested to secure compliance with the Supreme Court anti-segregation decisions."[1]

The association set up a timetable for the new round of litigation at a conference on school desegregation in Atlanta in February 1956. NAACP representatives from fourteen—mostly southern—states attended the gathering, as did the national NAACP leadership. As requested, southern state conference presidents and other leaders presented reports on the situation in their states, discussing where desegregation petitions had been filed, how state laws had changed, and what patterns of compliance or resistance had emerged. Most of the reports highlighted increasing white resistance.[2] It quickly became apparent that eight southern states, including Virginia, were resisting school desegregation absolutely, and the NAACP decided to concentrate its legal action in these states.[3]

Also in Atlanta, the national legal staff established a schedule for filing lawsuits in the chosen states. Based on Thurgood Marshall's suggestion, the NAACP chose to proceed state by state, starting immediately, with the association's attorneys essentially filing litigation in one and then moving on to the next. Localities within each state were chosen based on the level of commitment to school desegregation within the black community, the likelihood of white community resistance, the location of NAACP attorneys, and the case histories of southern federal judges, some of whom were more liberal than others. Among these considerations, the level of commitment within the black community and the location of NAACP attorneys were probably most important. The association expected white community resistance, and had chosen to focus on the most intransigent states, but carefully chose where to file its suits within these states—liberal or progressive locations were clearly preferred. The association sought to initiate litigation by June 1 in all of the eight states, including Virginia, which had completely resisted desegregation thus far.[4]

Perpetually short of funds and resources, the national office encouraged its representatives in states not chosen for litigation to continue negotiating with their local school boards. Delegates to the 1956 Atlanta Conference adopted a resolution stating that "much can be accomplished through further negotiations" in those states not explicitly chosen for legal action.[5] In June, delegates to the NAACP's 1956 annual convention reiterated the point—

state conferences other than the eight chosen were asked "to negotiate . . . to secure desegregation within a reasonable time and to proceed with such negotiations as long as the local board is acting in good faith. In those states legal action in the courts is only to be used as a last resort."[6]

White Virginia's resistance was certainly not in doubt. NAACP attorneys Oliver W. Hill and Spottswood Robinson, along with Executive Secretary W. Lester Banks and newly elected president Dr. E. B. Henderson, represented the Virginia State Conference at the Atlanta gathering, and Henderson outlined a clear pattern of noncompliance on the part of state officials. Most important, NAACP state conference desegregation petitions—fifteen had been filed with local school boards by the spring of 1956—had fallen on deaf ears. In correspondence with the national NAACP that winter, state conference officials had expressed their eagerness to begin litigation. In Atlanta, Henderson added that the Virginia NAACP was "ready to go ahead with as many law suits as would be necessary."[7]

The state conference legal team was well prepared for the task. From a handful of attorneys at the end of World War II, the Virginia State Conference legal staff had grown to twelve at the time of the *Brown* decision, largely as a result of the school equalization campaign. In 1954, J. Hugo Madison of Norfolk joined the team to help implement the historic decision. He joined Spottswood Robinson (Richmond), Martin A. Martin (Richmond), Roland Ealey (Richmond), S. W. Tucker (Emporia), Robert Cooley (Petersburg), Jerry L. Williams (Danville), Reuben E. Lawson (Roanoke), Victor J. Ashe (Norfolk), W. Hale Thompson (Newport News), Philip Walker (Newport News), and Edwin C. Brown (Alexandria). Oliver Hill remained head of the legal staff and Spottswood Robinson served as the group's liaison to the Legal Defense Fund. In the coming years, Hill and Robinson would oversee the implementation of *Brown* while their associates around the state helped by interviewing plaintiffs and witnesses, filing briefs and related paperwork, and making court appearances.[8]

In early 1956 the state of Virginia continued down the path of resistance. In a referendum held on January 9, 1956, voters supported changing the state constitution to allow tuition grants. African Americans throughout Virginia, including the NAACP, had opposed the referendum and called on Virginians to vote "no." In Richmond, members of the NAACP campaigned on radio stations WRVA and WRNL—stations that were popular with predominantly white audiences—against amending the constitution.[9]

The state conference and many branches also worked with labor unions, church groups, fraternal organizations, and public education organizations to stimulate voter turnout. Leading up to the referendum, these included the Virginia Society for the Preservation of Public Schools and the Virginia Council on Human Relations, the latter being the most racially liberal organization in the state and Virginia's only prominent biracial organization.[10]

Of the approximately eighty thousand registered black voters in Virginia in 1956, historians estimate that perhaps fifty thousand voted in the referendum, and local statistics suggest that the vast majority voted "no."[11] Roy Wilkins later congratulated the Virginia NAACP "on the vigorous and dignified campaign [it] conducted."[12] Despite this, the referendum passed by a margin of 2 to 1, and shortly thereafter the General Assembly passed legislation calling for a constitutional convention. In March 1956 this body met and altered the state constitution to legalize tuition grants. Virginia had placed itself in the forefront of growing southern opposition to desegregation.[13]

Most Virginians assumed the General Assembly would also adopt the remaining recommendations made by the Gray Commission in 1955, including provisions allowing local school districts to choose whether to begin desegregation voluntarily. Political leaders, including former governor John Battle and Congressman Watkins Abbitt, had given this impression during the referendum campaign, and members of the Gray Commission felt the referendum results endorsed this course of action. Senator Byrd, however, conspicuously refused to endorse the full Gray Plan in December 1955, leaving the door open for more sweeping resistance.[14]

The fear that Virginia's more liberal localities might launch school desegregation continued to trouble a number of high-ranking public officials. Shortly after the referendum, the issue of local option came to the forefront of Virginia politics. Assuming that the local option provisions would be put into effect, the Arlington County school board—which had received an NAACP school desegregation petition in 1955—voted unanimously to adopt a school desegregation plan for the coming fall. The county envisioned allowing a small number of black students into several of its previously all-white elementary schools. Alarmed and angered by the potential desegregation, however, the General Assembly revoked Arlington's right to have an elected school board.[15]

Rather than allow localities to integrate their schools if they chose to do so, state political leaders in the spring of 1956 increasingly spoke of maintaining segregation in every corner of the Commonwealth of Virginia. State senator and future governor Mills E. Godwin asserted that new laws were "needed as a deterrent to those localities in Virginia which have, or may indicate, a willingness to integrate."[16] Events outside Virginia, including the start of the Montgomery, Alabama, bus boycott in late 1955 (following the arrest of Rosa Parks) and the court-ordered admission of Autherine Lucy into the University of Alabama in February 1956 (following an NAACP lawsuit), fueled opposition to desegregation in Virginia. By February 1956, when U.S. senator Harry F. Byrd Sr. called for "massive resistance" to school desegregation throughout the South, he had the support of Virginia's leading politicians.[17]

On February 1, 1956, highlighting the growing acceptance of massive resistance within the state's political ranks, the General Assembly adopted a formal resolution of interposition, pledging to oppose the implementation of *Brown*. The vote was 36 to 2 in the Senate and 88 to 5 in the House of Delegates. Only one state, Alabama, had already passed an interposition resolution, and some say this was because Harry Byrd was waiting until the January 9 referendum before initiating the process in Virginia.[18] The General Assembly's resolution resembled statements adopted by other southern legislatures that spring, as well as the Southern Manifesto drafted with the support of Senator Byrd and endorsed by most southern members of the U.S. Congress in March.[19] The Virginia interposition resolution stated that the Commonwealth would use all measures "honorably, legally, and constitutionally available" to prevent the integration of its public schools. James J. Kilpatrick, its leading supporter, had previously written to Senator Byrd, "I would toss an old battle-cry back at the NAACP: Hell, we have only begun to fight."[20]

As Kilpatrick suggests, one reason for the rise of southern white massive resistance in 1956 was the actions of the NAACP itself. The organization's determination to bring about school desegregation in the years after *Brown v. Board of Education* stimulated great anger among white southerners. The filing of NAACP school desegregation petitions, the shift toward widespread school desegregation litigation in late 1955, and the filing of NAACP lawsuits in many areas of the South in early 1956 fueled this animosity. Politicians in Virginia—and the South as a whole—were responding to perhaps the greatest and most immediate threat to their segregated way of life.

In 1956, following the NAACP's announcement of school desegregation lawsuits, Virginia's political leadership began to increase pressure on the organization and its members. Many of the attacks focused on the state conference's ability to carry out legal action. On February 21, the *Richmond Times-Dispatch* reported on a bill introduced by Delegates Joseph J. Williams and John B. Boatwright. Boatwright, a Byrd Organization stalwart who had introduced the resolution of interposition into the General Assembly, would later chair a committee created by the General Assembly to investigate organizations promoting school desegregation within the state. In February, the proposed bill was meant to require organizations filing lawsuits against school boards to file affidavits proving they had the consent of everyone on whose behalf lawsuits were initiated, and to require statements of financial contributions from all sources related to such litigation. The bill did not expressly mention the NAACP, but Williams, "when asked if he was out to get the NAACP with the bill, answered: 'Yes.'" Further anti-NAACP actions would soon follow.[21]

Despite the growing opposition, the Virginia State Conference developed and filed its first new school desegregation lawsuits in Virginia in the spring of 1956. In April, NAACP representatives noted that nearly a year had passed since the organization announced its policy for implementing *Brown v. Board of Education.* As Oliver Hill and Spottswood Robinson explained to newspaper reporters, "No one seems to want to do anything. We have no alternative but to resort to the courts."[22] In April and May 1956, lawsuits were filed in federal district court against the school boards of Newport News, Norfolk, Charlottesville, and Arlington. In addition, litigation against Prince Edward County was renewed. In each case the NAACP sought to force the localities to operate their schools in accordance with *Brown v. Board of Education* and admit African American students into formerly all-white schools by September 1956.[23]

The four new localities that faced NAACP lawsuits shared important characteristics. For instance, they were all urban areas. For the NAACP, this offered the benefit of large branches that could offer financial and other support, in addition to large numbers of plaintiffs. Not surprisingly, the national office initially encouraged its state conferences to focus their implementation efforts on urban areas, and each of the four branches had submitted a desegregation petition to its school board in 1955.[24] In addition, three of the four branches included members who were also attorneys on the state conference's legal staff, which simplified the handling of litigation.[25] Another consideration was the relatively moderate beliefs of whites who resided in these communities. As national NAACP attorney James Nabrit Jr. explained, "Wisdom may dictate that we fight first where our chances of winning community support and compliance seem greatest."[26] The Newport News school board had expressed its preference for local option, and public officials in both Arlington and Norfolk had previously indicated their willingness to comply with *Brown* and begin plans for desegregation. In each case, local whites supported the maintenance of public education. As a member of the Arlington NAACP, Edith Burton, later explained, the NAACP's suits had been filed "where the first steps in desegregation would produce a minimum of community dislocation."[27]

Burton gives the impression the NAACP chose where to file its lawsuits, but NAACP protocol—developed by the national office and handed down to its state conferences—required that the state conferences wait for potential plaintiffs to ask for help before deciding whether to provide legal assistance or not. The association advertised its goals and intentions in various ways, and made it known that financial assistance was available to cover legal fees, but the organization did not handpick plaintiffs. Instead, when potential litigants came forward, the NAACP chose the best ones from those that presented themselves. This policy allowed the association the opportunity to refute the label of "outside agitator" and assured that its litigation came from plaintiffs who were strongly committed to school desegregation. It also allowed the NAACP's state conferences, in consultation with the national NAACP legal staff and the LDF, to determine which cases presented the best opportunities to establish legal precedents. The wealth of opportunities for legal action by the NAACP in Virginia in 1956 reflected the desire among African Americans around the state to see school desegregation begin.[28]

Other than granting the state conference permission to proceed, the national office of the NAACP played little role in the initial stages of the litigation. National NAACP attorneys did not prepare or direct the suits, though they did review briefs prepared by state conference lawyers and regularly made court appearances. This was partly because the national office sought to avoid being labeled an "outside agitator" who came into local communities to stir up trouble by filing desegregation lawsuits. Cases reaching the appellate level, however, automatically warranted the consid-

The NAACP and Massive Resistance | 51

eration of the national NAACP, and particularly important cases, or incompetent local attorneys, might also motivate the national office to become more involved. For the Virginia State Conference, modest involvement by the national office's attorneys and those of the Legal Defense Fund appears to have been standard operating procedure, both because of the personal connections between the NAACP attorneys and because the Virginia State Conference was viewed as one of the more responsible units of the association.[29]

State conference attorneys initially planned to supplement the four new cases with additional school desegregation lawsuits. In late February, Oliver Hill had noted that petitions in seven or eight new communities were almost ready to be filed, and state conference officials continued to prod Virginia branches to do so that spring and summer. In July a state NAACP representative announced that ten additional, "second line" lawsuits would be filed once court action in the five pending cases had "progressed far enough."[30]

The shift to widespread litigation was not without its drawbacks for the NAACP. Because the litigation cast the NAACP in the role of a more militant agitator, segregationists labeling the association "radical" were able to rally more supporters than previously. In Virginia and elsewhere in the South, segregationist activity increased as NAACP lawsuits were filed. Harassment of association members and supporters mounted, and even white liberals—fearing that the association's actions were fueling white opposition to desegregation—urged the NAACP to reconsider its approach. Looking back in 1961, Benjamin Muse wrote, "It is difficult to describe the intensity with which the NAACP was hated by white Virginians."[31]

Those involved in the NAACP's school desegregation lawsuits in Virginia knew this hatred well. In many localities, plaintiffs, lawyers, and others associated with the litigation faced threatening telephone calls, cross burnings, and other forms of intimidation. In July 1956, a segregationist from Arlington burned a cross on the lawn of the Sheraton-Park Hotel in Washington, D.C.—where Supreme Court chief justice Earl Warren resided. Several plaintiffs in the Charlottesville case lost their jobs, as did one in Alexandria, and two plaintiffs withdrew from the lawsuit in Arlington County because of the pressure. Oliver Hill's wife later recalled, "Every time something came out in the paper, we knew that was going to be a hectic night. I sat at the front door with a gun some nights after a particularly threatening call."[32] In 1996 Dorothy Hamm, a leader in the movement to integrate the schools in Arlington, remembered: "After that suit was filed, all hell broke loose."[33]

Government-sponsored attacks on the association also multiplied. Southern legislatures passed numerous laws in 1956 aiming to disrupt or shut down NAACP activities. Louisiana officials forced the organization to hand over the membership lists of several large branches; the state NAACP was "decimated."[34] Alabama shut down NAACP operations statewide, including the NAACP's regional office for the Southeast, in Birmingham, by late summer 1956. Arkansas, Mississippi, and other states created "sovereignty" commissions to investigate and undermine organizations that supported school integration.[35] Henceforth, as it pressed its school desegregation campaign, the NAACP also initiated an extensive legal campaign to preserve its right to operate in the South. As NAACP executive secretary Roy Wilkins laconically put it, "We have had our hands full." That fall the association began a special membership campaign to replace members, funds, and resources lost in these attacks.[36]

Officials in Virginia also moved against the NAACP. In the spring of 1956, state leaders introduced and debated various plans for dealing with the organization's litigation; among the more fantastic proposals was that of Congressmen Bill Tuck and Watkins Abbitt—to withdraw the state's consent to be sued. Attorney General Almond understood that more needed to be done, and immediately after the NAACP's school desegregation lawsuits were filed, he recommended that Governor Stanley call a special session of the General Assembly. Almond said that new legislation could forestall and perhaps even prevent the NAACP from succeeding. In early July, leaders of the Byrd Organization—including Byrd, Stanley, Gray, Abbitt, and Tuck—met secretly in Washington, D.C., and decided to press for legislation that would prevent school desegregation in Virginia. Shortly after returning to Richmond, the governor called the General Assembly to meet in special session in late August. The result would be markedly more radical than the modes of resistance the Gray Commission had proposed only six months earlier.[37]

Interestingly, Almond's plea for legislative action provoked bitter criticism from E. Blackburn Moore, a close Byrd confidant who served as Speaker of the House of Delegates (the lower body of the state legislature). As quoted in the *Richmond Times-Dispatch*, Almond had stated, "I have fought to the end of the legal rope and as counsel for the state it is my judgment that we must have state legislation on this subject in order to meet the attacks of the National Association for the Advancement of Colored People." Moore's response derided the attorney general for "making a public admission indicating that he was at 'the end of his rope' and thereby admit alleged weakness and give assurance to the NAACP while suits are pending."[38]

Two court decisions that summer encouraged the massive resisters to act. On July 12, in *Allen v. Charlottesville School Board*, in the first ruling on one of the NAACP's 1956 lawsuits, federal district court judge John Paul of the western district court of Virginia ordered the Charlottesville school board to begin operating desegregated schools that fall. Paul, a Republican who had served on the bench—the same as his father—since 1932, explained: "I would close my eyes to obvious fact if I didn't see that the state has been pursuing a deliberate, well-conceived plan of evasion." Making matters worse for Attorney General Almond, who participated in the hearing, Judge Paul asked if it was true that Almond had advocated new legislation as a means of avoiding compliance with the Supreme Court— as reported in the newspapers. Shortly thereafter, federal district court judge Albert V. Bryan of northern Virginia handed down a similar ruling. In *Thompson v. Arlington County School Board*, Bryan ordered the school board to begin operating its schools on a nondiscriminatory, desegregated basis no later than January 31, 1957. Both decisions were somewhat remarkable, in that few federal district court judges in the former Confederacy ordered immediate school desegregation in 1956. Both cases were appealed, suspending the court orders, but the victories served as a wake-up call to the state legislature.[39]

It was in this context that the Virginia state legislature convened in special session in late August. Historian Andrew Buni noted, "The Confederate flag-waving by spectators in the crowded galleries set the tone of the special session."[40] During the monthlong session, legislators who favored massive resistance, with the backing of the Byrd Organization, prevailed over a coalition of moderates and liberals. In the end, the body adopted twenty-three laws addressing school segregation. Together the measures, colloquially known as the Stanley Plan or the massive resistance legislation, mandated school segregation statewide.[41]

One law created a state Pupil Placement Board (PPB) charged with as-

signing all of Virginia's public school students. This removed the responsibility for pupil assignment from local school districts, which prevented
them from complying with *Brown*. It also meant the NAACP would need
to challenge the PPB's validity and tactics, as opposed to local school boards,
to bring about school desegregation in Virginia. This would delay the organization's push for school desegregation. As expected, the legislature
authorized this three-person board to assign students based on a variety
of factors that purported to be racially neutral—including test scores, academic performance, and residential location—but which in fact allowed
the body to avoid assigning black students to white schools. Though the
NAACP quickly challenged the pupil placement legislation in court, the
committee began its work in early 1957, and the Pupil Placement Board
continued to operate for nearly a decade.[42]

The General Assembly also passed legislation to prevent integration even
if its pupil assignment policies failed or were overturned by the courts. The
most important provisions were known as the school closing laws, a handful of related bills that authorized the governor to close any public school
ordered by the federal courts to integrate. Should federal courts order a
school board to enroll black students in a formerly all-white school, which
was considered the most likely path to integration, the governor would close
the affected white school(s), withhold all state funds from them, and begin
providing tuition grants (for enrollment in private segregated schools) to
the displaced white students.[43]

The massive resistance laws were Virginia's attempt to lead the South
in resistance to *Brown*, the NAACP, and the federal government. Most of
Virginia's white elected officials believed, and assumed their constituents
believed, that the state NAACP was threatening Virginia's way of life and
traditions, as well as those of the white South as a whole. In late August, at
an annual picnic attended by nearly two thousand guests on his farm near
Winchester, Senator Byrd vowed to fight "with every ounce of our energy
and capacity." With the special session of the General Assembly just days
away, he explained: "It's no secret that the NAACP intends first to press
Virginia. . . . If Virginia surrenders, if Virginia's line is broken, the rest of
the South will go down, too."[44]

Byrd's keen attention to the actions of the NAACP explains why the
General Assembly also adopted legislation aimed at the association and the
supporters of school integration in Virginia. Seven so-called anti-NAACP

laws were passed during the special session. David J. Mays, counsel for the Gray Commission, helped draft the legislation and explained in his diary that the intent was "to harass the NAACP in Virginia."[45] This legislation sought to undermine the organization's campaign for school desegregation by redefining commonly accepted legal practices related to the solicitation of clients and providing state legal aid to local school boards to defend against NAACP suits. The General Assembly also required the registration and public disclosure of NAACP members' names and created two legislative committees to investigate advocates of racial integration and their efforts.[46] Referring to the NAACP during the special session, Delegate James Thomson of Alexandria, a brother-in-law to Harry Byrd Jr., declared that with the new legislation "we could bust that organization wide open."[47] Roy Wilkins, executive secretary of the NAACP, added: "The intent of this legislation was clear: to destroy the NAACP in Virginia."[48] Firing back at its school desegregation litigation, the state of Virginia had declared war on the NAACP.

For its part, the Virginia NAACP actively opposed the legislative attempts to forestall school desegregation. A state conference press release in late July blasted Governor Stanley's support for massive resistance, calling it "another demonstration of his total incapacity to provide intelligent leadership to the people of Virginia during these significant times."[49] A number of NAACP supporters addressed the General Assembly during its special session, and the national NAACP also publicly criticized state officials.[50] But the NAACP had few defenders in the legislature, and those who supported compliance with the federal courts or the protection of the NAACP's right to operate were soundly defeated during the legislative session. Most of the massive resistance bills—and all the anti-NAACP legislation—passed easily. Only three members of the state legislature opposed all seven anti-NAACP bills.[51]

That fall, the new laws diverted the Virginia State Conference's attention from handling and expanding its desegregation lawsuits to defending its right to exist. In response to the General Assembly's actions, the state conference quickly initiated litigation testing the constitutionality of the new anti-NAACP and massive resistance laws, but the action became mired in the judicial system, where it would remain for years.[52] In a variety of federal and state courts throughout Virginia, the NAACP also repeatedly sparred with the two legislative committees, commonly referred as the

NAACP lawyers declined to furnish records and membership lists sought under a subpoena from the Thomson Committee, arguing that the committee had surpassed its legal mandate. Shown at the State Capitol in January 1958 are (*left to right*) Roland D. Ealy, Oliver W. Hill, W. Lester Banks, John B. Boatwright Jr. (head of the then merged Thomson and Boatwright Committees), Martin A. Martin, and John M. Brooks. (Courtesy of the *Richmond Times-Dispatch*)

Thomson Committee and the Boatwright Committee, set up to investigate the supporters of integration in Virginia. Attorneys for Virginia, recognizing that the anti-NAACP legislation would probably eventually be overturned by federal courts, still labored effectively to delay that outcome.[53] In subsequent years, as the NAACP won legal victories against the anti-NAACP and massive resistance laws in the courts, the General Assembly made subtle alterations to its legislation, prolonging the legal battle. In the end, the Virginia State Conference's legal campaign against the legislative attempts to destroy it was not complete until 1963.[54]

Over the next several years, largely as a result of anti-NAACP laws and policies, including requests for membership and financial information, the association would lose hundreds of branches in the South.[55] In Virginia, the damage was already evident by the end of 1956; national office records show the collapse of a disproportionate number of Virginia branches that year.[56] Publicly, the association argued that the anti-NAACP legislation had united the black community behind the NAACP, but, when pressed, NAACP officials conceded that the attack had cost the association members, money, and valuable resources.[57]

Massive resistance, however, did not shut down the NAACP in Virginia or force it to abandon its school desegregation campaign. To counteract the loss of members and funding, the state conference asked its branches to step up membership drives and fund-raising. A letter from state conference president Dr. E. B. Henderson in early 1957 entreated, "Never before has our NAACP needed the support of every Negro citizen as it has today."[58] To protect its finances, the state conference transferred its "principal monies" to New York, and to protect sensitive information, the state conference inquired about transferring its branch records to Washington, D.C. And perhaps most important, the association tried to maintain its supporters' morale with a stream of pronouncements and memoranda. One, written by Executive Secretary W. Lester Banks in early 1957, urged members to "keep on keeping on" until the organization's objectives had been achieved. Under the circumstances, it is doubtful Banks could have asked for more.[59]

In the meantime, the state conference's legal staff continued to push its school desegregation lawsuits through the federal court system. Given the complete recalcitrance of Virginia's political leadership, Oliver Hill and his assistants knew they had to rely on the courts to achieve school desegregation. In the fall of 1956 the state conference legal staff worked with attorneys from the Legal Defense Fund, including Thurgood Marshall and his assistant, Robert Carter, to defend their district court victories before the federal appeals court. In November the team celebrated another triumph when the U.S. Court of Appeals for the Fourth Circuit sustained the federal district court rulings handed down in the summer of 1956 requiring desegregation in Arlington and Charlottesville. As expected, however, both localities immediately appealed to the U.S. Supreme Court, suspending the desegregation orders.[60]

Moreover, the Fourth Circuit ruling came after the General Assembly's special session and its adoption of additional roadblocks to school desegregation. By concentrating the pupil assignment process in the hands of the newly created Pupil Placement Board, for example, the General Assembly ensured that the local school boards the NAACP had been suing became all but irrelevant in the struggle over school desegregation; racially separate schools would be maintained by state authorities. In response, the NAACP opened a new front in the legal war over school segregation: the association challenged the constitutionality of the new pupil placement law and the remainder of the massive resistance program.[61]

In the meantime, the association was forced to place the development of additional school desegregation lawsuits on hold. In the spring and summer, state conference attorneys had indicated that as many as fifteen additional lawsuits might be filed by the opening of school that fall. Attacks on the association and its supporters that summer, however, as well as the adoption of the state's massive resistance legislation, forced a change of plans— undoubtedly part of the intent. As the organization turned its attention to combatting the new massive resistance laws in late 1956, NAACP attorneys chose to hold off on any additional school desegregation lawsuits.[62]

In the end, the plethora of lawsuits the NAACP had to file to strike down the state's anti-NAACP legislation would occupy Virginia State Conference attorneys for several years. At the end of 1956, the road ahead of the association appeared fraught with difficulty and peril. Though *Brown v. Board of Education* had declared segregation in southern education unconstitutional, the implementation of that ruling in Virginia seemed distant at best. NAACP Executive Secretary Roy Wilkins later wrote, "Eventually we were able to cut through all these legal entanglements, but the fight took time, money, and energy that might otherwise have gone into more fruitful enterprises. In one sense, however, the harassment was rather flattering: it showed how pervasive our influence was—and how desperate the South was to stamp us out."[63]

FOUR

"Keep On Keeping On"
The Height of Massive Resistance, 1957–1959

In Virginia, the years between 1957 and 1959 brought grave hardships to the supporters of school desegregation. The size and power of segregationist organizations peaked in the late 1950s, as did state government efforts to prevent integration in the public schools. The Virginia NAACP, the preeminent supporter of integration in the Commonwealth, struggled to survive—even as it continued its efforts to bring about desegregation in Virginia's public schools.

Ultimately, in early 1959, state and federal judges overturned key elements of the Virginia General Assembly's massive resistance program. The rulings forced state leaders to choose between continuing outright resistance by crafting new massive resistance laws, or capitulating to the courts and allowing school desegregation to begin in the Commonwealth of Virginia. Governor Almond and a majority in the state legislature chose the latter.

On February 2, 1959, nearly five years after *Brown v. Board of Education*, school desegregation began in Virginia. That day, twenty-one African American students entered formerly all-white schools in Arlington and Norfolk. The process was generally peaceful, but the black students faced a variety of hardships in their new schools. After initial school desegregation, the Virginia State Conference of the NAACP sought—primarily through litigation—to increase the number of Virginia localities implementing desegregation and the number of black students admitted to white schools. State government leaders, shifting from outright defiance to token compliance, handed control of school desegregation to local officials and continued to aid those who wanted to preserve as much segregation as possible. Though the beginning of school desegregation was a historic NAACP victory, the state effectively minimized the amount of desegregation that followed in the early 1960s.

In the meantime, the General Assembly organized the two committees sanctioned by its massive resistance legislation of 1956. The House of Delegates created the Committee on Offenses Against the Administration of Justice (known as the Boatwright Committee), while the state senate established the Committee on Law Reform and Racial Activities (known as the Thomson Committee). Both panels were set up in early 1957 to impede and counteract the efforts of Virginians who wanted integration, primarily the NAACP, by questioning national and state NAACP leaders, intimidating plaintiffs and witnesses in the NAACP's cases, attempting to obtain the organization's membership lists and financial records, and challenging the credentials of the association's attorneys.[1]

The national office of the NAACP developed a flexible but coordinated strategy for handling attacks on the association mounted by Virginia and other southern states. Typical of the NAACP, most of the final decisions were made by the staff in New York City. In January 1957, following the Thomson and Boatwright committees' initial requests for information, Virginia State Conference officials journeyed to New York and met with national office leaders. The Virginia NAACP had already filed a lawsuit, *NAACP v. Almond*, against the state's anti-NAACP laws, and now its leadership discussed what actions to take while the courts considered their requests. The following month, the national board of directors of the NAACP chose to provide general information to Virginia's legislative committees but withhold the names and addresses of members and contributors, a move that was meant to preserve their anonymity and limit reprisals from white segregationists. That it was Executive Secretary Roy Wilkins who communicated the decision directly to the committees highlighted the association's concern.[2]

NAACP v. Almond, the Virginia State Conference's suit, had been filed with a three-judge federal district court in late 1956. The action sought to restrain Attorney General J. Lindsay Almond, and the Commonwealth's attorneys from areas sued by the NAACP, from enforcing the General

Assembly's anti-NAACP laws. The suit also contended that the anti-NAACP laws were unconstitutional, and sought to have them overturned. At the same time, the NAACP Legal Defense Fund filed a virtually identical lawsuit, as both organizations operated in Virginia and were subject to the legislation. Oliver Hill and Robert Carter handled the NAACP suit, while Spottswood Robinson and Thurgood Marshall oversaw the LDF litigation.[3] Between 1957 and 1959, the state conference legal staff worked regularly on this litigation, including the state's appeal of *NAACP v. Almond*, filed as *Harrison v. NAACP*, as well as *Scull v. Virginia* (1959), which resulted in a U.S. Supreme Court decision that overturned the contempt of court conviction of a white NAACP member from Virginia. By the fall of 1959, Oliver Hill noted that lawyers for the Virginia NAACP were handling at least six cases dealing with the disclosure of membership information. In the end, the litigation continued until the U.S. Supreme Court ruled for the NAACP in 1963 in *NAACP v. Button*.[4]

This litigation involved countless hours of legal preparation and hearings. As Robert Carter explained in 1957, "It appears that their plan is to keep us so busy working for them that we won't have time for other business." The NAACP's national board of directors established a separate fund to pay for the effort to overturn the anti-NAACP laws in Virginia, and NAACP records also show that attorneys' fees paid by the state conference skyrocketed in 1957.[5] In a report issued in 1960, the Boatwright Committee stated that "solely because of the NAACP and its affiliated person and organizations . . . the Committee has been required to obtain the assistance of various courts of the Commonwealth not less than fourteen times during a period of ten months." Virginia's taxpayers paid for the state's defense.[6]

While these cases were argued, the Thomson and Boatwright committees pressured the Virginia NAACP and its supporters. In late 1957, the committees, in formal reports to the General Assembly, accused the NAACP of engaging in the unauthorized practice of law. The following year the legislature directed the Boatwright Committee to take legal action against individuals or organizations violating Virginia's legal standards. In response, the committee launched proceedings to obtain an injunction against the legal operations of the Virginia State Conference, the national NAACP, and the NAACP Legal Defense and Educational Fund in Virginia.[7]

The legislative committees' focus on the national headquarters reflected a fundamental misunderstanding of the association. Committee members, like most white Virginians, believed the Virginia NAACP was merely doing the bidding of the association's national office in New York. Rather than recognize black Virginians' desire for change, white leaders assumed that black Virginians were being pressured, or bribed, by the national office. Speaking about the Virginia NAACP in 1958, Senator Byrd asserted, "They are told what to do by smart and ruthless outside leaders who have no regard for the fine relationship between the races which has existed in Virginia for so many years."[8]

In reality, Virginia's NAACP members and their leaders were as committed to the destruction of segregation as the organization's top officials, if not more so. Southern blacks suffered the indignities of segregation more than their northern counterparts, fueling a strong commitment to equal rights. Though claims of "outside agitators" stirring up trouble resonated with white southerners throughout the post-*Brown* era, the reality was that most black Virginians—and particularly NAACP members—were eager for the destruction of Jim Crow.

Senator Harry Byrd's opposition to the NAACP also induced him to attack the association's ability to function. In 1956, Byrd used his considerable influence as chairman of the U.S. Senate Finance Committee to convince the Internal Revenue Service (IRS) to investigate the NAACP's tax status. As he later explained, "I have asked the Internal Revenue Service for written justification of their action with respect to NAACP tax exemptions."[9] After an IRS investigation, and determination that the Legal Defense and Educational Fund had violated its tax-exempt status by sharing a chain of command with the national office of the NAACP, the IRS forced the two organizations to completely separate in May 1957.[10]

Under the new arrangement, the NAACP and the Legal Defense Fund developed separate administrative structures, boards of directors, and legal staffs. Thurgood Marshall continued as director of the Legal Defense Fund, while Robert L. Carter left the LDF payroll to become NAACP general counsel.[11] Virginia's NAACP attorneys continued to work with both organizations. As Oliver Hill later explained, "in our office, I would represent the NAACP and Spot [Spottswood Robinson] would be representative for the Legal Defense Fund."[12] Carter and the national legal staff were particularly important in defending the state conference from state government attacks by challenging the constitutionality of the General Assembly's anti-NAACP laws in court, and in other litigation related to the NAACP as an organization. In the legal campaign for school desegregation, state conference attorneys worked increasingly with the Legal Defense Fund, which largely oversaw the implementation of *Brown v. Board of Education* at the time.[13]

In the late 1950s, opposition to school desegregation, and pro-segregation organizations, expanded in the South. Polls showed that roughly 15 percent of white southerners agreed with the *Brown* decision in 1956, but the number dropped to 8 percent by 1959. The decline reflected the expansion of school desegregation in the region and segregationists' successful campaign to unite white southerners in opposition to *Brown*. In Virginia, the Defenders of State Sovereignty and Individual Liberties remained the largest pro-segregation group. By 1956 the Defenders had organized chapters throughout the state and claimed a membership of twelve thousand. The group also had access to the highest echelons of Virginia's government, including the allegiance of a number of legislators from Southside Virginia who supported massive resistance. In early 1956, a delegation of southern segregationists headed by Robert Crawford, president of the Defenders, met with Governor Stanley to promote interposition. Around that time, historian Robbins Gates wrote that "the Defenders and the [Byrd] organization seemed nearly as one."[14]

Like Byrd and other state officials, the Defenders of State Sovereignty attacked the NAACP. In October 1954, the Mecklenburg County Defenders unit had warned: "The question is whether we shall pass on to our children and grandchildren the proud heritage of the white race or whether we shall quietly submit to the dictates of [the] NAACP."[15] Between 1957 and 1959, the Defenders organized political rallies to pressure state leaders, harassed the proponents of integration with cross burnings and threatening phone calls and letters, and established tax-exempt foundations to create private segregated academies should the public schools be closed—or worse, integrated.[16]

As opposition to school desegregation swelled, the NAACP struggled. Southern attempts to secure NAACP membership lists as well as other attacks on the association led to a sharp decline in memberships in the South. These declines continued throughout the late 1950s. In January 1958, Thurgood Marshall and Roy Wilkins reported that memberships had dropped

14 percent, or forty-eight thousand members, in the previous year—the first decrease since the late 1940s.[17]

The Virginia State Conference's membership figures suffered as well. In the two years after *Brown v. Board of Education*, the organization had experienced significant growth. The Virginia State Conference's overall membership expanded from 16,032 at the end of 1954 to 30,354 at the end of 1955.[18] By the end of 1956, however, the state government's massive resistance policies began to take their toll, and the number of state conference members fell to 22,846. Afterward, Virginia State Conference memberships flattened out for the remainder of the decade—the association's membership totals for 1958 and 1959 were 21,168 and 21,777, respectively—before rising again in the early 1960s.[19]

As membership declined, so did the NAACP's income. Unlike other civil rights organizations, the majority of the national NAACP's revenue came from individual, annually renewed memberships; in 1958, such memberships supplied approximately 85 percent of the association's annual operating budget. As massive resistance led to a decline in memberships and also fewer donations to the NAACP, the association's income stagnated; after record-breaking income and budget surpluses in 1954 and 1955, the association's budget showed a deficit for 1957.[20]

The NAACP's protocol was that membership dues were sent to the national office, and then the national office paid its state conferences a percentage of the dues. After rising from approximately $13,000 in 1954 to nearly $40,000 in 1955 and almost $50,000 in 1956, the amount of membership income sent from the national office to the state conference fell below that level until the end of the decade, when it again began to climb.[21] As its income dropped, the state NAACP appealed to the national office for financial relief. In June 1957, Virginia State Conference executive secretary W. Lester Banks appealed to NAACP executive secretary Roy Wilkins: "We are still under the hammer." Requests for financial assistance from the national office—primarily for legal expanses—continued throughout the late 1950s.[22]

Massive resistance also led to reduced branch activity in Virginia. In its 1957 annual report, the Covington branch explained that much of its civil rights work had stopped. A handwritten addendum to national director of branches Gloster B. Current explained: "Our field of action has been narrowed considerably the last couple of years by the effects and pressure of the anti-N.A.A.C.P. laws and attempts by the state government of Virginia to secure branch membership lists." It concluded, "Rest assured that our branch is carrying on and doing its best under very difficult circumstances."[23]

The state conference, however, maintained its core programs and continued to press for school desegregation in Virginia throughout the late 1950s. The new dangers and hurdles failed to intimidate the organization's leadership. One NAACP supporter wrote of Virginia State Conference executive secretary W. Lester Banks, "When the timid begin discussions about going slow or stopping certain important projects, Les acts like a deaf man who has lost his hearing aid." Another penned a song about Banks, titled "The Iron Man."[24] In 1959, in addition to continuing its legal challenges against the massive resistance laws, state conference officials distributed more than 150,000 pieces of literature to "alert, inform and lend a feeling of security to our members and supporters." One brochure was pointedly titled "NAACP Membership and Contribution Lists Still Secure."[25]

As the anti-NAACP laws and segregationist attacks took their toll, national NAACP leaders also struggled to maintain the association's position as the nation's leading civil rights organization. Traditionally, though the NAACP cooperated with other civil rights groups and generally shared the same goals, the organization also jealously guarded its status and influence and feared new organizations that might challenge it. In the late 1950s and early 1960s, the very time when southern segregationists and state governments targeted the NAACP and its members, several new civil rights organizations were created—in part because of attacks on the NAACP—a development that threatened the NAACP's long-term preeminence and created angst within its leadership.[26]

Concern among national NAACP leaders increased as a result of the Montgomery, Alabama, bus boycott of 1955–56. Following Rosa Parks's arrest, the boycott was organized by the locally based Montgomery Improvement Association (MIA) and then led by that organization's president, the Reverend Dr. Martin Luther King Jr. While the Montgomery branch of the NAACP and the MIA shared many members, including King himself, friction existed between the two organizations from the beginning. The NAACP handled the MIA's legal work, but both during and after the boycott NAACP executive secretary Roy Wilkins downplayed the effectiveness of boycotts as a tactic for bringing about change. Ignoring the fact that the NAACP had organized similar economic boycotts in the past, Wilkins emphasized instead the importance of the U.S. Supreme Court decision that ended the boycott, and the NAACP's handling of the litigation.[27]

Wilkins also pointed out—correctly—that the boycott had encouraged the attack mounted by the state of Alabama on the NAACP. In June 1956 Alabama's attorney general launched one of the fiercest assaults on the NAACP in the region. Legislative action and judicial decrees shut down the Alabama State Conference as well as the organization's regional headquarters for the Southeast United States, which was relocated to Atlanta.[28] As Taylor Branch explains, Wilkins would long remember that "it was King's boycott that had put the NAACP out of business in the entire state, at a critical time in the school desegregation cases, and this handicap would grow more serious as other Southern states tried to follow Alabama's example."[29]

The birth of a new civil rights organization—the Southern Christian Leadership Conference (SCLC), led by Dr. King—in early 1957 intensified the NAACP's fears of lost influence in the region. Such fears were not unfounded; signs of King's influence would soon crop up in Virginia. In late 1956, shortly after Dr. King visited Petersburg for the Virginia State Conference's annual meeting, Wyatt Tee Walker, a leader of the local branch, suggested that a church-based civil rights group could replace the NAACP, should the organization become illegal in the state. "Call the NAACP by a different name," Walker explained, "but let its philosophy continue under the direction of the church." The state hosted its own "improvement associations" by 1957.[30] With the NAACP struggling to exist in many southern states, the creation of SCLC grated on Roy Wilkins and other national NAACP leaders. Though King attempted to maintain cordial relations and deliberately avoided confronting the NAACP's leadership, a close friend of Dr. King's commented that 1957 had been a virtual "year of disagreement."[31]

In the meantime, the Virginia NAACP's legal campaign to implement *Brown v. Board of Education* progressed. Two of the organization's five 1956 school desegregation lawsuits—in Arlington and Charlottesville—had won favorable rulings in federal district court and been unanimously upheld by the Court of Appeals for the Fourth Circuit in December 1956.[32] In February 1957, while the Fourth Circuit decision was appealed to the U.S. Supreme Court, Judge Walter E. Hoffman of the federal district court of eastern Virginia handed down a decision ordering that school desegregation in Norfolk and Newport News begin that fall. Hoffman explained that "by reason of the obvious lack of attempt to promulgate any plan looking forward to desegregation gradually or otherwise, there remains nothing for this court to do other than to restrain and enjoin the school board." Upheld by the Fourth Circuit Court in the summer of 1957, Hoffman's rulings were also appealed to the U.S. Supreme Court. In the meantime, segregated schools in Virginia would continue for the 1957–58 school year.[33]

Not all federal district judges in Virginia felt compelled to order the beginning of school desegregation at this time. Between 1956 and 1959, Judge Sterling Hutcheson, of Mecklenburg County, oversaw the Prince Edward County litigation. In early 1957, in the first ruling on Prince Edward County since the NAACP revived its litigation in 1956, Hutcheson refused to set a date for the beginning of desegregation. Late that year, the Fourth Circuit Court of Appeals reversed his decision and remanded the case back to the district court to set a deadline for desegregation. The following summer, Hutcheson determined that September 1965 was an acceptable date. After being reversed a second time by the appeals court, in 1959, Hutcheson resigned from the bench.[34]

In the fall of 1957, Virginia and the rest of the South took a backseat to news from Little Rock, Arkansas. Like the Virginia State Conference, the Arkansas State Conference of the NAACP filed a school desegregation lawsuit in early 1956 and won a federal district court ruling ordering school desegregation in Little Rock in 1957. Arkansas governor Orval Faubus, however, used the Arkansas National Guard to prevent the admission of nine African American students into Little Rock's Central High School in order to—as he put it—maintain order and prevent violence. Eventually President Dwight Eisenhower took control of the Arkansas National Guard and sent U.S. Army troops to help enforce the court order. Soldiers escorted the nine black students into the school and remained there for the entire year.[35]

The crisis in Little Rock reverberated throughout the South. In Virginia's gubernatorial campaign in the fall of 1957, Attorney General J. Lindsay Almond won a contest that focused largely on massive resistance to school desegregation. A stalwart segregationist, Almond branded his opponent, Republican Ted Dalton of Radford, an integrationist because of President Eisenhower's actions and Dalton's moderate views on desegregation; the Republican preferred segregation but supported compliance with *Brown*.[36] The Little Rock crisis, which broke less than two months before the election, sharpened white Virginians' concerns about integration and doomed Dalton's campaign. A poll conducted shortly after the incident revealed that two out of three whites in Virginia preferred closing schools rather than integrating them, and Dalton later concluded, "Little Rock knocked me down to nothing. It wasn't a little rock, it was a big rock."[37]

Also in the fall of 1957, the U.S. Congress passed civil rights legislation for the first time since Reconstruction. The Civil Rights Act of 1957 was meant to increase black voter registration in the South. It created the Civil Rights Division within the Department of Justice, and the United States Commission on Civil Rights. The commission consulted with local officials, set up state advisory committees, and subsequently issued a series of important reports related to voting and other civil rights issues, including school desegregation. Though many civil rights leaders rightly criticized the new legislation's provisions as weak, the passage of the Civil Rights Act of 1957 reflected changes in Congress that were slowly undermining the advantages that seniority and the Senate filibuster had traditionally afforded southern representatives. The vast majority of southern political leaders, including Virginia's delegation, denounced the legislation.[38]

In the spring of 1958, the Virginia General Assembly revised and expanded its massive resistance legislation. With support from now-governor J. Lindsay Almond Jr., the legislature adopted several so-called Little Rock bills, which required the closing of any school policed by federal troops and mandated that the federalization of the state militia be controlled by the governor. Responding to recent federal court rulings, the lawmakers also modified the Pupil Placement Act. In early 1957, as part of the Newport News and Norfolk school desegregation litigation, Judge Hoffman had ruled the act "unconstitutional on its face," and that summer the Fourth Circuit Court of Appeals agreed. The U.S. Supreme Court refused to review the appeals court's judgment in October, rendering the pupil placement law ineffective. To allow the PPB to continue school segregation without assigning students explicitly based on race, legislators in early 1958 allowed the body to consider additional nonracial criteria for student placement. Not surprisingly, state conference attorneys quickly challenged the measure in court.[39]

The General Assembly also amended its anti-NAACP laws. Delegate James Thomson sought to extend the life of his committee and expand its agenda to examine the racial beliefs of Virginia's schoolteachers, but

Governor Almond opposed the effort, fearing its effect on teacher recruitment. The General Assembly rejected Thomson's proposal and instead merged Thomson's committee with the Boatwright Committee. The investigation, and harassment, of the NAACP continued. That spring, the General Assembly also passed legislation requiring nonprofit organizations engaged in legal work to register with the State Corporation Commission, and ordered the Virginia State Bar to prosecute supposed violators of the state's legal ethics rules. Dozens of related measures sought to preserve segregation in the Commonwealth in various ways—in the sixty-day session, six hundred bills were passed, a new record. And though most legislators recognized, as did the *Richmond Afro-American,* that "the new laws will not stand the test of constitutionality," they would delay the beginning of school desegregation. In the spring of 1958, massive resistance was alive and well in Virginia.[40]

In the fall of 1958, litigation from the Little Rock crisis led to the first significant U.S. Supreme Court decision related to school desegregation since *Brown II* in 1955. Ruling on an appeal from the Little Rock school board for more time to implement its school desegregation plan, the high court in *Cooper v. Aaron* unanimously reiterated its commitment to *Brown v. Board of Education* and ruled that the threat of violence—and community resistance generally—did not excuse noncompliance. Still, although *Cooper v. Aaron* was "more forceful and condemnatory than *Brown,*" the decision did not significantly speed up southern school desegregation. In December 1958, only a few months after *Cooper,* the Supreme Court left standing a lower court ruling rejecting a challenge to Alabama's pupil placement law. During the five years after *Cooper,* the high court regularly refused to hear appeals of lower court decisions requiring only minimal compliance with *Brown,* thereby legitimizing the slow pace of school desegregation in the South.[41]

In the meantime, the NAACP continued to make slow progress in Virginia's courtrooms. After the U.S. Supreme Court allowed Judge Hoffman's decisions overturning the state's pupil placement law and ordering school desegregation in Norfolk and Newport News to stand, state conference attorneys sought to have school desegregation orders for those localities renewed. In the spring and summer of 1958, Judges Hoffman and John Paul complied, requiring school desegregation in Norfolk and Charlottesville, respectively, that September.[42] The Virginia NAACP also filed a sixth school desegregation lawsuit in Warren County, just north of Shenandoah National Park, in August 1958. The county had no black high school and instead transported students to a regional high school in Manassas. This case quickly resulted in a decision from Judge Paul ordering school desegregation there in September as well.[43]

With court-ordered desegregation pending, the NAACP made preparations for the fall opening of school. In June 1958, state conference officials traveled to New York to meet with representatives of the national NAACP. Robert Carter, who attended the gathering, had recently predicted that Virginia would be "one of the toughest tests in the whole desegregation fight in September." Those present—including Oliver Hill, W. Lester Banks, and recently elected state conference president Dr. Philip Wyatt, of Fredericksburg—agreed to dispatch national office education specialists June Shagaloff and Clarence Laws to the affected Virginia localities to help prepare the communities for desegregation, or for the closure of their schools, depending on the governor's response. A state conference memorandum the week after the gathering concluded: "It was the consensus that the above project is and must be the Number One Project in Virginia."[44]

Also that summer, at the end of August, U.S. senator Harry F. Byrd Sr. held his annual picnic at the family apple orchards in Berryville, Virginia. Before a record-breaking crowd at a traditionally well-attended event, on a bright, sunshiny Saturday, the senator called for continued massive resistance and denounced the proponents of school integration in Virginia. After noting that "the eyes of the world will soon be upon us," Byrd warned that the NAACP wanted "to bring Virginia to its knees first and then after conquering Virginia . . . they intend to march through the South singing hallelujah." Denouncing the organization and its efforts, Byrd proclaimed it was Virginia's duty to hold the line.[45]

During the fall of 1958, as Byrd predicted, the nation focused its attention on Virginia. In September, when federal court orders desegregating Virginia's schools were supposed to go into effect, Governor Almond closed nine affected public schools in Charlottesville, Norfolk, and Warren County. The closed schools were supposed to have enrolled African American students that fall. The remaining schools in each locale, and Virginia's public schools in other localities, remained open. Still, Almond's decision displaced nearly fifteen thousand schoolchildren—ten thousand in Norfolk alone. As the national media descended on Virginia, many of the affected white students enrolled in private schools that were hastily created with help from segregationist organizations.[46]

Underlying the media attention was the fact that what happened in Virginia would strongly influence the battle over school desegregation elsewhere in the South. This was particularly true in states that had not yet experienced desegregation. Quite simply, segregationists across the region hoped Virginia would hold the line. As Relman Morin put it in the *Richmond Times-Dispatch*, "In effect, other Southern states are telling Virginians, 'If you go down, there is little hope for the South.'"[47] In James Jackson Kilpatrick's view, the state's importance as the first American colony and the capital of the Confederacy had convinced the NAACP to focus its attack there, and the organization simply had to be defeated. In the fall of 1958, Kilpatrick wrote: "The next few weeks will be bitter weeks for Virginia. We have sacrifice ahead, and some exhausting labor, and a terrible harvest of worsening race relations. But we also have an opportunity to defend, before the whole country, constitutional principles held precious in Virginia for more than a century and a half."[48]

That same fall, the Virginia NAACP filed litigation challenging the school closings in Virginia and the legislation that had authorized them. In October, Oliver Hill submitted a motion to Judge Paul for further relief in the Warren County case and asked Judge Hoffman to force the Norfolk school board to reopen the schools. Also in Norfolk, a predominantly white, moderate organization known as the Norfolk Committee for Public Schools filed a lawsuit, *James v. Almond,* challenging the state's school closing and tuition grant laws. Judge Hoffman convinced the state NAACP to withdraw its suit in favor of the committee's case, which represented all the pupils whose schools had been closed rather than only the black plaintiffs who had been assigned to desegregated schools. While the litigation worked its way through the courts, the schools remained closed.[49]

The rise of the Norfolk Committee for Public Schools was part of a broader save-the-schools movement that reflected an important shift among Virginia's white population. Facing the prospect of closed public schools throughout the state, a growing number of white Virginians began calling for the state to maintain and protect its public schools, even if doing so required token, or minimal, school desegregation. These white moderates believed that maintaining segregated schools was not worth abandoning public education. Some also pointed to the negative economic repercussions of school closures, specifically the challenge of attracting employers to locations without public schools. The previous fall, the ever-prescient Oliver Hill had noted that if school closures were needed to "bring Virginia to its senses, then the sooner we reach that crisis the better." In December 1958 the growing acceptance of this perspective in Virginia led white moderates from around the state to create the Virginia Committee on Public Schools, an organization committed to reopening closed public schools and preventing future school closures in the Commonwealth.[50]

The stalwart supporters of segregation, however, pressed state officials to continue massive resistance even as the school closings created an atmosphere of crisis. Former governor William Tuck and U.S. congressman Watkins M. Abbitt Sr. came out against any modifications to the state's program, and the Defenders of State Sovereignty and Individual Liberties and other segregationists created private segregated school systems in the affected localities. The organization also began to make similar plans elsewhere in Virginia. In December, the board of directors of the Defenders resolved that "since Virginia . . . is the battleground upon which the eternal fight for the liberties of America must be waged, let us not falter, let us not yield."[51]

With the pressure mounting, Governor Almond considered his options. Senator Byrd and the Democratic political machine supported the continuation of massive resistance, but Almond knew that a growing number of white Virginians felt that statewide school segregation should be abandoned if public school closings were the inevitable result of that policy. Governor Almond would not defy the massive resisters lightly, but a crucial question now arose of whether a new political coalition including moderates, liberals, and former Byrd supporters, preferring minimal compliance with *Brown* rather than massive resistance, was viable.

As an attorney, Almond also understood the likelihood that Virginia's massive resistance laws would eventually be overturned by federal courts. In the fall of 1958, Governor Almond asked Attorney General Albertis Harrison to initiate a test case in the state courts to assess the constitutionality of the school closing laws and tuition grant system Virginia had created in 1956, and modified the previous spring. Perhaps the governor sought to transfer some responsibility for school desegregation in Virginia to the court system. Hearings were held that fall on *Harrison v. Day*, which would be decided in early 1959 along with the Norfolk Committee for Public Schools' federal district court suit.[52]

As tensions reached the boiling point, the Virginia NAACP helped to stage the state's largest civil rights demonstration of the 1950s, reportedly the first mass demonstration of its kind in the South. In Richmond on Emancipation Day—January 1, 1959—more than a thousand people marched in the Pilgrimage of Prayer for Public Schools, organized by the state NAACP, the Congress of Racial Equality (CORE), and the Southern Christian Leadership Conference (SCLC). The goal was to bring about national pressure on Virginia's leadership over the school closures, and a resolution delivered to the State Capitol called for "a change of heart and a change of policy." Martin Luther King Jr. was supposed to attend the event, but King was stabbed in September in New York City.[53] In a letter encouraging the marchers, however, he noted: "As Virginia goes, so goes the South, perhaps America, and the world."[54]

The protest highlighted the rapidly changing civil rights milieu in Virginia. Desperate to make inroads in Virginia, CORE—a northern-based civil rights organization that specialized in nonviolent direct action—sent field-workers to the state to organize branches in late 1957 and again in early 1958. By late 1958, during the school closing crisis, CORE's efforts led to the creation of branches in Norfolk, Portsmouth, Suffolk, and Petersburg. Though its branches sought the same goals as the NAACP, namely desegregation of education and other areas of life, they also advocated a more direct approach, as represented by the march.[55]

In Virginia and elsewhere in the South, members of the various civil rights organizations cooperated, although not as kindly as one might expect. One of the principal organizers of the march was Wyatt Tee Walker, pastor of Gillfield Baptist Church in Petersburg and a protégé of the Reverend Vernon Johns, Barbara Johns's uncle. In late 1958, Walker, who also served as president of the Petersburg NAACP branch, suggested the Emancipation Day march to CORE representatives. Within a year Walker was serving as the state director of CORE in Virginia. By early 1960, he also served as head of the Petersburg Improvement Association, an organization that was related to the Montgomery Improvement Association and Dr. King's SCLC. He also continued to work with the Petersburg NAACP, and attended the national NAACP's 1960 annual convention. Late in the summer of 1960, Walker joined SCLC full-time as its executive director, a position he held until 1964. His success organizing the January 1959 Pilgrimage of Prayer for Public Schools in Richmond had caught Dr. King's attention.[56]

Shortly after the Prayer Pilgrimage, the NAACP's pending school desegregation litigation in Virginia came to a successful conclusion. On January 19, 1959, a special three-judge federal court, ruling on the Norfolk Committee for Public Schools' lawsuit, declared the state's school closing law unconstitutional. The court explained that it was unlawful for the state "to close one or more public schools in the state solely by reason of the assignment of children of different races or colors, and, at the same time, keep other public schools throughout the state open on a segregated basis."[57] That same day, in a 5 to 2 ruling in *Harrison v. Day*, the Virginia Supreme Court ruled on Attorney General Harrison's test case, holding that Virginia's constitution prevented it from closing schools and cutting off state funds to avoid desegregation. Shortly thereafter, the Fourth Circuit Court of Appeals upheld the admission of black students in Arlington, and the same three-judge district court that had voided the school closing law on January 19 enjoined officials in Norfolk from further conspiring to prevent school desegregation.[58]

Virginia's state government now needed to choose a different path, and the decision fell largely on Governor Almond's shoulders. Though extreme segregationists and the Byrd Organization encouraged Governor Almond to continue massive resistance, the governor declined. Before a special session of the Virginia legislature the following week, Almond called for the abandonment of massive resistance and the development of new policies related to segregation in public education. The governor had decided to steer Virginia in the direction of token, or minimal, compliance with *Brown v. Board of Education*. At his urging, a newly created coalition of moderates and liberals in the General Assembly prevented the passage of new massive resistance legislation and secured the repeal of the state's 1956 school closing law in late January. Upon Governor Almond's recommendation, the legislature also made tuition grants available for students who wanted to transfer into nonsectarian private schools. Shortly thereafter, authorities reopened the closed schools in the affected localities and on February 2, 1959, nearly five years after the original *Brown* decision, twenty-one black students first entered formerly all-white public schools in Virginia.

Desegregation took place first in Arlington, followed by Norfolk that same afternoon, and Alexandria the following week. Charlottesville was allowed by Judge Paul to delay school desegregation until the fall.[59]

Representatives of the Virginia NAACP celebrated the breakthrough. While cautioning that the "spirit of massive resistance is by no means dead," John B. Henderson, vice president of the state conference, allowed: "It seems that once again the voice of moderation is being heard in Virginia. This is a welcome development."[60] In Norfolk, Vivian Carter Mason, former president of the National Council of Negro Women and chairwoman of the state conference's education committee, said that "the educators, city officials, and children seemed to have joined in a spiritual union today to make this a smashing success, and we salute the people of Norfolk on this momentous and historic occasion."[61]

As might be expected, Virginians who continued to support massive resistance expressed outrage over Governor Almond's actions. Delegate Sam Pope of Southampton County called February 2 "one of the blackest days Virginia has faced since reconstruction."[62] Later that month, in a letter to one of the founders of the Virginia Committee for Public Schools, Governor Almond wrote, "I have been held up as a traitor, a Benedict Arnold, and subject to epithets too vile to mention to a gentleman."[63] On April 10, after days of "foul, abusive threats," the governor survived an assassination attempt on the Capitol grounds; the assailant was never caught.[64]

That spring, with Senator Byrd's blessing, massive resisters in the General Assembly attempted to revive the school closing legislation. The effort revealed a schism within the Virginia Democratic Party and definitively alienated Almond and his supporters from the Byrd Organization and Virginia's segregationists. Also that spring Senator Byrd refused to return Governor Almond's phone calls, and political battles between the two would occur repeatedly during the coming years. The hardliners' efforts to revive massive resistance in the spring of 1959 failed, but some of the votes were extraordinarily close—a law granting localities control over school desegregation passed the state senate 20 to 19.[65]

The new policy of Virginia's elected officials was token compliance; they sought to minimize the amount of school desegregation that would take place in the coming years. The legislature enacted a school program, promoted by Almond, known as "freedom of choice of association," which combined pupil placement policies, private school tuition grants, and locally enforced compulsory education policies. In later years, "freedom of choice" would refer to desegregation plans that allowed parents, both black and white, to choose which school their children would attend within the district in which they lived. "Freedom of choice of association," adopted in 1959, was a set of legislative policies that preceded this, which was meant to preserve as much segregation as possible and to allow parents to opt out of desegregated schools if they preferred to do so.[66]

A new pupil placement law allowed localities to begin making their own pupil assignments starting March 1, 1960, if they so desired. If not, the new pupil assignment law permitted the state Pupil Placement Board to continue its discriminatory assignment policies by removing all references to race.[67] The state's new tuition grant system also avoided any mention of race, in an effort to survive judicial scrutiny. The program allowed the state to distribute money, now called scholarships, to families with children who were enrolled in private, nonsectarian schools or in public school outside of the district in which they lived. No mention of segregation or desegregation was made, meaning that much of the disbursed money went to families whose children attended private schools for reasons other than avoiding desegregation. Modified over the years, the state's tuition grant program continued to exist until 1969.[68]

Prince Edward County, Virginia, refused to accept even token desegregation. The NAACP had renewed its school desegregation lawsuit against the county in 1956, but failed to receive adequate remedy before Judge Sterling Hutcheson. In May 1959, however, the Fourth Circuit Court of Appeals reversed the district court judge's latest ruling and ordered that desegregation begin in the county no later than September 1959. The court explained, "The proceedings of the District Court . . . and the total inaction of the School Board speak so loudly that no argument is needed to show that the last delaying order of the District Judge cannot be approved, and that it has become necessary for this Court to give specific directions as to what must be done."[69] Facing a federal court order to desegregate its schools in the fall, the board of supervisors in Prince Edward County discontinued funding for the public schools that summer, thus closing them for the indefinite future. New legislation adopted by the General Assembly in the spring of 1959, including laws allowing districts to use public school buses to transport children to private schools and allowing tax-exempt donations to private schools, tacitly supported that decision. A private school foundation, organized largely by the Defenders of State Sovereignty and Individual Liberties, created a private academy, Prince Edward Academy, for the county's white students. Many African American students went without schooling, or left the district to be educated. The county's schools remained closed until 1964, when the U.S. Supreme Court ordered them reopened.[70]

After initial desegregation in 1959, the Virginia State Conference of the NAACP continued to press for more extensive school desegregation throughout Virginia. State conference attorneys filed litigation contesting Prince Edward County's school closings, which launched the legal battle that culminated in the Supreme Court's *Griffin v. Prince Edward County* decision in 1964. Additional school desegregation lawsuits were filed in Richmond and Petersburg in 1958, and in Galax, West Point, and Hanover County in 1959. Many more school desegregation suits would follow in subsequent years, as the NAACP sought to expand the implementation of *Brown v. Board of Education* in Virginia. Local NAACP attorneys shouldered an increasing amount of the workload by preparing legal briefs, making court appearances, and working with plaintiffs. Oliver Hill, head of the Virginia State Conference's legal team, oversaw the process. For the next several years, he did so with less input from the national office, as the NAACP's struggle for desegregation shifted to the Deep South, where white resistance remained most acute.[71]

Unfortunately for the NAACP, federal judges generally accepted even the most modest desegregation plans in the late 1950s and early 1960s, in Virginia and elsewhere. This was partly because the Supreme Court showed little preference for increasing the pace. In late 1958 the U.S. Supreme Court rejected a challenge to Alabama's pupil placement law, which effectively legitimized placement policies that were used to limit school desegregation. The following year the high court refused to review Nashville's desegregation plan, which had ordered desegregation within a "grade-a-year" time frame (something Thurgood Marshall had denounced as "legally and morally wrong") and which included a transfer option that allowed white students to withdraw from desegregated schools. In the late 1950s, the high court's decisions made it difficult for the NAACP to litigate against southern school boards that often worked diligently to minimize its impact. Speaking of the Supreme Court, Michael Klarman writes, "In the late

1950s, the Court did nothing to condemn this tokenism and was widely perceived to have endorsed it."[72]

Lower federal courts and judges, of course, followed the high court's lead, accepting school plans that barely began the desegregation process. Despite the NAACP's best efforts, the result was that token desegregation remained the norm in Virginia and much of the South throughout the 1950s and well into the 1960s. In Virginia, only 4 of 128 school districts had desegregated by May 1959, and only two additional districts desegregated during the 1959–60 school year. The number of black children in desegregated schools in the state climbed at an equally slow pace, from thirty in the spring of 1959 to eighty-six in September 1959, out of a total black student population of more than two hundred thousand.[73]

As 1959 drew to a close, the Virginia State Conference of the NAACP celebrated the accomplishment of a significant victory—the initial desegregation of Virginia's public school system. Its attorneys had broken through the legislative bulwark of massive resistance and forced Virginia's leaders to accept the mandate of *Brown v. Board of Education* for the first time. Still, a vast amount of work remained. The state conference continued to face government-sponsored attacks on its leaders and supporters, which strained its resources and diverted attention from the implementation of *Brown v. Board of Education.* While it labored to defeat the state's anti-NAACP laws, the association also sought to convince the federal courts of the legitimacy of its position—that school segregation should be eliminated as rapidly and completely as possible.

FIVE

Battling Tokenism
Direct Action Protest and the Campaign for School Desegregation, 1960–1963

The early 1960s ushered in a new era of the civil rights movement. Frustrated by the slow pace of change in the late 1950s, a new generation of civil rights activists, aided by their elders, took to the streets between 1960 and 1963, launching nonviolent direct action protests against segregation throughout the nation, but especially in the South. Part of what motivated these activists, of course, was the slow pace of southern school desegregation, but their actions largely targeted segregated public businesses and facilities. During this period the Greensboro sit-ins, the Freedom Rides, the Birmingham campaign, and the March on Washington occurred. Nonviolent protests, their influence magnified by media coverage, put increased pressure on the federal government to take a stand; partly as a result, the Kennedy administration became more directly involved in civil rights issues than previous administrations.

Segregation in elementary and secondary education, however, largely continued throughout this period. Though initial desegregation had occurred in public schools in Virginia in 1959 and in every southern state except Mississippi by late 1963, the number of black students attending integrated schools remained minuscule. Between 1960 and 1963, while direct action protests confronted segregation in restaurants, theaters, transportation facilities, and other areas of southern life, the battle for school integration took place largely in southern courtrooms. And though federal court orders in the South increased the extent of desegregation taking place in public schools, the gains were small, and frustration with the slow pace of change grew in the black community.

The resilience of segregation and discrimination after *Brown v. Board of Education* had fueled some direct action protests in the late 1950s. The most notable was the bus boycott organized in Montgomery, Alabama, discussed in chapter 4. Not long after, in August 1958 in Oklahoma City, members of the local NAACP youth council demanded service at downtown lunch counters and refused to leave when denied. The youths desegregated thirty-nine businesses that year. Members of an NAACP youth council in Wichita, Kansas, carried out similar protests in the late 1950s, as did members of an NAACP college chapter in St. Louis. In Mississippi, African Americans bravely conducted a wade-in at a Gulf Coast beach in 1959. In Virginia, youth delegates to the Virginia State Conference's 1957 annual meeting presented a skit "on how to break down discrimination in department stores which have large numbers of Negro customers."[1]

One of the most important instances of nonviolent direct action of this era were the sit-ins in Greensboro, North Carolina, in 1960. On February 1, four black students from the Agricultural and Technical College of North Carolina entered a local variety store, bought several items, sat at the lunch counter, and asked to be served. When they were denied service, the four refused to leave and sat until the store closed. The following day they returned with supporters. In the coming days, similar protests occurred in cities and towns throughout North Carolina before spreading to neighboring states. By April, sit-ins had taken place in seventy-eight cities throughout the South, including Virginia.[2]

The rapid spread of the sit-ins that spring posed challenges for the NAACP. Never a mass-based organization, the association only occasionally utilized organized protest, and when it did, it generally avoided situations that led to arrest. Picketing and boycotts were acceptable techniques, but trespassing, disorderly conduct, and related activities were generally discouraged.[3] Although at least two of the original four participants in the Greensboro sit-ins were members of the youth council of the Greensboro NAACP, when the four youths contacted the head of the local NAACP—seeking advice and support on the night of the first sit-in—the NAACP leader contacted CORE on their behalf.[4]

Initially, the national NAACP criticized the sit-ins, but the association quickly changed its position. When first asked to defend arrested protestors in court, Thurgood Marshall reportedly "stormed around the room proclaiming . . . [that] he was not going to represent a bunch of crazy colored students who violated the sacred property rights of white folks. . . ."[5] Within a month, however, after the protests quickly spread and after NAACP branches and local leaders gave their backing, the national office gave its full support to the sit-in movement. In March 1960, Roy Wilkins and eighty-two-year-old NAACP president Arthur Spingarn picketed in New York City. That same month, following a conference with southern NAACP attorneys, Thurgood Marshall promised to vindicate the legal rights of student participants, by taking cases to the U.S. Supreme Court if necessary. By then the Legal Defense Fund and cooperating attorneys were representing more than twelve hundred students.[6]

Throughout Virginia, NAACP members and branches participated in sit-ins and similar protests in 1960, though the amount of NAACP involvement varied from place to place. In Richmond in late February, Virginia State Conference president Robert Robertson picketed with a sign reading, "We are in full support of the students." A week later, at a mass meeting organized to support the sit-ins, Oliver Hill added, "We must be willing to do picket duty, not leave it to just these students."[7] Hill and his wife subsequently picketed, and state conference attorneys represented arrested Virginia Union University students in court. In March, also in Richmond, the arrest of former state conference president Dr. J. M. Tinsley's wife, Ruth, made national news when photographers captured an image of her being arrested for refusing to obey orders: the image depicted Mrs. Tinsley being dragged across the street by two policemen, one with a police dog at his side.[8] In Norfolk, NAACP members helped plan demonstrations, and Milton Gay, president of the state conference's youth councils and college chapters, led them.[9] In other Virginia localities, however, such as Lynchburg, the NAACP largely avoided involvement in the sit-ins initially.[10]

To learn about the sit-in movement and monitor the situation in the South, the national office requested regular reports from its state conferences. In late May 1960, W. Lester Banks reported protest activity in eight Virginia communities, and proudly added that the demonstrations had been under the surveillance of the state conference from the beginning. That fall, Banks and state conference president Robert Robertson reported: "Since February 1960, some desegregation [in public accommodations] has been accomplished in Roanoke, Lynchburg, Charlottesville, Danville,

Petersburg, Richmond, Norfolk, Portsmouth, Newport News, Hampton, Williamsburg, Prince William County, Fredericksburg, Alexandria, Fairfax and Arlington Counties."[11] In October, at the Virginia State Conference's annual meeting, college student members led a workshop on sit-ins, featuring Frank Pinkston, a leader in the Richmond sit-in movement. Herbert Wright, the national NAACP's youth secretary, addressed the delegates of the youth councils and college chapters at the same gathering. Sit-ins and related activities would henceforth supplement the NAACP's legal efforts to secure racial equality in Virginia and throughout the South.[12]

In the spring of 1960, the sit-ins led to the creation of a new civil rights organization, the Student Nonviolent Coordinating Committee (SNCC). Organized by student leaders and sit-in participants in April in North Carolina, SNCC represented a youthful, protest-oriented wing of the civil rights movement. During the early 1960s the organization played a major role in nonviolent protests and voter registration campaigns, particularly in the Deep South.

Nonetheless, SNCC's relationship with the national NAACP was volatile and difficult. After it endorsed the sit-ins, the NAACP—as did other civil rights groups—attempted to align itself with the student leaders and, in effect, oversee their efforts.[13] Though most of SNCC's founders respected the NAACP and its achievements, they also found shortcomings in its operations. Julian Bond, later chairman of the board of directors of the NAACP, wrote in his introduction to Roy Wilkins's autobiography: "For me and many of my movement-mates, our first introduction to civil rights had come from a parent who was an NAACP activist or a community leader in the organization Roy Wilkins helped to build. My father's Life Membership plaque held an honored position on our living room wall." But, Bond continued, "As a young self-described militant in the Student Nonviolent Coordinating Committee in the early '60s, I agreed with and cheered on those who thought Wilkins and the NAACP passé. We wanted action today!"[14] At SNCC's founding conference, held in Raleigh, North Carolina, James Lawson criticized "middle-class conventional, half-way efforts" to challenge segregation, a thinly veiled critique of the NAACP. Roy Wilkins was reportedly "shocked" by the criticism, which he blamed on Martin Luther King and SCLC, who had called the conference. Over time, the relationship between the national NAACP and SNCC worsened.[15]

The NAACP's relationship with other civil rights organizations also became increasingly strained in the early 1960s. In the spring of 1960, CORE reported that "everywhere under the surface there were conflicts between the NAACP and other race relations organizations."[16] In 1961 Roy Wilkins called CORE's major campaign—the Freedom Rides—"a big mistake" and discouraged NAACP branches from helping the riders, who were using nonviolent direct action to push for the desegregation of transportation and transportation facilities in the South.[17] Wilkins later complained that in 1962, "S.C.L.C., C.O.R.E., and S.N.C.C. were all in full-fledged competition with the N.A.A.C.P., when cooperation and solidarity were obviously needed."[18]

In Virginia, other civil rights organizations were increasingly active in the early 1960s, buttressing Wilkins's concerns. The outbreak of the sit-ins helped their cause; so did the state government's attacks on the NAACP. In February 1960, CORE led workshops in Portsmouth related to the sit-ins.[19] The following year the Freedom Rides passed through Virginia, stopping in Fredericksburg, Richmond, Petersburg, Farmville, Lynchburg, and Danville. CORE's national director, James Farmer, had spent time in many of these locations in 1960—while working as program director for the national NAACP. Despite that, and the fact that the rides grew out of a lawsuit handled by the Virginia NAACP (*Boynton v. Virginia*, which voided segregation in bus and train stations), the state conference did little to help the riders.[20]

SNCC also sought to gain a foothold in Virginia. By 1962 the group had about twenty staff members, though the vast majority—and later staffers as well—worked in Arkansas, Mississippi, Alabama, and Georgia. In Virginia, the organization was mainly supported by black college students.[21] In 1961 students arrested during sit-ins in Lynchburg held "jail ins," in which the arrested students chose to stay in jail rather than accept bail, similar to those being organized by SNCC in Rock Hill, South Carolina. The "Student Non-Violent Movement" of Lynchburg also carried out protests in 1963 against a variety of segregated businesses.[22] The same year in Farmville, SNCC workers helped organize marches and demonstrations targeting segregated businesses and churches.[23] Several years later, as part of its Black Belt Project, volunteers from SNCC and related organizations, including the Virginia Students' Civil Rights Committee, registered black voters in Southside Virginia.[24]

In the early 1960s, Martin Luther King's SCLC was the most active new civil rights organization in Virginia. "Improvement associations," modeled on the Montgomery (Alabama) Improvement Association, had sprung up in several locations around Virginia in the late 1950s, and these were often converted into SCLC chapters. As elsewhere, many of the early SCLC branches in Virginia were created by individuals who had previously supported the NAACP, including Wyatt Tee Walker of Petersburg and Curtis Harris of Hopewell.[25] A statewide organization—the Virginia Unit of SCLC, or VCLC—was created in Petersburg in 1960. Although the VCLC initially concentrated on voter education and registration, over time the organization broadened its scope both tactically and geographically. King traveled to Virginia repeatedly between 1960 and 1963, and SCLC and its surrogates launched direct action protests in Hopewell, Petersburg, Danville, and Lynchburg, among other places. In late 1962, Virgil Wood, chairman of the board of the Virginia SCLC, wrote to King: "Although we do not seek to make gain from the ineptness of other State Civil Rights organizations, yet we do have a unique and unparalleled opportunity and responsibility in Virginia at this time."[26]

In Virginia, however, the NAACP remained the largest and most active civil rights organization throughout the 1960s. Strategically, the state conference cooperated with other civil rights groups when their interests were aligned, for instance, in the 1959 Pilgrimage of Prayer for Public Schools and the provisional education of African Americans in Prince Edward County while the county's schools remained closed. However, the Virginia NAACP also worked to prevent other organizations in the state from supplanting the association. After the sit-ins began, for example, the state conference allowed its youth members to organize protests with other organizations so long as the protests were "planned and guided" with help from the NAACP.[27] In Prince Edward County in 1961, Lynchburg in 1961–62, and Danville in 1963, the Virginia NAACP openly jockeyed with representatives of other civil rights organizations for influence and publicity.[28] As the *Richmond Afro-American* reported in 1962, "As in previous years, the rights fight still is spearheaded by the NAACP. The difference now is many other organizations have joined the fray."[29]

To counteract the rise of new civil rights organizations and the growing acceptance of direct action, the Virginia NAACP also became more militant over time. From Prince Edward County, Reverend L. Francis Griffin prodded the state conference's leadership to "step up our activity" in

National, state, and local NAACP representatives at an NAACP-sponsored rally at the Prince Edward County courthouse, located in Farmville, on May 21, 1961. Shown (*left to right*) are Oliver W. Hill, Roy Wilkins, and the Reverend L. Francis Griffin. (Courtesy of the *Richmond Times-Dispatch*)

1961; a mass protest at the county courthouse featuring Roy Wilkins took place shortly thereafter. In NAACP branches around Virginia, younger and more aggressive members took leadership positions in the early 1960s. In New Kent County, for example, Calvin Coolidge Green, a Korean War veteran, helped reorganize the local branch of the NAACP and became its president in 1960, in part because he was inspired by the sit-ins. Green went on to file a lawsuit demanding school desegregation in New Kent that led to an important U.S. Supreme Court decision in 1968.[30]

The national office and the state conference also supported a more assertive approach. State conference executive secretary W. Lester Banks was arrested for violating a segregation ordinance in a restaurant at the Lynchburg train station in late 1961, immediately following the Virginia State Conference's annual convention.[31] In 1963, L. Francis Griffin—by then president of the Virginia State Conference—helped organize and lead direct action protests in Farmville. There, members of the local NAACP youth council, together with SNCC activists, launched a series of sit-ins, marches, and other demonstrations aimed at overcoming segregation and discriminatory employment practices.[32] Protests such as this allowed the NAACP to maintain its position of leadership by helping to bring about the dismemberment of segregation in public facilities throughout the Commonwealth. They also ensured that the NAACP was not easily eclipsed by younger organizations in Virginia.[33]

Focusing on its strengths, the Virginia NAACP also accelerated its campaign to bring about public school desegregation in the early 1960s. After the first instances of desegregation in February 1959, the organization sought to bring about additional school desegregation, even as its attorneys challenged the state's anti-NAACP laws in state and federal courts. The result was extremely slow, but steady, growth in the number of African American students attending formerly all-white schools in Virginia in the early 1960s—a situation that frustrated both the NAACP and Virginia's segregationists.

State government officials continued to impede the NAACP's school desegregation efforts throughout the early 1960s. Having accepted token desegregation on a minimal scale when ordered to do so by federal courts, the state now sought to maintain as much segregation as possible in the public schools. The new, "moderate" policies—adopted in the spring of 1959 and adjusted in subsequent years—allowed small, or token, numbers of African American students to gain admission into formerly white schools in Virginia after a rigorous application process. At the same time, the state continued its attacks on Virginia State Conference leaders, attorneys, and supporters.

The new law allowing local school districts to make pupil assignments themselves (rather than giving that power to the state Pupil Placement Board) went into effect in March 1960, but only a handful of localities chose to take control of the process within the first year. Not surprisingly, these localities—including Arlington County, Falls Church, Fairfax County, Norfolk, and Newport News—were more accepting of school desegregation than most Virginia communities.[34] Most applications for transfer in Virginia continued to be forwarded to the state Pupil Placement Board with the locality's recommendation and, as before, the state board rejected most black applicants, citing aptitude test scores, residential requirements, and academic qualifications. Approved by federal courts in the early 1960s, this process assured that only small numbers of black students—the most academically qualified and supposedly the least disruptive—were admitted to white schools.[35]

Separate legislation passed by the General Assembly strengthened state support for Virginia's nonsectarian private schools. Such schools served as an outlet for white students fleeing Virginia's public schools in order to avoid desegregation. In 1960, donations to private schools became tax deductible, and the legislature allowed localities to provide free transportation to private school students. Other legislation exempted private school buildings from zoning and building code laws for two years and permitted the sale of surplus school property to private school foundations.[36]

At the same time, the General Assembly updated its tuition grant system to continue to allow white students who were assigned to integrated schools the opportunity to attend private segregated schools at no cost instead. By the early 1960s tax-supported "scholarships" were available to any student who wished to attend a nonsectarian private school, whether attendance was related to desegregation or not. As a result, tuition grants cost the state and localities (who shared part of the financial burden) more than one million dollars a year by the early 1960s. Paid directly to parents in an effort to shield the fact that they were the "financial life blood" of segregationist academies, the tuition grants were of questionable legality, and by then, NAACP legal efforts were under way to have them declared unconstitutional.[37]

Continued attacks on the Virginia NAACP also challenged the association's school desegregation efforts. In February 1960, as the sit-ins began, so did disbarment proceedings against Virginia State Conference attorney S. W. Tucker. For years, state officials, including the Boatwright Committee, had pressed the Virginia State Bar to do something about the NAACP's attorneys. Accused by the Fourth District Committee of the State Bar of violating Virginia's code of legal ethics for the improper solicitation of clients, Tucker faced the revocation of his law license before a three-judge court in Emporia, Virginia. The national NAACP came to his defense, sending Chicago-based attorney Robert Ming to represent Tucker in court. Other NAACP officials, including Executive Secretary Roy Wilkins, attended court hearings. After two years of legal wrangling, in early 1962 the Greensville County circuit court dismissed the charges against him. W. Lester Banks wryly commented, "The mountain labored and brought forth a mouse." In 1987, when he received a civil rights award from the Virginia State Bar, Tucker noted the irony.[38]

Despite the victory, defending Tucker had cost the NAACP both time and money at a time when both were in short supply—undoubtedly one of the reasons behind the segregationists' attack. Linking their endeavor to the implementation of *Brown v. Board of Education,* state conference attorneys continued to challenge the constitutionality of Virginia's anti-NAACP laws in court. Though federal judges had overturned several of the statutes in the late 1950s, a divided U.S. Supreme Court decided in June 1959 that Virginia's state courts should have been allowed to rule on the ordinances first.[39] The continuation of this litigation—initiated in 1956 against Virginia attorney general J. Lindsay Almond as *NAACP v. Almond*—forced the NAACP and LDF attorneys to return time and time again to state and federal courts in Virginia in the early 1960s. After the state courts refused to overturn the remaining anti-NAACP laws, NAACP attorneys again appealed to the U.S. Supreme Court, which held arguments in November 1961 and October 1962.[40] Commenting on the length of the struggle, Oliver Hill later noted that "by the time the litigation ended . . . the case had carried the names of [Virginia] Attorneys General [Albertis] Harrison, [Kenneth] Patty, [Frederick] Gray, and [Robert] Button."[41] Finally in January 1963, in *NAACP v. Button,* the U.S. Supreme Court held the last of Virginia's anti-NAACP laws unconstitutional. Roy Wilkins called it "one of the most important civil rights decisions handed down by the high court," and the *New York Times* predicted the ruling "is certain to have a wide impact."[42] For the state NAACP's legal team, the decision was instrumental in ratcheting up the association's campaign for school desegregation in Virginia.

As its campaign against Virginia's anti-NAACP laws wore on, the state NAACP experienced turnover on its legal staff. In 1960 Spottswood Robinson left the state conference to become dean of the Law School at Howard University and then a member of the United States Commission on Civil Rights. In 1964 he became the first African American appointed to the U.S. District Court for the District of Columbia, and in 1966 the first black appointed to the U.S. Court of Appeals for the District. In the meantime, in 1961 Oliver Hill took a job as assistant to the commissioner of the Federal

Housing Administration for Intergroup Relations in the Kennedy administration; he would not return to Richmond full-time until 1966.[43]

After a brief period during which Martin A. Martin chaired the state conference legal staff, S. W. Tucker took over in late 1962. Martin had served as vice chairman for several years under Oliver Hill, and may have given up the chairmanship for health reasons. A native Virginian who had been active in the state NAACP since his youth, Tucker was well qualified—and supremely motivated—to press for equal rights for African Americans in Virginia. A Howard University graduate, Tucker read for the bar on his own and passed, along with Oliver Hill, in late 1933—the two prepared for the examination together. Quiet and unassuming, Tucker was nonetheless a force in Virginia's courtrooms. After being cleared of any wrongdoing in 1962, he threw his energy into the campaign for school desegregation. He would remain head of the state conference's legal team through the late 1970s.[44]

Following the departures of Hill and Robinson, the remaining attorneys on the state conference's legal staff picked up the slack. From a height of fifteen in the late 1950s, however, their number now dropped to ten, and the organization would lose another when Martin A. Martin passed away in April 1963. Fortunately for the state conference's legal program, the all-important cadre of attorneys would grow again in the mid-1960s. By late 1965 their number had increased to seventeen, and by late 1967 to twenty-one—just as the state conference undertook some of the most important legal actions in the organization's history.[45]

Throughout the 1960s and 1970s, Tucker's principal cocounsel was Henry L. Marsh III. Marsh, a native of Isle of Wight County, alumnus of Virginia Union University, and graduate of Howard Law School, had joined Tucker and Hill's law firm in the spring of 1961. Before he took the job, Tucker warned Marsh: "Look, I'm a target. If you want to disassociate yourself from me, it will be okay." Marsh refused, and spent much of the next two decades handling civil rights cases throughout the state, even as he entered into Virginia politics. He would later serve as Richmond's first African American mayor, and then as a long-standing member of the General Assembly.[46]

Also in the early 1960s, the national NAACP updated its legal protocol. The goal was to clarify the relationship between attorneys for the NAACP and those of the Legal Defense Fund, and to formalize the division of legal work handled by the two organizations. Following the separation of the two organizations in 1957, their relationship had become confusing and, at times, difficult.

The outbreak of direct action protests and mass arrests in the early 1960s undoubtedly prompted the changes in the NAACP-LDF relationship, but turnover at the Legal Defense Fund may have played a role as well. In 1961, Thurgood Marshall departed the organization after being appointed to the federal bench by President Kennedy. Marshall served on the U.S. Court of Appeals for the Second Circuit until 1965, and then as U.S. solicitor general. In June 1967 President Johnson nominated Marshall to the U.S. Supreme Court, and he was confirmed that August, becoming the first African American to serve on the high court. In the meantime, Jack Greenberg, a Legal Defense Fund attorney since 1949 and one of the organization's few white staff members, was picked to succeed Marshall, apparently with his blessing.[47]

Even before Marshall's departure, the NAACP had begun examining the relationship between the NAACP's legal team and that of the Legal Defense Fund. In 1960 and 1961, longtime associates of both organizations, William Hastie for the LDF and Robert Ming for the NAACP, worked to develop a plan that would allow the two organizations essentially to divide the legal caseload of the civil rights movement. As Roy Wilkins explained to Carl Murphy in mid-1961, "I am in hearty agreement with the view that a harmonious and workable plan be adopted. This is no time for the NAACP family to be separated by technicalities, personalities or psychologies."[48]

In late 1962 an agreement between the two organizations was finalized, and Roy Wilkins communicated its terms to the NAACP's members and supporters. In a letter to the presidents of the organization's branches, state conferences, and youth groups, Wilkins explained that many aspects of the NAACP legal effort would not change. For example, the NAACP's general counsel would continue to handle matters having to do with the internal affairs of the NAACP, including lawsuits involving officers or units of the organization and laws or regulations affecting the NAACP as a body. Cases that differed from those, and cases with implications beyond routine matters—particularly those that offered the possibility of developing legal precedents—would continue to be handled by the Legal Defense Fund. Wilkins's letter also explained several important changes. Rather than send requests for assistance directly to the LDF, NAACP units were told to send such correspondence to the national office, which would then forward it to the Legal Defense Fund if needed. In addition, and more important, a new arrangement was put into place to coordinate the legal affairs of the two organizations at the national level. Henceforth, the chairman of the NAACP's board of directors would attend the meetings of the Policy Advisory Committee of the Legal Defense Fund's board of directors, while the executive secretary and general counsel of the NAACP would serve as advisers to the same committee. The Policy Advisory Committee's reports would also be made available to the NAACP's board of directors. It was hoped that this arrangement would allow for continued cooperation between the two organizations, particularly as related to litigation, even as the organizations remained formally separate.[49]

The Virginia State Conference's attorneys continued to conduct legal work with both organizations, but over time their relationship with the Legal Defense Fund grew more important. In the early 1960s, the NAACP's general counsel, Robert Carter, and his team remained a key partner while the Virginia State Conference continued to defend itself from state government attacks. Carter often worked with Oliver Hill, and later with S. W. Tucker. It was Carter and Hill who took *NAACP v. Button* on the path to the Supreme Court. The Legal Defense Fund also participated in anti-NAACP litigation, in part to develop precedents against southern laws. This work was handled by Thurgood Marshall initially, and later by Jack Greenberg, who worked with L. Douglas Wilder, among others.[50] In 1969, Wilder was elected Virginia's first black state senator since 1890 and later Virginia's first black governor. After the state's anti-NAACP laws were finally struck down by the high court in 1963, the state conference's relationship with the Legal Defense Fund proved more important. In the mid-1960s and beyond, state conference attorneys and those of the Legal Defense Fund worked diligently to obtain greater school desegregation in Virginia and legal precedents that would speed up the process nationwide.[51]

Also in the early 1960s, a new administration took the reins in Washington, D.C. President John F. Kennedy's election in 1960 had raised hope among African Americans, but over time many blacks became disillusioned with Kennedy's civil rights policies. Oliver Hill had campaigned for Kennedy in 1960, and Roy Wilkins noted that "everyone expected him to come in and tear up the pea patch for civil rights." Dependent on the votes of southern Democrats in Congress for passing federal legislation and on the votes of southern white citizens should he run for re-election, however, Kennedy was hesitant to press for racial equality. As president, Kennedy was also distracted by the Cold War, especially in 1961–62 when the Bay of Pigs invasion and then the Cuban Missile Crisis took place. Nevertheless, Oliver Hill lambasted the president for taking two years to sign an executive order, which he had pledged to do when running for president, banning segregation in federally funded housing.[52] Roy Wilkins, who worked closely with the president, concluded, "I did not for a moment doubt his moral fervor, and his sympathy for black Americans was real enough as well, but getting him to turn those emotions into tangible political action was a matter of an entirely different order."[53]

The pace of school desegregation remained slow during Kennedy's presidency, though the administration did take some important steps. In February 1961 President Kennedy denounced the use of school closures to avoid school desegregation, and that spring Attorney General Robert Kennedy attempted to join the NAACP's school desegregation litigation against Prince Edward County, Virginia, as a co-plaintiff, the first time the federal government had done such a thing. Unfortunately for the NAACP, which welcomed the move, federal district court judge Oren Lewis denied the request.[54] That fall the president appointed Thurgood Marshall to the federal bench, a bold move that angered southern congressmen. However, several of Kennedy's other judicial appointments angered African Americans, particularly his appointment of Harold Cox to a federal judgeship in Mississippi.[55] In 1962 the U.S. Justice Department, led by President Kennedy's younger brother Robert, filed a school desegregation lawsuit against Prince George County, Virginia, for operating segregated schools that affected U.S. military personnel, part of a flurry of similar suits filed mainly in the Deep South.[56]

Southern federal judges continued to play the most important official role in the school desegregation process in the early 1960s. Although a slowly growing number of school districts integrated voluntarily, particularly in the border states and Upper South, desegregation in the former Confederacy occurred primarily because of court decisions. Each of the eleven school districts in Virginia that desegregated between February 1959 and September 1960, for example, did so under court orders.[57] This situation highlighted the importance of the NAACP in the school desegregation process, as the association represented the principal litigants. On the other hand, the NAACP could do little without favorable court rulings. Oliver Hill later commented, "Reporters and others constantly questioned us regarding when we thought schools would be desegregated. I consistently replied that desegregated schools would exist when we got judges who would order that Negro children attend white schools."[58]

One challenge was that the lower federal courts continued to operate with little guidance from the U.S. Supreme Court prior to 1963. During the early 1960s, the Supreme Court refused to hear appeals of most lower court rulings related to school desegregation, including cases that could have provided guidance to the lower federal judges. Many legal historians argue that the Supreme Court did so deliberately because of the controversial nature of school desegregation. The lack of guidance, however, allowed for varied interpretations of "with all deliberate speed" throughout the region. As federal district court judge Walter Hoffman noted in 1957: "I haven't the slightest idea what the words 'with all deliberate speed' mean." While some southern federal judges expanded the amount of school desegregation required in the early 1960s, other courts allowed the continuation of complete segregation—as in the Deep South.[59]

Even without guidance from the U.S. Supreme Court, federal courts outside of the Deep South generally demanded more effective desegregation measures over time. Frustrated with continued southern intransigence, and prodded by NAACP attorneys, a growing number of federal judges overturned state and local pupil placement decisions and allowed blacks to skip time-consuming administrative procedures established by the states to slow desegregation. Black plaintiffs were also allowed to file more class action suits, which allowed federal judges to apply their rulings more broadly. By 1962, minority transfer provisions, which allowed whites to transfer out of integrated schools, and which had been accepted by most federal courts in the late 1950s, were often viewed unfavorably as well. The United States Commission on Civil Rights reported at the time, "It is increasingly the demand of Federal courts that an accelerated time schedule be adopted in new desegregation plans."[60]

Fortunately for the NAACP, the U.S. Supreme Court reentered the school desegregation fray in 1963, on the side of those seeking more rapid school desegregation. Just four months after it overturned the last of Virginia's anti-NAACP laws, the high court in *Watson v. City of Memphis* warned against school desegregation plans that "eight years ago might have been deemed sufficient." Justice Arthur Goldberg explained: "The basic guarantees of our Constitution are warrants for the here and now and unless there is an overwhelmingly compelling reason, they are to be promptly fulfilled."[61] A week later, in *Goss v. Board of Education of Knoxville,* the court invalidated a transfer provision it had declined to review in 1959. Also in 1963, the court waived the requirement that litigants exhaust all administrative remedies before suing in federal court. The Supreme Court now encouraged southern federal judges to demand more effective school desegregation plans to implement *Brown v. Board of Education.*[62]

The shifting judicial winds resulted in a noticeable increase in school desegregation in the South in the early 1960s. In the District of Columbia and seventeen states that formerly required segregation, the number of school districts integrating for the first time grew from 14 in the fall of 1960, to 31 in 1961, 52 in 1962, and 113 in 1963. Within these states there were approximately 3,000 school districts with both black and white students, and 979 had experienced some desegregation by August 1963.[63] South Carolina and Alabama joined the list of newly desegregated states that fall. Only Mississippi—the "last holdout" in the words of historian Charles Bolton —had yet to integrate a single public school. Nonetheless, the percentage of black children who attended desegregated schools climbed much more slowly—for the seventeen-state South the figure in August 1963 was just 8 percent.[64]

For its part, the Virginia State Conference of the NAACP continued to press for more, and more rapid, school desegregation—on a voluntary basis, through the state Pupil Placement Board, and in the courts. In 1960 the organization sought to create Education Committees in each of its local branches, in part to "encourage, stimulate, prepare and guide the applications of more students [to formerly all-white schools] throughout the state." A statewide Education Committee composed of state conference leaders oversaw the effort, in conjunction with national office staff including James Farmer, later the national director of CORE.[65] At its twenty-fifth annual meeting in the fall of 1960, the state conference resolved that "a strong and consistent program to increase applications [by parents of black pupils] to non-integrated schools and those already integrated is the number one problem of the Conference and the Virginia community."[66]

The goal was to increase both the number of desegregated localities and the amount of desegregation in areas where the process had begun. To accomplish this, state conference officials encouraged blacks from around the state to file applications to transfer into formerly white schools. In October 1960, Roy Wilkins highlighted the allure of better-funded white schools to encourage applicants. State conference officials also educated potential applicants about the process, including the annual May 31 deadline for transfer applications and the latest PPB placement policies. In the fall of 1962 approximately six hundred black students applied for transfers to formerly white schools in Virginia, and in 1963 W. Lester Banks reported that the number of applications was expected to double.[67]

When African American students applied for such transfers and were rejected, the state conference often filed a school desegregation lawsuit. As a result, the state conference's legal program picked up considerably in the early 1960s. After NAACP attorney S. W. Tucker was cleared of charges related to the improper solicitation of clients in 1962, the state conference launched a "a statewide drive to get rid of Jim Crow schools in Virginia." That year alone, the state conference legal staff filed new school desegregation lawsuits against York, Powhatan, King George, Frederick, Chesterfield, and Shenandoah counties and against the cities of Hopewell and Fredericksburg. The following spring, suits against Greene and Albemarle counties were added. In February 1963, after a one-day planning conference devoted to speeding up desegregation in the state, the NAACP announced it had more than thirty-two school desegregation cases pending in Virginia.[68]

During this period, the NAACP's lawsuits sought the admittance of African American students into formerly white schools and also the elimination of schemes designed to minimize school desegregation. The latter included local school board policies governing assignment of pupils as well as pupil placement policies overseen by the state Pupil Placement Board. As one NAACP press release explained in late 1962, "The NAACP is attempting to overcome barriers placed by Virginia's pupil placement laws which hold integration to a bare minimum."[69] Broadly speaking, the NAACP pressed local school boards to eliminate segregation and sought the right for black students to enroll in white schools should they desire to do so.

As the association's legal campaign progressed, NAACP attorneys employed innovative methods to compel compliance with *Brown*. One tactic was to seek court injunctions preventing or overseeing school construction projects in segregated, or mostly segregated, districts. In late 1961 state conference attorneys adopted this approach in a suit against Arlington

County, which had initiated desegregation in 1959 but continued to do so on a token basis. Hoping to reverse the county's practice of allowing white students to transfer out of desegregated schools while requiring black students from throughout the county to attend all-black schools, NAACP attorneys including S. W. Tucker's brother, Otto, petitioned the federal courts to police the county's construction plans. Similar arguments related to site selection and proposed school construction would be utilized by the state NAACP against a variety of Virginia localities in the coming years.[70]

The NAACP's lawsuits also sought more, and more rapid, desegregation over time. Levels of compliance that had been accepted by the association in the late 1950s, as the best to be obtained, were now rejected.[71] Thus, while a growing number of white Virginians hesitantly supported grade-a-year desegregation plans, which started integration with one grade and integrated one additional, succeeding grade per year, the association called for plans that allowed students of all ages to choose the school of their choice. When blacks in Lynchburg demanded such a "freedom of choice" plan in early 1962, one leader noted that "the Negroes in Lynchburg would have accepted the grade-a-year plan in 1954 but now 'cannot conceive anything but . . . complete and immediate integration.'" By the mid-1960s, the NAACP itself would reject "freedom of choice" plans in favor of more substantial desegregation.[72]

The national office of the NAACP continued to aid the Virginia State Conference in its effort to speed up the rate of school desegregation. Members of the state conference's legal staff had easy access to the national office legal staff and attorneys for the Legal Defense Fund. Virginia's NAACP leaders also traveled regularly to New York to meet with national office staff. In early 1960, after attending the national NAACP's annual meeting in New York, W. Lester Banks reported that "activities in all phases of the Association's program placed Virginia far ahead of her sister southern states and significantly, Virginia's production and program placed high among the rest of the Association's units."[73] At the same time, national representatives regularly traveled to the Old Dominion to meet with state conference leaders and branch officials, and national NAACP leaders attended the Virginia State Conference's annual gathering each year. In May 1962, Roy Wilkins journeyed to Virginia to celebrate the eighth anniversary of *Brown v. Board of Education* in Richmond. Alongside S. W. Tucker, W. Lester Banks, and L. Francis Griffin, Wilkins noted that the Virginia

State Conference had more branches than any other NAACP state confer-ence and continued to be one of the most important units of the national organization. Turning his attention to school desegregation, the executive secretary added, "Virginia has more token integration than any other state. You are making slow but steady progress."[74]

National NAACP school desegregation specialists also regularly visited Virginia. Special Education Assistant June Shagaloff, a social worker on the staff of the Legal Defense Fund who assisted the Charlottesville branch during its school closing crisis in 1958, also took part in planning sessions in Virginia in 1962 and 1963.[75] Determined to bring about the implemen-tation of *Brown v. Board of Education* throughout the South, the national NAACP resolved in 1962: "With a sense of immediate urgency, the Asso-ciation pledges itself to rededicate every effort toward meaningful desegre-gation by vigorously challenging the 'token' and less than token admission of a few Negro pupils to formerly all-white schools, grade-a-year and pupil assignment plans, and all other delaying plans so clearly intended to evade the May 17th decision."[76]

Over time the NAACP's efforts paid off. In the early 1960s, under NAACP pressure, the state Pupil Placement Board permitted the trans-fer of growing numbers of black students into formerly all-white schools. The U.S. Civil Rights Commission reported that the agency approved 137 applications for the fall of 1961 (even as it rejected 266). The board also began approving transfer requests from African American students located in school districts not facing NAACP litigation.[77] In mid-1962, the head of the Pupil Placement Board, E. J. Oglesby, announced that black first graders seeking to transfer to white schools would henceforth be accepted if they lived closer to a white elementary school than the nearest black elementary school. Not surprisingly, the state NAACP sought to round up as many relevant transfer applicants as possible.[78] In the summer of 1963, during school desegregation proceedings before the U.S. Court of Appeals for the Fourth Circuit, Oglesby added that the board would no longer consider academic qualifications in making school assignments. The predominant consideration for transfer applications would now be school district bound-aries and the locations of residences and schools. Though residential segre-gation patterns and other considerations meant the number of black student transfers remained small throughout the early 1960s, it grew over time, as did the number of school districts ordered to desegregate by the agency.[79]

Prodded by the NAACP, the federal courts in Virginia also gradually demanded more school desegregation, though the pace of change remained maddeningly slow in the eyes of the association. As of the fall of 1960, NAACP litigation had resulted in some school desegregation in eleven Virginia localities.[80] In April 1961, the Court of Appeals for the Fourth Circuit denied a group of black students the right to transfer into Charlottesville's formerly white schools, but warned that the city's administration of its court-approved desegregation plan "which appears to contradict its express provisions, cannot indefinitely continue."[81] When four black students applied to white schools in Lynchburg in 1961, the PPB rejected their applications because the students lived closer to black schools. As federal district judge Thomas Michie pointed out, however, numerous whites in Lynchburg lived closer to black schools, but did not attend them. Two of the black students were admitted, and the following year Michie approved a grade-a-year desegregation plan for the city.[82] In 1961 in Norfolk, federal district court judge Walter Hoffman rejected an NAACP attempt to outlaw the school board's use of academic tests — for black students only — as part of the transfer process. However, the judge added that the tests would be slowly abandoned and school desegregation would occur "gradually and pleasantly."[83]

Following the U.S. Supreme Court's 1963 school desegregation decisions in *Watson v. City of Memphis* and *Goss v. Board of Education of Knoxville*, S. W. Tucker pressed Virginia's federal courts to take heed of the high court's rulings, declaring that "the time of shadow boxing, technicalities and the labyrinth of administrative procedures has passed." Before Judge John D. Butzner in June 1963, Tucker stated it was time for Virginia localities "to get down to serious business and begin desegregating schools."[84] Judges complied, overturning grade-a-year plans and minority transfer provisions in Charlottesville and Lynchburg. In Richmond, after being reversed by the Fourth Circuit Court of Appeals in June 1963, federal district court judge John Butzner overturned dual, racially defined attendance zones and so-called feeder schools, which funneled students to racially identifiable campuses.[85]

As a result of the NAACP's litigation, state Pupil Placement Board actions, local school board decisions, and federal court rulings, school desegregation in Virginia increased during the early 1960s. In the fall of 1960, 208 black students attended school with whites in 11 districts around the state. The number of desegregated districts rose to 20 in the fall of 1961, and 29 in the fall of 1962, when approximately 1,100 of Virginia's 225,000 black schoolchildren attended school with whites. By the fall of 1963, 55 of Virginia's 130 school districts had admitted African American students to at least one formerly all-white school. Still, only 3,700 black pupils, or 1.6 percent of the state's black schoolchildren, attended school with whites that year. Though the pace of change exasperated the state NAACP and its supporters, given the South's long history of discrimination and segregation the expansion of school desegregation in Virginia represented a major accomplishment.[86]

Virginia's demographics strongly influenced the school desegregation process. In northern Virginia, white community acceptance of black students came less grudgingly, and political opposition to desegregation was less widespread, than elsewhere in the state. There, perhaps because of its proximity to Washington, D.C., or because the schools contained fewer African American students, whites were more likely to comply with *Brown* than to resist. As mentioned previously, Arlington County initially planned to desegregate its schools before the adoption of massive resistance, and after the General Assembly allowed localities to retake control of the pupil assignment process, several northern Virginia school boards promptly did so. Moreover, as desegregation increased in northern Virginia, earlier than elsewhere in the state, the number of children attending public schools remained essentially the same; no substantial movement for segregated private schools developed.[87]

The same was generally true of Southwest Virginia, which—like northern Virginia—contained few African American students. In Floyd County, the first locality in Southwest Virginia to desegregate its schools (under court order in 1960), the process was carried out "with extraordinary ease." The county school board and superintendent planned for the adjustment, even preparing the county's white pupils for desegregation, and the process was "quiet" and "orderly." Speaking of Southwest Virginia more broadly, the *Roanoke World-News* concluded that the white population would accept desegregation "with the same calm and good sense shown by the Floyd County people yesterday." As in Floyd County, however, the NAACP generally had to resort to the federal courts to bring about school desegregation in Southwest Virginia in the early 1960s.[88]

Desegregating schools in Southside and Tidewater Virginia was a more challenging endeavor. Because blacks represented a larger proportion of the population in these two regions (a majority in a handful of counties), opposition to desegregation among whites was more common and vehement. The decision of the Prince Edward County board of supervisors, in Southside, to close the county's public schools rather than integrate under court order in 1959 serves as one example of the depth of feeling (albeit not one replicated anywhere else); Prince Edward's schools would remain closed for five years, and other localities in Southside considered similar action in the early 1960s. Partly as a result, the NAACP filed fewer school desegregation lawsuits in Southside than in other areas of the state. The NAACP also hesitated to focus too much attention on Southside because of the challenges involved in recruiting black plaintiffs in that part of the state. Both the Pupil Placement Board and Virginia's federal courts, moreover, accepted the idea that Southside Virginia would need more time to prepare for desegregation than would localities elsewhere in the state. Though school desegregation began in a handful of Southside localities in 1963, the region—like the Deep South—largely avoided school integration in the early 1960s. Substantive school desegregation in this area—which W. Lester Banks described as "Virginia's most reactionary section"—would not come until the middle of the decade.[89]

Central Virginia, fittingly, occupied the middle ground between the grudging acceptance of school desegregation in northern and western Virginia and the near-total opposition in the Black Belt. Most whites in central Virginia opposed desegregation and often resisted it, but few called for resistance at any cost. By the early 1960s it was obvious that local desegregation would eventually be ordered by the federal courts, and the debate focused on the extent of desegregation required and the long-term viability of private academies. Most whites in central Virginia preferred token desegregation over having to send their children to private schools, and in the early 1960s, desegregation occurred in many localities in this region.[90]

Regardless of the region, race relations in Virginia's urban areas differed considerably from its rural counties. Generally speaking, the anonymity of city life and the large number of black residents allowed for greater black activism in urban areas. Cities boasted the state's largest NAACP branches and, therefore, commanded much of the organization's early school desegregation efforts. In the early 1960s, patterns of school desegregation in

Virginia reflected this dynamic. By 1963 black students had entered formerly all-white schools in nearly every city, including Norfolk, Alexandria, Charlottesville, Richmond, Hampton, Newport News, Fredericksburg, Lynchburg, Winchester, and Virginia Beach.[91]

Irrespective of the location, school desegregation in the early 1960s affected black students who changed schools more than it did white students. After all, white students were not transferred to black schools during the early years of school desegregation in Virginia. It was not until 1963 that the Virginia Pupil Placement Board—under judicial pressure—assigned white children to formerly black schools for the first time. This was in Hopewell, and even then the white students refused to go.[92] As a result, the first black integrators—black students admitted to formerly white schools—generally attended school without access to most of their friends, sympathetic teachers, or symbols of pride important to the black community. Many of these black students regularly faced harassment, sometimes by teachers and administrators.[93]

The experience of Carol Swann, one of two African Americans chosen to desegregate the public schools in Richmond in 1960, is indicative of the challenges faced by these pioneering black students. Swann, then twelve years old, integrated the eighth grade of Chandler Junior High School. Fortunately there was no outright violence, but decades later Swann easily recalled the resentment and animosity of her white peers: "No one dragged you out and beat you up. It was more like little tortures each day. There was name calling, and people would spit on you or trip you up. They would take the top of their ink pen and squirt the ink all over your clothes." Normally, of course, students would be punished for such actions, but Swann added: "If any adults saw it, they did nothing. The teachers didn't intervene. They didn't want us there."[94]

Attending white schools often required other sacrifices from black students in Virginia in the early 1960s. In the fall of 1961, the superintendent of schools in Charlottesville cancelled the homecoming dance after four black students at the mostly white Lane High School asked permission to invite nonstudent escorts. The following summer the school board in nearby Albemarle County voted to discontinue sports and other social activities in any school that desegregated—although none had. That same year, when the first black students attended Stafford County High School, they were asked to voluntarily forgo participating in sports or social activities. When the black students refused, the school board held the junior-senior prom off campus and cancelled the senior class trip to New York.[95]

In the meantime, as the campaign for school desegregation progressed, the broader civil rights movement picked up momentum. In 1963 black frustration with the pace of change spilled into the streets of the South as never before. In Birmingham, Alabama, SCLC-organized protests and mass arrests culminated in nonviolent protestors being attacked by police with dogs and firemen with high-powered water hoses. Press coverage, images, and film footage of the protests helped convince President Kennedy to deliver a televised speech in support of federal civil rights legislation in June 1963.[96]

The most visible result of Birmingham was the outbreak of similar nonviolent direct action campaigns throughout the South in the spring and summer of 1963. African American civil rights protestors took to the streets in their largest numbers yet, demanding the desegregation of all public businesses and public spaces, fair hiring practices, equal access to health care, and legal equality in general. More than one hundred thousand people participated in demonstrations in hundreds of cities and towns. By the one hundredth anniversary of the Emancipation Proclamation, the goal among activists was expressed in a common protest phrase—"Freedom Now."[97]

In Virginia, protests took place in many communities in 1963. Historian Paul Gaston, a professor at the University of Virginia at the time, described the beating he suffered during demonstrations at a restaurant in Charlottesville, and protests also took place in Richmond, Farmville, Lynchburg, Petersburg, Norfolk, and other locations across the state.[98] The largest campaign in Virginia took place in Danville. In early June, in a scene eerily reminiscent of Birmingham, police and newly inducted deputies attacked demonstrators with water hoses and billy clubs; dozens of protestors were injured. As national representatives from SCLC, SNCC, CORE, and the NAACP converged on the city, Martin Luther King said, "I have seen some brutal things on the part of policemen all across the South in our struggle, but very seldom, if ever, have I heard of a police force being as brutal and vicious as the police force here in Danville, Virginia."[99]

The NAACP embraced the expanded goals and techniques of the 1963 campaigns. At its 1963 annual convention, held in June in Chicago, the organization adopted a Direct Action Resolution ordering branches to initiate "picketing, sit-ins, mass action protests, selective-buying campaigns, and all appropriate constitutional means of attacking discrimination and segregation in public accommodations, housing, education, employment and political action." To encourage its less militant branches, the resolution continued: "In cases where such direct action in support of our resolutions are resisted, or hindered by any NAACP unit, immediate corrective action shall be requested of the Committee on Branches of the National Board of Directors."[100] In Jackson, Mississippi, in May, Executive Secretary Roy Wilkins had been arrested for picketing with Medgar Evers, head of the Mississippi NAACP, and at the annual convention Wilkins encouraged the NAACP to "accelerate, accelerate, accelerate" its attack.[101] In late June the Virginia State Conference of the NAACP adopted a new Direct Action Program and organized a statewide "program of application." In July, Executive Secretary W. Lester Banks was again arrested, this time for attempting to eat at a white restaurant near Halifax, Virginia. NAACP members participated in protests in Charlottesville, Danville, Farmville, and many other locations around the state.[102]

The largest demonstration of the era took place on August 28, 1963, in Washington, D.C. Two hundred and fifty thousand people took part in the March on Washington, seeking equal job opportunities and federal legislation protecting civil rights. All the major civil rights organizations participated, but beneath the surface were growing rivalries and disagreements among the civil rights groups. The Virginia NAACP encouraged its members to attend and arranged transportation for a small fee, but Roy Wilkins agreed to participate only after other march leaders promised to avoid arrests, and John Lewis of SNCC was prevailed upon to temper his remarks.[103]

Ironically, public opinion was growing more supportive of equal rights even as the civil rights organizations drew apart. After Birmingham, national polls showed a clear shift in favor of civil rights legislation. Support among southerners, however, was lacking, and this sharply reduced the initiative's chances in Congress. Kennedy appealed to governors, including Virginia's Albertis Harrison, to support federal civil rights legislation. Governor Harrison responded by telling the president, "local action and cooperation would be more effective and lasting than new federal legislation in the civil rights field."[104] Before the nation could learn whether the changes of 1963 would lead to congressional action, however, President Kennedy was shot and killed in Dallas, Texas, on November 22.[105]

That same month, Martin Luther King Jr. returned to Danville, Virginia. The summer's large antisegregation demonstrations had subsided and a tense calm had returned. Much of the city remained segregated, including the downtown business district. Tucked away quietly in the city's predominantly white schools, however, were eleven African American students who had been admitted that fall by the state Pupil Placement Board after requesting a transfer into the white schools. Their enrollment in the first desegregated schools in the midst of a tense and otherwise largely segregated city highlighted both the accomplishments of and the challenges facing the state NAACP. Fortunately for the association, its campaign to implement *Brown v. Board of Education* in Virginia was about to get significantly easier.[106]

SIX

A New "Holy Prerogative"

Freedom of Choice and School Desegregation
in Virginia, 1964–1967

The implementation of *Brown v. Board of Education* in the South picked up noticeably during the mid-1960s. Continued litigation pursued by the NAACP and growing pressure from the federal government accelerated school desegregation, as did direct action protests and demonstrations. In 1964 Mississippi became the last southern state to begin the desegregation of its public schools, and by the fall of 1966, 16.9 percent of black students in the eleven states of the former Confederacy attended desegregated schools, up from 2 percent in the fall of 1964. On the other hand, even as late as 1967 desegregation had yet to begin in many southern school districts, particularly in the Deep South, and the number of African American students attending desegregated schools within localities where it had begun remained small.[1]

The executive branch of the federal government played an increasingly important role in civil rights issues in the mid-1960s, although President Lyndon Baines Johnson's background did not suggest a powerful commitment to civil rights. Born and raised in the South, Johnson was elected to represent Texas in the U.S. Congress in the 1930s. After moving from the House of Representatives to the Senate in 1949, Johnson became Senate Majority Leader in 1955. In the spring of 1956, he was one of only three senators who refused to sign the Southern Manifesto, but Johnson was not a proponent of school desegregation. After John F. Kennedy defeated Johnson for the Democratic presidential nomination in 1960 and then asked the well-connected Texan to join the ticket as the vice presidential nominee, Roy Wilkins noted that it was to "nearly everyone's dismay."[2] That fall, addressing the Virginia State Conference's annual convention, Wilkins added, "His negative civil rights record is a long and consistent one."[3]

As president, however, Johnson defied expectations. Building on President Kennedy's ideas, and growing white support for civil rights nationwide, Johnson pressed Congress to enact major civil rights legislation, including the historic Civil Rights Act of 1964 and the Voting Rights Act of 1965. The former, passed after a nearly two-month filibuster by southern congressmen, banned discrimination in employment and in public accommodations, including hotels, restaurants, theaters, and retail stores. It had an immediate impact throughout the nation. The following year the Voting Rights Act established federal oversight of elections in much of the South and prohibited the use of procedures that had the effect of disqualifying voters based on race or color.[4] It too was monumental. President Johnson's judicial appointments—including Spottswood Robinson and Thurgood Marshall of the NAACP—also demonstrated a commitment to diversity and long-term change greater than that of any previous president. In the end, Roy Wilkins concluded, "Johnson became the greatest civil rights president in our lifetime."[5]

The Civil Rights Act of 1964 also targeted school segregation. Title IV authorized the U.S. attorney general to file lawsuits seeking desegregation, and Title IX authorized the Justice Department to intervene in lawsuits brought by private parties if it felt that doing so was in the public interest. By the spring of 1967 the agency was involved in more than one hundred such cases.[6] More important, Title VI prohibited discrimination by entities receiving federal funding, including school districts. School systems that continued to segregate could lose that money. Moreover, in April 1965 Congress passed the Elementary and Secondary Education Act, which increased the amount of federal financial support available to southern schools. The United States Commission on Civil Rights reported that in some cases federal aid made up more than 30 percent of local school funding, "so significant a portion of school budgets that it cannot be disregarded."[7]

To enforce Title VI of the Civil Rights Act, the U.S. Department of Health, Education, and Welfare (HEW) issued compliance guidelines explaining what southern school districts needed to do to avoid the loss of federal funding. The first version of the guidelines was released in April 1965 by HEW's Office of Education. In conjunction with the guidelines, HEW required all U.S. school districts to submit compliance documents by July. HEW officials would review these documents and determine if individual school districts were in compliance. For districts that had already begun to desegregate, HEW simply required the submission of a compliance assurance form. For those that had not, HEW required a locally developed desegregation plan meeting certain criteria, or documentation indicating that the district was in compliance with federal court orders.[8]

For districts submitting their own desegregation plan as a means of compliance, HEW's guidelines laid out the minimal requirements. To ensure the assignment of children on a nondiscriminatory basis, HEW encouraged districts to choose one of three pupil assignment systems: geographically based attendance areas, a choice of school "freely exercised by the pupil and his parents or guardians," or some combination of the two. Nondiscriminatory admission was required for at least four grades by the fall of 1965, and for all grades by the fall of 1967. HEW also directed localities to begin assigning teachers and administrators without regard to race, and to take steps to eliminate existing teacher segregation.[9]

For white authorities in the South, freedom of choice plans provided the most desirable means to comply with HEW, and these plans were adopted by the majority of school districts. Essentially, freedom of choice allowed districts to assign students to segregated schools unless black parents chose to enroll their children in white schools. This perpetuated segregation because many black families, faced with intimidation or hesitant to subject their children to potentially hostile conditions in white schools, chose not to demand the admission of their children into desegregated schools. By the beginning of the 1965–66 school year, 92 percent of school districts from the southern and border states had submitted compliance paperwork to HEW, and most had adopted some form of freedom of choice plan.[10]

Despite HEW's relatively modest requirements, some southern school districts refused to comply. The vast majority of noncompliant districts were small and rural, with large percentages of African Americans. As of August 1965, about four hundred districts—almost all in the Deep South —had failed to submit paperwork or had indicated they would not comply with HEW's guidelines. That fall the department began proceedings against fifty-four noncompliant districts. By August 1967 HEW had issued citations, for failing to submit acceptable assurance documents or taking inadequate steps to desegregate, to more than three hundred school boards, and more than fifty districts in the South had been deemed ineligible for federal aid because of segregation-related policies.[11]

In spite of such resistance, HEW's efforts to accelerate southern school desegregation proved more successful than the rulings of federal courts during the mid-1960s. Although federal judges in the South overturned discriminatory placement plans more regularly than before, their decisions applied less broadly and required less of a result than HEW's mandate. HEW required conformity from all southern districts in 1965 and then revised its desegregation guidelines in 1966 to demand plans that demonstrably eliminated dual school systems. The agency also proposed numerical target figures for compliance in 1966, suggesting that districts meet specific desegregation goals based on the amount of school desegregation they experienced in the 1965–66 school year.[12] In 1966 the agency highlighted the importance of results: "The single most substantial indication as to whether a free-choice plan is actually working to eliminate the dual school structure is the extent to which Negro or other minority groups have in fact transferred from segregated schools."[13]

For most of the mid-1960s, the Office of Education within the U.S. Department of Health, Education, and Welfare effectively oversaw the southern school desegregation process, as federal judges deferred to its efforts to implement *Brown v. Board of Education.* As the *Richmond News Leader* noted in 1965, "Federal courts, for 10 years the battleground over the desegregation question, slowly are stepping aside and letting the U.S. Office of Education set the pace."[14] Largely as a result of HEW's implementation requirements, when the 1965–66 school year began, 7.5 percent of black students in the former Confederacy attended school with whites, as compared to 2 percent in 1964—the largest year-over-year percentage increase since *Brown v. Board of Education.* The following year the figure rose to 16.9 percent.[15]

Despite this increase, however, concern over the effectiveness and constitutionality of freedom of choice grew over time. In 1967, the United States Commission on Civil Rights reported that freedom of choice plans "had failed" to eliminate dual school systems in the South. That same year, Judge John Minor Wisdom of the United States Court of Appeals for the Fifth Circuit expressed concern that freedom of choice plans illegally placed the burden of school desegregation on African American parents and their children. Judge Wisdom wrote that "boards and officials administering public schools have the *affirmative duty* under the Fourteenth Amendment to bring about an integrated, unitary school system in which there are no Negro schools and no white schools—just schools."[16] In 1968, frustration with the pace of change and concern about the legality of freedom of choice led the U.S. Supreme Court to retake the lead in determining federal school desegregation policy from HEW.

In the meantime, school districts throughout Virginia, fearful of losing federal funding, notified HEW of their plans to comply with the agency's desegregation guidelines in 1965. Because federal funds were paid initially to the states, and then distributed to localities, Virginia public education officials now also encouraged compliance. Motivated to secure more than sixty million dollars in federal aid for Virginia's education system for the 1966 fiscal year, the Virginia Department of Education submitted its own compliance documents, publicized HEW's guidelines, facilitated meetings between local and federal officials, and submitted paperwork from localities to HEW. By April 1965, only 5 of the 130 school districts in Virginia had failed to submit assurance forms, desegregation plans, documentation showing that they were complying with court orders, or some combination thereof to HEW. That fall, for the first time, every school district in Virginia operated on a desegregated basis.[17]

The state Pupil Placement Board also adjusted its policies to meet federal desegregation requirements in the mid-1960s. Under pressure from both federal courts and HEW, the state PPB began to approve most student transfer requests, increasing the number of black students in formerly white schools throughout Virginia, and in some cases, such as when local desegregation plans were based on geographic attendance zones, ordering white students to attend formerly black schools. In 1964, the *Washington Post* reported that the state PPB "now virtually is a funnel for the admission of Negroes."[18] Some school districts now attempted to maintain segregation by withdrawing from the PPB's oversight and establishing their own assignment policies, but most localities knew such steps would not prevent desegregation for long. Instead, most school districts in Virginia remained under the jurisdiction of the state PPB and grudgingly complied. The General Assembly, recognizing the Pupil Placement Board had outlived its usefulness, allowed the board to expire in June 1966.[19]

As in much of the rest of the South, freedom of choice plans had their heyday in Virginia in the mid-1960s. A few districts had adopted freedom of choice prior to 1965, but the vast majority adopted the arrangement in 1965 to comply with HEW's guidelines. In May 1965, the Williamsburg–James City County school board adopted a freedom of choice plan and promised "the elimination of race" in the selection and assignment of teachers and staff and the "termination of segregated buses."[20] Later that month, Nottoway County became the first in Southside Virginia to implement a freedom of choice plan. By 1968, freedom of choice plans had been adopted by approximately 90 percent of Virginia's school districts. Although local officials vocally opposed HEW's desegregation requirements and the intrusion of the federal government, the relatively modest impact of freedom of choice on school attendance patterns provided consolation.[21]

Resulting from HEW's guidelines and NAACP litigation, the pace of school desegregation increased substantially in Virginia in the mid-1960s. In the fall of 1963, fewer than 4,000 of the approximately 230,000 black students in Virginia, or about 1.6 percent, went to desegregated schools in the Commonwealth.[22] By the fall of 1964, the figure in Virginia had risen to more than 6,000, and by the fall of 1965 to more than 26,000. The latter figure amounted to more than 14 percent of the state's black students, far more than the eleven-state average of 7.5 percent.[23] By the fall of 1966, the percentage of black students attending desegregated schools in Virginia had risen to nearly 25 percent, again higher than the regional average of 17 percent. In the summer of 1967, the United States Commission on Civil Rights reported, "The Southern States with the largest percentage of Negro pupils going to school with whites are Texas, Tennessee, and Virginia."[24]

This is not to suggest that school desegregation came easily to Virginia. Several localities initially resisted HEW's mandates. Amelia County, between Prince Edward County and Richmond, was the last to submit compliance paperwork in 1965. County officials initially insisted segregated schools were more important than federal assistance, though the county would have forfeited about $240,000 of a school budget of $575,000. However, after black residents of the county filed a school desegregation lawsuit with help from the NAACP, local leaders realized that ignoring HEW would not preserve segregation in the schools. In June 1965, the county announced the adoption of a freedom of choice plan and submitted compliance paperwork to HEW.[25]

Other Virginia locales also resisted the demands of HEW. Mecklenburg County, in Southside, adopted a freedom of choice plan in 1965, but local black children who transferred into formerly all-white schools reported harassment and intimidation on the school buses. Then, in early 1967, a local black resident reported that someone had fired a gun at his home after his two grandchildren transferred to a white school. In the spring of 1967, HEW cited a number of Southside school districts, including Mecklenburg, for "poor performance"—only 1.14 percent of Mecklenburg County's black students attended desegregated schools at the time. At the end of that school year, twelve Virginia school districts had yet to comply fully with HEW's directives, and in 1966–67 HEW began enforcement proceedings against ten Virginia school boards for violations of Title VI of the Civil Rights Act.[26]

The resurgence of the Ku Klux Klan in Virginia in the mid-1960s also challenged the proponents of school desegregation. State officials had long opposed the Klan because of its extralegal methods, and Klan activity, though not unheard of, was less common in Virginia than states farther south. In the mid-1960s, however, the organization experienced a reawakening in the Commonwealth, concentrated in central and Southside Virginia. In September 1966 the Virginia State Conference highlighted its concern in a letter to branch leaders, noting "the rapidly increasing menace of the Ku Klux Klan in Virginia." The letter reported harassment and physical attacks directed at NAACP leaders, as well as those representing other civil rights groups. Confirming reports in the press, the state NAACP concluded: "Last year the KKK began its revival program in Virginia's black belt and now the Klan is getting bolder and bolder moving into our metropolitan areas demonstrating in Richmond, Portsmouth and other cities."[27]

The Klan's rebirth in Virginia was linked to the initiation of voter registration projects and the slow expansion of school desegregation in Southside. One center of Klan activity was Lunenburg County, where NAACP branch president Nathaniel Lee Hawthorne carried out an extremely active civil rights agenda. Despite "constant harassment from [the] KKK" and nine threats to his life in 1966 alone, Hawthorne canvassed door-to-door seeking black students willing to transfer into the county's white schools. The number of African American children enrolled in the county's mostly white schools that year climbed from 15 to 110 as a result. Hawthorne also successfully pressed for the transfer of black teachers to the white schools, and vice versa, as well as integrated school buses—despite a series of Klan rallies and suspicious shootings in the vicinity.[28]

In Southside and elsewhere, the Virginia State Conference of the NAACP loudly criticized the rate of school desegregation in the Commonwealth in the mid-1960s. Although HEW and the federal courts accepted freedom of choice school desegregation plans as a legitimate means of compliance with *Brown*, the NAACP strongly opposed freedom of choice and sought measures that would come at the initiative of school officials and bring about greater integration. Before the ink had dried on HEW's 1965 school desegregation guidelines, NAACP officials attacked the agency and its recommendations. As W. Lester Banks put it, freedom of choice was neither fair nor effective, but rather "a continuation of Virginia's 11-year effort to stave off school integration."[29]

While State Conference attorneys undertook legal action against freedom of choice plans in federal courts, Executive Secretary W. Lester Banks announced an acceleration of the NAACP's efforts "to bring about complete desegregation of public schools" in Virginia. In May 1965, Banks asked branch officers to "step up your efforts" to convince parents to "overcome indifference, fear and complacency" and request that school officials transfer their children into formerly white schools. In areas where school officials had adopted freedom of choice plans, Banks said parents should enroll their children in white schools at all grade levels—even if authorities had established limits on what grades were eligible (HEW initially only required that freedom of choice be applied to four grades). The state conference also distributed sample school assignment forms to educate blacks about the transfer process. Pleading for action, Banks concluded, "Let us rescue as many of our Negro children as we can while we await the Court's determination that 'Freedom of Choice' is not enough and that the school board must totally desegregate the school system." Judging by the growing number of African American students who applied for admittance into formerly white schools in Virginia in the mid-1960s, the state conference executive secretary's entreaties were successful.[30]

As Banks encouraged members, supporters, and parents to press for school desegregation, the state conference increased its legal efforts. The litigation fell largely on the shoulders of the chairman of the legal staff, S. W. Tucker, and his protégé, Henry L. Marsh III, but the two were assisted by old and new members of the state conference legal team. At the Virginia State Conference's fall 1965 annual meeting, five new attorneys joined the unit, representing important cities throughout the state. The following year, Ruth Harvey, the first female member of the legal staff, was elected, and in 1967, the membership grew to twenty-one. By then, Oliver Hill had returned from Washington, D.C., and rejoined the legal staff.[31]

The state NAACP won a key victory against Prince Edward County in 1964. County officials, ordered by federal courts to begin school desegregation in 1959, had closed the county's public schools rather than desegregate. Shortly thereafter, local whites created a private segregated academy, Prince Edward Academy, and white students enrolled in droves—paying tuition, at times, with taxpayer money provided by the state. Left without public schooling and unwilling to turn to segregated private schools as an alternative, the black community worked with the Virginia Teachers Association, the American Friends Service Committee, and a host of other organizations and individuals to meet the needs of its children. The Virginia NAACP provided financial assistance and helped establish temporary private schools, and state conference lawyers sued to reopen the public schools and to prevent the use of public money for the operation of private, segregated schools. The litigation dragged on for years, alternating between state and federal courts, before the U.S. Supreme Court conclusively ruled against county officials in May 1964. In *Griffin v. County School Board of Prince Edward County*, the justices held that the board of supervisors had violated the Fourteenth Amendment by denying funding to, and thus closing, the schools. County officials were forced to reopen the public schools in the fall of 1964, and black students returned to the public schools. However, school integration proved elusive—most local white children continued to attend the Prince Edward Academy, at their parents' expense.[32]

The NAACP had opposed the use of taxpayer money to fund segregated education in Virginia since the tuition grant program had been activated by the state legislature in 1959. Virginia's program provided financial support to parents with children enrolled in private schools, or public schools in a district other than their own, because of desegregation in their home district. In 1960, state legislation went into effect authorizing localities to provide free transportation to private school students and making donations to private schools tax deductible (from local real estate and property taxes). Other legislation allowed private school teachers to tap into the

A delegation from Prince Edward County after a hearing at the federal court building in Richmond, Virginia, on June 2, 1962. Among those pictured are (*back left*) Virginia State Conference executive secretary W. Lester Banks, (*one row from back, left to right*) NAACP attorneys Henry L. Marsh III, S. W. Tucker, and Robert L. Carter, and (*third from right*) the Reverend L. Francis Griffin of Farmville. (Courtesy of the *AFRO-American Newspapers* Archives and Research Center)

Three NAACP lawyers involved in the Prince Edward County school litigation, June 1964. Shown are (*left to right*) Frank D. Reeves, Henry L. Marsh III, and S. W. Tucker. (Courtesy of the *Richmond Times-Dispatch*)

state's pension program and permitted the sale of surplus school property to private school groups.[33] The General Assembly sought to allow white students who were enrolled in desegregated schools the option to attend adequate private, segregated schools at little to no cost instead. The creation of a number of new private schools in Virginia, many founded to avoid school integration, indicated that legislators had achieved their desired result.[34]

Initially the state NAACP linked its assault on the tuition grant program with its suit to reopen the public schools in Prince Edward County, but in 1964 state conference attorneys launched a broad attack on the tuition grant program by filing a lawsuit against the Virginia Board of Education (which administered it), the Superintendent of Public Instruction, and a number of local school boards that were engaging in the practice. *Cochyese Griffin v. State Board of Education,* or the "omnibus tuition grants case" as the suit was known, marked the beginning of another long legal battle. In a brief filed in late 1964, attorneys Tucker and Marsh emphasized the role that tuition grants played in the maintenance of school segregation. The attorneys pointed out that nearly twelve thousand white children had received tuition grants to attend private schools in Virginia during the previous school year. Many of them attended schools whose creation "followed assignment of Negro children to 'white' public schools in the community where the private school was located." Despite this, in 1965 a federal district court approved tuition grants, so long as they did not make up the preponderant source of income of a segregated school, and the state continued to operate the program. In the mid-1960s, NAACP attorneys, led by S. W. Tucker, continued with suits against individual school districts—to prevent them from utilizing tuition grants to avoid desegregation—and pursued an appeal on the legality of tuition grants in general.[35]

State conference attorneys also focused on faculty and staff desegregation in the mid-1960s. HEW supported this effort, requiring southern school boards to eliminate racial considerations in their assignment of teachers and staff. As a result, some Virginia districts, such as Williamsburg–James City County in 1965, adopted freedom of choice plans that included school employees. In many other localities, however, concerns about black staff members overseeing white students prevailed, and the NAACP was forced to turn to the courts. In their lawsuits and in court hearings in the mid-1960s, NAACP lawyers asked that teachers and administrative staff be desegregated along with the student bodies. As a result of the NAACP's efforts, the U.S. Supreme Court ruled in favor of faculty and staff desegregation in *Bradley v. School Board of the City of Richmond* in 1965. In *Bradley,* the justices directed lower federal courts not to approve desegregation plans without addressing claims of discrimination in faculty and staff assignments.[36]

In many cases the issue of faculty and staff desegregation was linked to the consolidation of schools. Facing mandatory desegregation in the mid-1960s, some southern school districts began to consolidate their dual school systems into unitary biracial systems. Especially in localities with small numbers of black students, this was generally accomplished by closing the formerly black schools and transferring the black students into previously white schools. Faced with the loss of community landmarks, African Americans often protested such closures, but often without success. In fact, the policy was promoted by federal agencies, including HEW, which reasoned in 1966: "In some cases, the most expeditious means of desegregation is to close the schools originally established for students of one race, particularly where they are small and inadequate, and to assign all the students and teachers to desegregated schools." Regardless of the cause, the closure of historically black schools was a trial that numerous black communities in the South were forced to confront during desegregation.[37]

The closure of black schools, and southern school desegregation in general, also displaced African American teachers, administrators, and staff. Rather than retain (or hire) black teachers to instruct white students, southern white school boards often preferred to employ white teachers. When Giles County, in Southwest Virginia, consolidated its schools in 1964, the change resulted in the dismissal of seven black schoolteachers. The Virginia NAACP, with the help of the Virginia Teachers Association (the African American counterpart to the all-white Virginia Education Association), sought their rehiring. NAACP attorneys filed a lawsuit in federal district court. In 1965 in *Franklin v. Giles County*, Judge Michie agreed that the rights of the teachers had been violated, but refused to require their reinstatement. On appeal, however, the Fourth Circuit Court of Appeals—ruling after the Supreme Court's *Bradley* decision—ordered the teachers rehired.[38]

Not surprisingly, the widespread adoption of freedom of choice plans in the mid-1960s was also of concern to the NAACP. Though deemed an acceptable means of school desegregation by HEW and most federal courts, the NAACP maintained, as S. W. Tucker put it, that "freedom of choice is still massive resistance, no matter what you call it."[39] Tucker felt this way because freedom of choice continued to place the burden of school desegregation on the parents or guardians of black schoolchildren. This mechanism was, therefore, not only ineffective, the NAACP believed, but also unconstitutional.

In response, the NAACP initiated a broad legal attack on freedom of choice school desegregation plans. Prior to the mid-1960s, state conference attorneys had attacked freedom of choice in localities as part of ongoing litigation, such as in Fredericksburg and Richmond in 1963. In 1965, however, state conference attorneys partnered with the Legal Defense Fund to file more than a dozen virtually identical school desegregation lawsuits in U.S. District Court for the Eastern District of Virginia. The litigation targeted Amelia, Brunswick, Charles City, Gloucester, Goochland, Greensville (home of S. W. Tucker), Halifax, Hanover, Middlesex, and New Kent counties, as well as the city of Petersburg. After the *Richmond Times-Dispatch* reported that the number of suits might grow to fifty, the *Richmond Afro-American* proclaimed, "This massive attack upon segregated public school education is believed to be the largest and most inclusive action ever undertaken to eliminate dual school systems based on race."[40]

The suits individually and collectively challenged the constitutionality of freedom of choice and the slow pace of school desegregation. The association contended that faculty and staff segregation, harassment within schools, and other considerations minimized the rate of desegregation under freedom of choice. NAACP attorneys also argued that choice plans violated *Brown II* by placing the burden of desegregation on the shoulders of African Americans; the high court had given that responsibility to the local school boards. As the NAACP explained that spring, "The suits seek to force the various school boards to adopt and implement plans for school integration, including the ending of all forms of discrimination regarding its employment policies, transportation and pupil assignment."[41]

In some cases, in place of freedom of choice plans, NAACP attorneys suggested that localities adopt geographic zoning plans. Under these plans, which were also accepted by HEW as a means of compliance with the Civil Rights Act, children generally attended the schools nearest their homes. School boards were supposed to determine the boundaries of the school zones based on nonracial criteria, and students living in a certain zone would attend schools in that area, regardless of race. The issue of housing segregation, of course, blunted the effectiveness of such arrangements in achieving desegregation, particularly in urban areas. Later, the NAACP would demand the widespread busing of pupils to establish uniformly integrated schools in districts throughout the nation, but in the mid-1960s geographic zoning plans were accepted by the NAACP—as long as the mandate to arrange and implement such plans was imposed on the school board, and as long as they were implemented fairly.[42]

The association's willingness to accept geographic zoning plans in the mid-1960s was indicative of the evolving nature of school desegregation. As shown in previous chapters, the NAACP's school desegregation objectives changed over time, as did those of federal judges and government officials from both the state and localities. Initially the NAACP sought simply the abandonment of policies enforcing segregation, as Thurgood Marshall had argued before the U.S. Supreme Court in the proceedings leading to *Brown v. Board of Education.* Then, Marshall had said, "The only thing that we ask for is that the state-imposed racial segregation be taken off, and to leave the county school board, the county people, the district people, to work out their own solution of the problem to assign children on any reasonable basis they want to assign them on." The South fought this in the 1950s, but by the mid-1960s southern whites had essentially embraced this concept in the form of freedom of choice plans. Then, as the NAACP sought, and the federal courts required, more deliberate integration measures in the late 1960s and 1970s, the South again found itself on the defensive.[43]

In localities throughout Virginia, blacks associated with the NAACP fought against the adoption of freedom of choice plans in 1965. When Albemarle County, in west-central Virginia, adopted a freedom of choice plan in the summer of 1965, a leader in the Charlottesville branch of the NAACP castigated the school board. Eugene Williams pointed out that faculty and staff segregation would continue under the board's plan, as would the existence of many all-black schools. Instead, Williams urged, the county should consider a geographic plan similar to the one adopted by the city of Charlottesville, "where districts have been revised without regard to race, and all children in a given district are assigned to one school in that area."[44]

With help from the NAACP Legal Defense Fund, state conference attorneys reached a court-approved settlement with the city of Norfolk on its school desegregation plan in 1966. The agreement, announced in March, came after ten years of litigation, and was negotiated with assistance from the U.S. Justice Department. The city agreed to abandon its previous desegregation plan, based on a combination of freedom of choice and geographic zoning, and set up nonracial school attendance zones for pupils. All faculty and staff working in the city's schools would also be desegregated, starting with the 1966–67 school year. Legal Defense Fund director Jack Greenberg called the agreement "an encouraging example of what can be accomplished if the parties to a school desegregation suit realistically face up to the issue and meet to settle their differences," and hoped the suit might serve as an example for the "other 180 communities in which the Legal Defense Fund has school desegregation suits pending."[45] While LDF attorneys sought new legal precedents by pressing forward with a small number of carefully chosen test cases, the organization hoped to reach school desegregation settlements, similar to that of Norfolk, with other localities.

While the Legal Defense Fund focused on southern school desegregation, the NAACP's national legal staff pursued separate but related objectives. Under the leadership of general counsel Robert Carter, the national legal staff initiated an elaborate assault on school segregation in the northern and western United States, even as it continued to defend the NAACP from legal attacks on its southern operations. By the mid-1960s, with the anti-NAACP laws outlawed by the federal courts, the number of actions facing the association dropped considerably, but a trickle continued to demand the attention of the national legal staff. In the mid-1960s in Virginia, for instance, the association was sued for damages resulting from an NAACP-supported selective buying campaign related to Klan violence in the town of Victoria, in Lunenburg County. The case, *Hornstein v. NAACP,* was the only Virginia case on the national legal department's docket between 1965 and 1967, and in mid-1967, it was resolved in favor of the NAACP.[46]

At the same time, attorneys for the Legal Defense Fund had their hands full in Virginia. By early 1966, the LDF boasted an annual budget of nearly two million dollars and claimed to handle 95 percent of all southern civil rights litigation not handled by the U.S. Justice Department. Partly because of its assault on freedom of choice plans, waged in conjunction with attorneys for the Virginia State Conference, the LDF was handling more than 175 mostly southern school desegregation cases by early 1966. On its docket that fall were 22 Virginia school desegregation cases, including all of the recently filed lawsuits challenging the constitutionality of freedom of choice plans.[47]

The most important new school desegregation case filed by the Virginia State Conference, in conjunction with the Legal Defense Fund, arose in New Kent County, just east of Richmond. The local NAACP branch, which was separated from the two-county Charles City–New Kent branch in 1960 at the request of Calvin Coolidge Green, had pressed county officials to begin desegregation in the early 1960s, to no avail. Instead, county officials continued to bus children of both races long distances to attend segregated schools. Shortly after the passage of the Civil Rights Act of 1964, however, Green attended an NAACP meeting in Richmond. At that gathering, state conference attorneys explained their desire to file a new round of school desegregation lawsuits throughout Virginia. Green, a Richmond school-teacher with three young sons, volunteered to sponsor such a suit in New Kent County. In March 1965, after local school officials rejected a petition to begin desegregation, state conference lawyers filed *Charles C. Green v. County School Board of New Kent County*, named after Calvin Green's youngest son, in federal district court.[48]

As expected, the filing of the *Green* lawsuit angered New Kent County's white population. Local officials, and even conservative New Kent blacks, pressed Green to withdraw the suit. When he refused, the county chose not to renew his wife's contract as a teacher, though she had been employed by the county for ten years. The decision placed the family in financial jeopardy. Threats and intimidation against other New Kent black leaders also increased, and several, including Green, made it known that they would defend themselves in the event of physical attacks.[49] Green explained, "I knew from history and other kinds of things that people who filed suits were in great danger and we soon . . . we found ourselves in it."[50]

Faced with the NAACP lawsuit and pressure from HEW, county officials grudgingly adopted a freedom of choice plan in the summer of 1965. The plan allowed students to choose between the county's heretofore all-black school, the George W. Watkins School, and the county's all-white school, the New Kent School. In August 1965, thirty-five black students enrolled in the latter for the first time. Over the course of the next several years, however, most blacks in New Kent County continued to enroll their children in the all-black Watkins School. African American enrollment in the formerly all-white school rose to 111 in 1966 and 115 in 1967. Still, this represented only 15 percent of the county's black student population, and no white student transferred to the black school. In New Kent County, as elsewhere around the South, freedom of choice did not lead to substantial school desegregation.[51]

The reasons for the failure of freedom of choice in New Kent County mirrored its failure in other locales. First, the desegregation process was hard on black students, and by extension, on their parents. Some white students threw spitballs at the black students in New Kent; others pushed them in the hallways. Many white students simply ignored their new classmates. One of the first black students to attend the New Kent School, Cynthia Gaines, recalled: "I tried out for the girls' basketball team, and I was the first black girl to ever play basketball for New Kent. But . . . no one would sit by me on the bus the entire basketball season; I don't care if we went to Mathews, Middlesex, Yorktown, for miles no one would sit by me on the bus. And they would sometimes sit three in a seat to keep from sitting by me on the bus, so after a while you just had to make things funny so you wouldn't be hurt. So I would cross my legs, stretch out on the seat, put my suitcase up, and prop my feet up and just ride."[52]

Adding to the difficulties, white teachers and administrators often showed little inclination to help, or even to teach, the African American students—in New Kent and elsewhere. Shortly after the 1965 school year began in Franklin, Virginia, the president of the local NAACP branch wrote NAACP executive secretary Roy Wilkins to express concern over the actions of a white teacher. Glaring at one of the new African American students, the teacher had demanded: "What do you want me to call you, colored or nigger?" By contrast, in the black schools most students knew the teachers and staff, and recollections of segregated black education during this era often include fond reminiscences of teachers who cared for and mentored their students. Many black students also preferred attending school with their friends, with whom they could study and enjoy school functions. In the white schools, a feeling of hostility and resentment often prevailed, and those blacks who were the first in their communities to desegregate formerly all-white schools remember the experience as a trying one. As Dr. Francis Foster, whose daughter Carmen attended Thomas Jefferson High School in Richmond in 1965, put it, "I guess I would describe myself as the father of a sacrificial lamb."[53]

Lawyers for the Virginia State Conference developed and handled the *Green* case, with assistance from Jack Greenberg and James Nabrit Jr. of the Legal Defense Fund. S. W. Tucker and Henry Marsh did much of the work, though they were joined by Oliver Hill when he moved back to Richmond and rejoined the state conference legal staff in 1966. In the original suit, the NAACP attorneys pointed out that the county's schools remained 100 percent segregated eleven years after *Brown*; subsequent iterations of the suit pointed out that the county had adopted its freedom of choice plan in the fall of 1965 only under duress. More to the point, the plan was not producing appreciable school desegregation, even as late as 1967.[54]

The NAACP hoped that questions about the effectiveness and constitutionality of freedom of choice would sway the federal courts, which were divided on the acceptability of such plans in the mid-1960s. Though most federal judges continued to endorse freedom of choice plans, a growing number were critical of this form of pupil assignment. Judge Thomas J. Michie of the federal district court of western Virginia fell into the former category. When NAACP attorneys asked in 1965 that he order the school board of Frederick County to take the initiative in desegregating the county's schools, meaning that the court require the board to develop and implement a proactive desegregation plan, Michie responded, "It is clear that the plaintiffs in this case are simply asking this court to force the school authorities to force Negro students into totally integrated county schools which they have voluntarily chosen not to attend." Michie denied the NAACP's request.[55]

Also in 1965, however, in *Bradley v. School Board of the City of Richmond*, Judges Simon Sobeloff and J. Spencer Bell of the United States Court of Appeals for the Fourth Circuit wrote that "the initiative in achieving desegregation of the public schools must come from the school authorities. . . . Affirmative action means more than telling those who have long been deprived of freedom of educational opportunity, 'You now have a choice.'" The two judges partially dissented in *Bradley*, arguing in favor of faster faculty and staff desegregation while giving the city the opportunity to determine whether its freedom of choice plan would achieve the desired result. The following year, Judge John Minor Wisdom of the United States Court of Appeals for the Fifth Circuit added a stinging criticism of freedom of choice plans in a ruling that ordered the New Orleans school board to abandon such policies, which had failed to desegregate the local schools.[56]

Still, federal district court and appeals court judges hesitated to overturn freedom of choice without precedent, or guidance from the Supreme Court, and so the federal judiciary continued to endorse such plans throughout the mid-1960s. The courts may also have accepted freedom of choice plans because they were clearly an improvement over previous methods of school desegregation. Questions of legality aside, freedom of choice plans led to more school desegregation in the South in the mid-1960s than any earlier assignment policies. In the New Kent County case, the federal district court ruled against the NAACP in 1966, as did the United States Court of Appeals for the Fourth Circuit the following year. Both courts ruled, not incorrectly, that the county's desegregation plan fulfilled currently accepted judicial (and HEW) standards.[57]

Despite the amount of school desegregation achieved under freedom of choice, the lower court rulings in *Green v. New Kent County* were disappointing to the NAACP. Following the United States Court of Appeals for the Fourth Circuit's decision in June 1967, the association's attorneys debated whether to take the *Green* case to the U.S. Supreme Court. By then, state conference attorneys had a number of related civil rights cases before the federal courts, and it was important to choose carefully which cases to appeal. As a test case, to show that current desegregation programs — including "freedom of choice" — were not working, *Green* had a lot to offer. Until 1965, the school board deliberately maintained segregation by busing children of both races long distances to attend racially designated schools. Subsequently, the county's freedom of choice plan had not substantially altered the racial makeup of the schools, so the case against the effectiveness of freedom of choice was strong. "We had all these school cases, and we wanted to get a case to be the pilot case so the Supreme Court could really break the logjam," former state conference attorney Henry L. Marsh III later recalled. "New Kent was the logical choice." The NAACP filed an appeal in *Green v. New Kent County* with the U.S. Supreme Court in October 1967, and two months later the high court agreed to hear the case.[58]

SEVEN

The *Green* Light

The NAACP and School Integration in Virginia, 1968–1974

By the late 1960s, the Virginia State Conference of the NAACP had helped to bring about a dramatic rise in the amount of school desegregation in the Commonwealth. Supported by the Civil Rights Act of 1964, and subsequent compliance guidelines issued by the U.S. Department of Health, Education, and Welfare (HEW), a growing number of African American students had entered formerly white schools in Virginia during the mid-1960s. In the spring of 1968, HEW ranked Virginia second of the eleven states of the former Confederacy, behind only Texas, in the percentage of black students attending desegregated schools. Still, like the national NAACP, the members and leaders of the Virginia State Conference sought greater racial mixing in the state's public schools. By the late 1960s, their goal had advanced beyond the elimination of segregation from education; now the NAACP sought judicial decrees requiring districts to proactively develop and implement plans to eliminate any vestiges of dual school systems. In the language of today, the desired end had shifted from desegregation to integration, meaning school systems that could not be distinguished by race, in which black and white students commingled and interacted as equals.[1]

In May 1968 the Virginia State Conference legal staff, with help from the NAACP Legal Defense Fund, won yet another major U.S. Supreme Court victory. With *Charles C. Green v. County School Board of New Kent County*, the high court reentered the desegregation fray and demanded that school boards throughout the South initiate plans that would lead to quick and complete desegregation. Afterward, the Virginia State Conference of the NAACP used the *Green* decision to convince federal court judges to require more effective and comprehensive integration plans throughout the Commonwealth.

One means of achieving school integration, however, greatly angered many white Virginians during this era. By the early 1970s, the busing of students, which had been used to maintain segregated schools for generations, was sometimes required by federal judges to integrate school districts —particularly in urban areas where residential segregation resulted in mostly white and mostly black schools. For many whites, however, busing meant long-distance rides and enrollment in predominantly black schools. Busing imposed parallel hardships on blacks, which generated some opposition to busing among African Americans, but the likelihood of gaining access to better educational opportunities limited African American concerns. In Virginia and elsewhere, a large and vocal movement against busing developed, supported by white segregationists, moderates, and even white liberals. Over time, opposition to busing fueled a backlash against school integration that challenged the accomplishments of the Virginia NAACP and the civil rights movement more broadly.

As explained in the previous chapter, the expansion of school desegregation during the mid-1960s came about because of growing pressure on the South from the federal courts and the federal government, both of which were pushed by the NAACP. During these years, however, the amount of desegregation in the South was limited by the fact that both the federal courts and HEW approved of the use of freedom of choice school desegregation plans. In the spring of 1968, by HEW's own estimate, only 14 percent of the black pupils in the eleven former states of the Confederacy attended desegregated schools. Though the agency calculated this figure in a different manner than the United States Commission on Civil Rights, making a precise comparison with earlier years impossible, it was clear that freedom of choice plans had failed to bring about school integration. The critics of freedom of choice plans added that it was unfair—and illegal—to place the burden of school desegregation on the shoulders of African Americans, as such plans did.[2]

Questions about the effectiveness and the legality of freedom of choice plans led the federal government to demand new methods of school deseg-

regation in the late 1960s. In the latest iteration of its school desegregation guidelines, announced in March 1968, HEW suggested that districts
adopt geographic attendance zones, not based on race, instead of freedom
of choice plans, as a means of complying with the Civil Rights Act of 1964.
As HEW noted, freedom of choice plans had proven largely ineffective at
bringing about unitary school systems. The agency added that southern
school districts that had not ended segregated schooling by the start of the
1969 school year would face a cutoff of federal funds for education.[3]

Just two months later, the U.S. Supreme Court offered additional support
for abandoning freedom of choice plans, handing down the first of three
significant school desegregation decisions that altered education policies
throughout the United States. By addressing school desegregation issues
after a long period of relative noninvolvement, the high court reclaimed
control of the desegregation process for the federal judiciary and provided
guidance to lower-level federal judges. As S. W. Tucker explained it, the
high court had "cleared away the smoke and let the lower courts see what
they meant." HEW, which had led the campaign to increase southern
school desegregation since 1965, now began to play a more supportive role
while federal judges largely determined school desegregation policy in the
late 1960s and 1970s. On the fifteenth anniversary of *Brown v. Board of
Education*, Hamilton Crockford of the *Richmond Times-Dispatch* noted,
"The justices had finally caught up with what HEW had been maintaining
all along."[4]

The first major Supreme Court decision of the late 1960s affecting school
desegregation was *Charles Green v. New Kent County, Virginia*. Filed in
federal district court in Virginia in the spring of 1965, *Green* asked federal
judges to force New Kent school officials to initiate and implement a plan
that would lead to greater school desegregation than had been accomplished
under the county's freedom of choice system. After losses at the federal
district court and circuit court of appeals levels, Virginia State Conference
and Legal Defense Fund attorneys took *Green* to the U.S. Supreme Court
in 1967. The Supreme Court heard oral arguments in *Green* the day before
the assassination of Martin Luther King Jr. and handed down its decision
on May 27, 1968.[5]

The ruling was a significant victory for the NAACP. In *Green*, the Supreme Court found that New Kent County had deliberately violated *Brown*
and *Brown II* for more than a decade by operating two school systems, one

black and one white, down to "every facet of school operations — faculty, staff, transportation, extracurricular activities and facilities." Furthermore, and more important, the court found that the county's freedom of choice plan — adopted under pressure from the NAACP and HEW in 1965 — had failed to produce significant desegregation, and that "rather than further the dismantling of the dual system, the plan has operated simply to burden children and their parents with a responsibility which *Brown II* placed squarely on the School Board."[6]

In the unanimous ruling, the justices also expressed frustration with continued attempts by southern whites to prevent or minimize school desegregation. Discussing New Kent County's freedom of choice plan, for instance, Chief Justice William Brennan, author of the opinion, wrote, "It is relevant that this first step did not come until . . . 10 years after *Brown II* directed the making of a 'prompt and reasonable start.'" The justices unambiguously ordered the county school board to develop a plan that "promises realistically to work, and promises realistically to work now."[7]

The justices in *Green* did not rule that freedom of choice plans were in and of themselves unconstitutional. However, they did say that, where other methods of desegregation promised to be more effective, they were preferable. In most southern school districts this meant that more effective techniques, such as geographic zoning, unitary school systems, or busing, would be required. Justice Brennan explained that "if there are reasonably available other ways . . . promising speedier and more effective conversion to a unitary, nonracial school system, 'freedom of choice' must be held unacceptable." In addition, the court made it clear that it was the school board's responsibility to develop and implement such plans, as opposed to placing the burden on the shoulders of African American parents or their children, as freedom of choice had done.[8]

In *Green* and in subsequent rulings, the Supreme Court also emphasized the importance of results. In other words, starting in 1968 the legality of school desegregation plans would depend largely on their effectiveness in promoting integration in the local schools. In *Green,* the court listed six factors that could be used to measure success: the composition of the student body, faculty, and staff; and the accomplishment of integration in school transportation, extracurricular activities, and facilities. The goal, wrote Justice Brennan, was "a system without a 'white' school and a 'Negro' school, but just schools."[9]

Importantly, the *Green* decision altered how school desegregation was defined and what the process entailed. As defined in *Brown v. Board of Education*, desegregation meant removing or eliminating mandatory segregation. To comply, school districts were required to remove racial distinctions and discrimination from their pupil assignment policies. As Spottswood Robinson argued in court proceedings on school desegregation in Prince Edward County, Virginia, in 1955, the NAACP sought "desegregation, in the sense of removing the stipulation of race as a factor in public school operations, rather than integration, which he called the 'compelled mixing of pupils.'"[10] *Green*, however, transformed *Brown*'s prohibition of segregation into a requirement that school boards develop and implement ways of bringing about racial integration in their schools. As the *Los Angeles Times* reported, "In *Green v. New Kent County*, racial considerations have somehow been restored."[11] The change was based on the high court's continued frustration over southern resistance to school desegregation and was influenced by the appointment of new justices (such as Thurgood Marshall in 1967) to the Supreme Court. The new interpretation of *Brown* was different from the original, and widely recognized, interpretation, and the change prompted Supreme Court justice William H. Rehnquist to later refer to *Green* as a "drastic extension of *Brown*."[12]

Although they had been hesitant to accept freedom of choice desegregation plans in the mid-1960s, white southerners had grown to support freedom of choice over time. The approach did not lead to significant school desegregation, yet it preserved the flow of federal funds into southern schools. By June 1968, the *Norfolk Journal and Guide* reported that 90 percent of all southern schools were using freedom of choice plans.[13] Not surprisingly, when the Supreme Court demanded that southern officials develop more effective desegregation plans, white southerners rallied around freedom of choice as never before. Legal scholar J. Harvie Wilkinson III noted the irony: "What was unthinkable five or six years ago suddenly assumed, in light of more threatening alternatives, the status of holy prerogative."[14] James Jackson Kilpatrick predicted that "the court, in its own omnipotent fashion, might as well undertake to reverse the orbit of the earth around the sun."[15]

Many whites in New Kent County were also distressed by the opinion. Almost immediately, a number of local teachers and students threatened to leave the county's public schools for nearby private, segregated academies. In the end, about 30 percent did. Shortly after the decision, when Calvin Green and other plaintiffs held a celebration dinner at the all-black Watkins School, a cross was burned on the front lawn.[16] School superintendent H. Kenneth Brown struggled to preserve the county's public school system by complying with the Supreme Court's decision, but at a pace more palatable to the white population. In June 1968, county officials announced a new school desegregation plan that would integrate the county's teachers and school workers that fall, but would not integrate the students until the fall of 1969. Federal district court judge Robert R. Merhige initially rejected the timetable, but the judge then visited the county to investigate. The trip convinced Judge Merhige that local whites were sincere in their efforts to comply, and he later noted that some local black leaders also accepted the delay. After touring New Kent County's schools and holding discussions with school personnel in August, Judge Merhige approved the county's desegregation plan.[17]

The plan adopted by county officials created a unitary school system using a technique many rural southern districts would emulate in the coming years. Starting in 1969, the county's formerly white school served as the middle and high school, and the formerly black school served as the county elementary school. All students, regardless of race, now attended one school or the other, depending on their age. This eliminated the formerly racial identities of the county's schools. In rural areas throughout Virginia, and elsewhere in the South, compliance with the Supreme Court's mandate in *Green* was accomplished similarly.[18]

Increasingly, however, school integration came at a cost to African American communities, in Virginia and around the nation. The process was usually overseen by white public officials, and decision making was not always evenhanded. In New Kent County, without input from citizens, officials stripped the formerly black school of its name in 1969. Presumably they did not want white children attending a school named for George W. Watkins, a well-respected black leader and longtime principal. At about the same time, Prince Edward County officials renamed the formerly all-black Robert Russa Moton School, which had been named after Booker T. Washington's successor as head of Tuskegee Institute, who was a native of the county. The following year the Bedford County NAACP branch held a mass meeting and submitted an appeal to the school board to protest the renaming of Susie G. Gibson High School. Though the board refused to rescind its decision, it agreed to name the school's auditorium in honor of the former supervisor of the county's black schools.[19]

Elsewhere in Virginia black schools were closed or converted into lower-level schools as a result of integration, and black teachers and administrators suffered. In Lynchburg, local blacks protested when Dunbar High School, which had been central to the black community for decades, was converted to a middle school. As the U.S. Civil Rights Commission reported in 1972, "Minority schools have been closed in carrying out desegregation plans while previously white schools have remained in use. Often it has been the minority senior high school that has been converted to a desegregated junior high school."[20]

Furthermore, African American teachers and administrators were often fired or demoted when formerly black schools were converted, closed, or integrated. The NAACP often contested this development, as in the case of Giles County, Virginia, discussed previously. Nonetheless, one federal study found that the number of black secondary school principals in Virginia declined from 107 to 17 between 1965 and 1971, and in Fredericksburg, one longtime educator later recalled that as a result of integration, "Many African American administrators were demoted."[21] In early 1969 in Spotsylvania County, the NAACP branch protested the school board's policies for hiring and promoting teachers. Claiming the procedures were discriminatory, branch president Charles Franklin noted that the percentage of black teachers in the county's schools had dropped from 26 percent to 13 percent and that black teachers were being replaced by whites "at an alarming rate."[22]

Even when districts were supposedly integrated, problems within schools often plagued black students. In the early 1970s, the Virginia State Conference and the Legal Defense Fund worked diligently to address such matters, which were sometimes referred to as "second-generation problems." In Greensville County in 1970, for instance, the mostly white school board continued to maintain segregated school buses, assign African American students to all-black classrooms, and confine a disproportionate number of black schoolchildren to the county's special education building. In Hanover County, the NAACP branch successfully interceded to change the name

An all-black seventh grade class at Robert Russa Moton High School in Farmville, Virginia, in March 1969. The U.S. Supreme Court ordered Prince Edward County to reopen its public schools in 1964, but most of the county's white residents continued to send their children to a segregated private academy. In 1969, the county's population was roughly 36 percent African American, but its public school enrollment was approximately 99 percent African American. (Courtesy of the *AFRO-American Newspapers* Archives and Research Center)

of the football team; not surprisingly, black players objected to playing for the Confederates.[23]

   The continued struggle for fair treatment and equal educational opportunities led to frustration, and resentment, among African Americans. Nearly twenty years after *Brown v. Board of Education,* the fight demanded patience and fortitude beyond what might have been reasonably expected. One result, especially common among younger African Americans, was to question the value of integration. This was not a new phenomenon, of course; some African Americans had questioned the value of integration in previous generations, and others questioned the NAACP's commitment to *Brown v. Board of Education.* In the late 1960s, the state and national NAACP continued to strongly promote the need for school integration—not to attend school with whites, but to obtain the best educational opportunities. At times, however, the vehemence of their arguments belied the fact that growing numbers of African Americans questioned the approach.

One letter to the editor in the *Richmond Afro-American* in early 1970 pointed out simply that "a lot of black people have soured on the concept of integration."[24]

Despite these challenges, the Virginia NAACP pressed immediately for statewide implementation of the *Green v. New Kent County* ruling. S. W. Tucker, chairman of the Virginia State Conference legal staff, said, "We hope that the school boards will implement the law all over the state of Virginia with the beginning of the next school session."[25] The day after *Green* was handed down, Tucker paid a visit to federal district court judge Robert R. Merhige in Richmond. The high court had ordered the district court to maintain oversight of the *Green* case, and the NAACP attorney brought with him an armful of similar desegregation cases he wanted reopened in the wake of *Green*. In August, however, Tucker was disappointed when Judge Merhige allowed New Kent County to delay full integration until the fall of 1969. That summer, the NAACP attorney initiated litigation seeking complete school integration in more than a dozen Virginia localities, all of which operated under freedom of choice, as quickly as possible—by the fall of 1969 at the latest.[26]

Tucker's effort to bring about complete school integration in Virginia at the earliest practicable date mirrored the efforts of national NAACP attorneys. Like Tucker and Marsh, Legal Defense Fund attorneys expressed deep satisfaction with the new mandate, particularly the fact that it shifted the burden of implementation to local school boards and emphasized results. In New York, Jack Greenberg happily explained that "the time for deliberate speed has expired." Greenberg added that the *Green* case would be used to reopen most of the organization's two hundred pending school desegregation suits in the South.[27]

As the NAACP's new, and renewed, school desegregation litigation wound its way through the federal courts, the impact of the *Green* decision spread beyond the borders of New Kent County. Because it altered what school desegregation entailed and emphasized the role of the federal judiciary, *Green v. New Kent County* transformed the school desegregation milieu of the late 1960s. Afterward, the number of southern black students attending integrated schools skyrocketed. One study of school desegregation in the United States explains: "The results were startling. In 1968–69, 32 per cent of black students in the South attended integrated schools; in 1970–71, the number was 79 per cent."[28] Acknowledging the

Federal district court judge Robert R. Merhige Jr. chats with students at Peabody High School in Petersburg, Virginia, in March 1969. Merhige was making an inspection of Petersburg's high schools as part of court deliberations following *Green v. New Kent County*. (Courtesy of the *Richmond Times-Dispatch*)

decision's impact, historian and legal scholar Davison Douglas calls *Green* "the Court's most important school desegregation opinion since *Brown*."[29]

Across Virginia, school boards adjusted their policies to achieve the Supreme Court's new mandate in the late 1960s. Virginia NAACP attorney Henry Marsh later recalled: "That's when we had real meaningful desegregation—all over in 1968. Before we had the [*Green*] decision, desegregation was stymied because you only had desegregation where you had black applicants willing to run the gauntlet in white schools. After *Green v. New Kent*, as long as 'freedom of choice' was not working, it was unlawful. So . . . that was a crucial case."[30] Using geographically based school zones in which the entire district constituted a single zone, as in New Kent County, a number of school boards integrated their schools in 1968, including the city of Fredericksburg and Spotsylvania and King George counties, all to the north of Richmond. Other localities waited to integrate until ordered by the courts, which generally delayed the process until the fall of 1969. After losing a court battle to maintain its freedom of choice plan, for example, Powhatan County, a short distance west of Richmond, merged its black and white schools in the autumn of 1969. The result of *Green v. New Kent County* was a substantial rise in school integration in Virginia at the end of the decade.[31]

In the meantime, separate Virginia State Conference litigation ended Virginia's tuition grant program, which since 1959 had provided taxpayer-funded financial support to parents with children enrolled in public schools outside their district or in private schools. Perhaps the most famous such institution was Prince Edward Academy, created in 1959 when the county closed its public schools rather than desegregate under court order, but dozens of other "segregation academies" had been created in Virginia since the 1950s. Predictably, the NAACP challenged the right of the state to fund such segregated institutions indirectly, particularly since part of the tax money involved came from the state's black citizens.

In 1964, NAACP attorneys had launched a broad-based legal attack on the tuition grant program by bringing suit against state and local officials that were engaged in the practice. Subsequent court rulings on the case restricted the use of tuition grants to schools that obtained the majority of their funding from other sources, but failed to end the program. As a result, tuition grants continued in Virginia into the late 1960s, even as federal courts in other states invalidated similar programs. In response, Virginia State Conference and Legal Defense Fund attorneys used legal action against individual school districts to prevent them from utilizing tuition grants to avoid desegregation, while also challenging the legality of the tuition grant program in federal courts. Finally, in February 1969, the same panel of three federal judges in Virginia that had approved the program in 1965, with caveats, found the state's tuition grant program unconstitutional. Basing its decision on federal court rulings in the intervening years, the court explained that "any assistance whatever by the State towards provision of a racially segregated education exceeds the pale of tolerance demarked by the Constitution." After ten years and twenty million dollars in grants, the program ended on June 30, 1969.[32]

The NAACP's campaign to bring about school integration in the South benefitted from support from HEW and the Department of Justice in the period after *Green v. New Kent County* was handed down. Shortly after the decision was rendered, the Department of Justice asked federal courts to require 160 southern school districts to abandon their freedom of choice plans in favor of more effective measures. In Virginia, the agency sued 2 school districts in late 1968, with the same goal in mind. At the time, both Sussex County and the city of Franklin continued to operate school systems in which more than 90 percent of black students attended all-black schools.[33] The following year, the department filed an unprecedented lawsuit seeking to bring about integration throughout the entire state of Georgia, leading James Jackson Kilpatrick to conclude: "Plainly, the government means business."[34] HEW, too, ratcheted up its pressure on southern school boards after *Green,* by withholding federal funds from districts that refused to adopt unitary school systems. By June 1968 funds had been cut off to 52 districts in the South and another 107 districts had been cited for noncompliance—meaning that the process of cutting off federal funds had been initiated. In May 1968, the *Richmond Times-Dispatch* reported that federal school aid had been cut off to 7 Virginia districts and that cutoffs were pending in another 4 districts.[35]

Over time, however, political considerations affected the NAACP's campaign for southern school desegregation. In the presidential election campaign of 1968, Republican candidate Richard M. Nixon employed a "southern strategy" to win the support of southern white voters. Nixon expressed support for freedom of choice desegregation plans despite the U.S. Supreme Court's decision in *Green,* and claimed to support a "middle course on integration" as opposed to "immediate integration" or "segregation forever." The approach worked, and five southern states, including Virginia, handed their electoral college votes to the Republican candidate—part of a broader realignment of southern white politics following the passage of the 1965 Voting Rights Act. Like many other African Americans, however, Roy Wilkins of the NAACP expressed chagrin: "It was beyond me how he could talk about 'instant integration' when we were fifteen years beyond the *Brown* decision."[36]

Despite Wilkins's displeasure, and that of African Americans nationwide, Nixon's administration withdrew the federal government's long-standing support for far-reaching school integration in the South. During the president's first term, HEW and the Justice Department moderated their school desegregation activities to be more acceptable to white southerners, leading to grumbling and staff turnover within both departments. A U.S. Civil Rights Commission report on school desegregation between 1966 and 1975 concluded: "Starting in 1965, HEW started to play a decisive role in initiating enforcement in hundreds of highly segregated districts. This enforcement continued until 1970, when the administration withdrew substantial support from the desegregation effort."[37] Political scientist Gary Orfield, a historian of school desegregation, reported that by 1971 HEW had abandoned its policy of withholding federal funds from school districts not in compliance with judicial mandates. Much to the dismay of the NAACP, the Department of Justice followed a similar path. Once an ally of integrationists, the department now "gave low priority to school cases and sometimes led the opposition to legal theories advanced by civil rights lawyers." In the early 1970s it was common for Justice Department lawyers, who had sided with the NAACP on school desegregation cases since the 1950s, to support the opponents of integration in school desegregation cases before federal courts.[38]

In his defense, Nixon's policies on school desegregation were not meant to halt the process or to roll back the gains of the previous generation. Indeed, during his presidency, the numbers of African Americans attending integrated schools continued to grow. Rather, the president sought to give comfort to white southerners who had undergone dramatic and discomforting alterations to their way of life. Moreover, Nixon's policies in other civil rights fields, such as affirmative action and the status of other minority groups, included important initiatives.[39]

With the executive branch less inclined to promote school integration during the Nixon presidency, the federal courts assumed a more active role. In the summer of 1969, HEW asked the United States Court of Appeals for the Fifth Circuit to allow several dozen school districts in Mississippi to delay implementation of their desegregation plans until December—the first time HEW had supported a desegregation delay before the federal courts. With support from the Justice Department, the Fifth Circuit Court of Appeals granted the delay, but in October 1969 the Supreme Court prevented the postponement and reiterated its position on school desegregation in the second of its major school desegregation decisions of the late

1960s, *Alexander v. Holmes County Board of Education.* As J. Harvie Wilkinson III noted, "The Court that once badly needed executive support now moved in the face of executive opposition."[40]

In *Alexander,* the Supreme Court unanimously held that the *Green* decision had to be implemented immediately. The court's decision directed the lower federal courts to order southern school districts "to terminate dual school systems at once and to operate now and hereafter only unitary schools."[41] Subsequently, federal judges throughout the region ordered school boards to bring about complete school desegregation at the earliest possible date. In many cases, their rulings required major changes in the middle of the 1969–70 school year. Virginia, which had experienced a notable increase in integration following the *Green* decision in 1968–69, now underwent another wave of change as localities across the state responded to the new mandate. In December 1969, ruling on the desegregation plans of Halifax and Amherst counties, the United States Court of Appeals for the Fourth Circuit declared: "Further delays will not be tolerated in this circuit. No school districts may continue to operate a dual system based on race." By the 1970–71 school year, the Virginia Department of Education estimated that 87 percent of black students in the Commonwealth were attending schools with whites, a 50 percent increase over the year before.[42]

In urban areas throughout the nation, however, achieving unitary school systems posed greater challenges than in rural communities. Whereas rural school districts could often integrate their schools by adopting nonracial geographic school zones, cities contained numerous segregated neighborhoods and the racially identifiable schools that served them. Geographic attendance zones in urban areas would therefore mirror, rather than counteract, widespread residential segregation. As a result, integration in urban areas often required more proactive measures, such as busing large numbers of students. Transporting black students to predominantly white schools and vice versa allowed a district to determine the racial makeup of individual schools, offering a direct and effective way of bringing about school integration in cities. Recognizing this fact in the late 1960s, HEW suggested busing in some localities as a means of compliance with its desegregation requirements, and some federal judges in the South began to order desegregation plans that included busing provisions.[43]

In cities throughout Virginia in the late 1960s and early 1970s, busing became a central issue in the NAACP's campaign for school integration.

Discussing the ramifications of the *Green* decision in 1968, S. W. Tucker had predicted that Virginia's counties would be largely desegregated by the fall of 1969, but that "big difficulties" remained to overcome the effects of segregated housing patterns in the state's urban areas.[44] In early 1970 state conference attorneys asked federal district court judge Robert R. Merhige, in *Bradley v. School Board of the City of Richmond*, to require the Richmond school board to develop and implement a proactive and effective desegregation plan in light of the *Green* and *Alexander* decisions. Sixteen years after *Brown*, the city still had a handful of all-white schools, more than thirty predominantly white schools, and twenty-six all-black schools. The city's long history of segregated neighborhoods meant that a geographic-based student assignment system would only replicate these divisions. After discussions with the school board that summer, Judge Merhige approved an interim plan that included busing, pending the development of a more substantial plan after the school year began. As a result of this decision, Richmond began to bus thirteen thousand black and white students in the fall of 1970, out of a total school population of roughly fifty thousand.[45]

In Richmond as elsewhere, the decision to use busing to overcome segregation was angrily contested by many whites. In addition to subjecting schoolchildren to long bus rides, busing often meant the enrollment of white students in predominantly black schools with largely black administrations and staffs (Richmond's school population was approximately 35 percent white in 1970). Instead, many white parents supported the idea of neighborhood schools. Richard Kluger explains that "bussing to maintain segregation had been happily countenanced by white parents, but the prospect of bussing their own youngsters for the purpose of integration produced bared teeth."[46] In Richmond, some whites avoided busing by moving to the surrounding counties, which were not part of the busing plan. Anger toward the NAACP and Judge Merhige also boiled over. Although Judge Merhige sought protection from federal marshals for nearly two years, his guest house was burned to the ground and his dog shot. "I would say there was a time when he [S. W. Tucker] and I were two of the most hated men in the entire Commonwealth," Merhige later recalled—noting that Tucker was not afforded federal protection.[47]

Despite the uproar against busing, the Virginia NAACP continued to press for school integration statewide, including busing when appropriate.

A young girl at an antibus-
ing rally in Richmond in
July 1970. (Courtesy of the
Richmond Times-Dispatch)

In the fall of 1969, S. W. Tucker predicted that all the schools in Virginia would be integrated within two years.[48] With compliance in the state's rural areas growing, the organization now focused its legal strength on Virginia's cities. During the summer of 1970, state conference attorneys juggled desegregation lawsuits against Richmond, Norfolk, Roanoke, Lynchburg, and Newport News. Largely because of *Green* and *Alexander*, the NAACP's work was noticeably easier than before. With the onus now on local school boards to produce and implement desegregation plans resulting in unitary schools, the NAACP attorneys focused on pointing out deficiencies in the plans produced by Virginia's urban centers.[49]

NAACP attorney Henry Marsh pointed out, for instance, that Norfolk's latest desegregation plan, which had been approved by federal district court judge Walter Hoffman in 1969, failed to address faculty segregation or completely eliminate student segregation. The Virginia State Conference and the U.S. Department of Justice had both opposed Hoffman's ruling, leading to a swift appeal. In the summer of 1970, the United States Court of Appeals for the Fourth Circuit agreed with their arguments in *Brewer v. School Board of the City of Norfolk,* noting that "white schools remain predominantly white; black schools remain black." Highlighting their frustration with the local school board, Justices Sobeloff and Winter added that the suit had been "frustratingly interminable . . . because of the unpardonable recalcitrance of the defendants." In the end, the court ruled that, if the school board could not integrate the city schools because of residential segregation, then "the school board must take further steps." The result that fall, as in Richmond, was busing.[50]

With little time to prepare, school officials in Norfolk scrambled to implement the court-ordered plan. Although the city had long bused some of its students (approximately eight thousand students per day, out of a total student population of fifty-six thousand, in 1969–70), the new plan increased that number by 50 percent. Because Norfolk owned no school bus fleet of its own, students were forced to buy "school tickets" from the Virginia Transit Company, which operated the city bus system. Though all students received a discounted rate for school transportation, the greatest burden for integrating Norfolk's schools fell again on African American parents.[51]

Cities in western Virginia also faced court-ordered busing in 1970. In Lynchburg, like Norfolk, one difficulty was that the school board owned no school buses or bus facilities. This situation had circumscribed desegregation under the city's freedom of choice plan (as it had in other Virginia cities), but in 1970 it proved an even greater obstacle to integration, in that it prevented busing. In subsequent years, federal judges would order localities to purchase buses to increase desegregation, but that step was not considered acceptable in 1970. Despite that, the state conference argued that busing was the best means of truly integrating the city's schools. In late summer 1970, Judge Merhige reluctantly approved a temporary, small-scale busing program combined with other desegregation measures; full desegregation, he noted, would be expected within thirty days. The judge added, "If you need transportation, you had better get it."[52]

Farther west, in Roanoke, the NAACP pointed out in *Cynthia Green v. School Board of the City of Roanoke* that Roanoke had also failed to develop an effective plan to shift to a unitary school system. Federal district court judge Ted Dalton, who had succeeded Judge John Paul on the bench in 1959, refused to order substantial busing, which he considered "harmful" to children. In the summer of 1970, however, the United States Court of Appeals for the Fourth Circuit assigned a fall deadline for the school board to develop a plan to bring about a unitary school system; the ruling led to the adoption of busing in Roanoke in the fall of 1970 as well.[53]

Meanwhile, a federal district court judge in North Carolina grappled with the same challenges facing the proponents of school desegregation in Virginia's cities. Like many cities in Virginia, Charlotte, North Carolina, had operated under a geographic assignment desegregation plan until shortly after *Green v. New Kent County,* when federal district court judge James McMillan—in his first major ruling from the bench—recognized that the "rules of the game have changed," and that the city's desegregation plan failed to meet the new constitutional requirements. After rejecting several revised plans offered by the school board in 1969, Judge McMillan adopted a remedy proposed by one of the expert witnesses in the case—busing. The United States Court of Appeals for the Fourth Circuit, however, rejected McMillan's decision in May 1970, ruling that the judge had gone too far. Holding that "not every school in a unitary school system need be integrated," the judges concluded, "if a school board makes every reasonable effort to integrate the pupils under its control, an intractable remnant of segregation, we believe, should not void an otherwise exemplary plan for the creation of a unitary school system."[54]

The U.S. Supreme Court, however, disagreed, and the high court affirmed Judge McMillan's decision in *Swann v. Charlotte-Mecklenburg* on April 20, 1971. Writing for the unanimous court, Chief Justice Warren Burger agreed that implementing *Green* often required new school desegregation guidelines. The high court shied away from requiring a specific remedy, such as busing; instead, it reiterated its long-held policy that local circumstances should determine the nature of desegregation plans, leaving the question of remedy to lower-court judges. In some locations, geographic zoning or even freedom of choice might lead to "the greatest possible degree of actual desegregation," said the court. In other cases, however, particularly in cities, busing might represent a legitimate and necessary remedy.[55]

Following the *Swann* decision, school integration increased in urban areas throughout the South. The high court did not require each school within a district to match the racial composition of the district as a whole, but the justices did note that racial ratios might be considered a "starting point" in shaping remedies, including busing. As a result, lower-level federal judges would struggle with the question of appropriate remedy in coming years. Nonetheless, the high court's acceptance of busing expanded its use in the South in the early 1970s.[56]

School officials in urban areas throughout Virginia adjusted their integration plans in accordance with the high court's mandate. In some cases, this meant expanding or purchasing fleets of buses to accommodate the growing number of students to be transported. Not surprisingly, the percentage of Virginia students bused to school daily climbed. Other localities, including Richmond, sought to annex surrounding areas to increase their population of white students; this made the realization of an integrated school system simpler. Regardless of the method employed, the sharpest increases in integration in Virginia's public schools in the early 1970s occurred in the state's urban areas.[57]

As expected, President Nixon opposed the *Swann* decision. The president publicly denounced busing as "forced integration" and asked officials in the Department of Justice to draw up a constitutional amendment to nullify the Supreme Court's decision. He also reiterated his support for neighborhood schools and argued that the primary goal of any public school was to educate, not to integrate. Richard Kluger described the president's actions with regard to school integration in the early 1970s as "downright obstructionist," and argued "it was not just neglect that Nixon offered the Negro; it was downright opposition." Many white southerners, however, were pleased, and for this and other reasons they rewarded Nixon with a record number of votes in the 1972 presidential election.[58]

More important, Nixon's appointments to the U.S. Supreme Court began to dramatically affect the struggle over school desegregation, and the controversy over busing in particular. Between 1969 and 1971, Nixon appointed four justices to the high court: Chief Justice Warren Burger and Justices Harry Blackmun, Lewis Powell, and William Rehnquist. He also had two Supreme Court nominees rejected by Congress—southerners G. Harrold Carswell and Clement Haynsworth. In subsequent years, the four confirmed justices voted together more often than any bloc of justices since the

1950s. Their conservative views shifted the Supreme Court's perspective on school integration, leaving more liberal justices, including Thurgood Marshall, isolated.[59]

In the meantime, Marshall's former colleagues at the NAACP used the *Swann* decision to expand their campaign for school integration. In New York, the NAACP's Legal Defense Fund "moved swiftly to follow up the *Swann* breakthrough by pushing similar cases elsewhere."[60] In Virginia, *Swann* legitimized Judge Merhige's decision to require busing in Richmond, as well as similar court orders applying to other Virginia cities, by declaring the technique an acceptable remedy.

Outside of the South, federal courts and agencies, including the Department of Health, Education, and Welfare, increasingly required school boards in the northern and western United States to eliminate dual school systems as well. This was based on the recognition that non-southern school segregation—easily discernable in attendance statistics—had been perpetuated by deliberately discriminatory policies such as creating racially identifiable school attendance zones and building schools near racially identifiable neighborhoods (to reduce the likelihood of racial mixing in the schools). Widespread segregation, in other words, was at least partly the result of deliberate choices made by school and city officials. In many non-southern urban areas, this realization brought about court decisions in the early 1970s requiring the adoption of desegregation plans that included busing.[61]

Still, busing faced a growing challenge throughout the nation because of the phenomenon known as "white flight"—the exodus of whites from inner cities to surrounding suburbs in the mid- to late twentieth century. Signs of this phenomenon extended back into the early twentieth century, but white flight had picked up during the massive suburbanization that followed World War II, promoted by improvements in transportation, housing construction, and the desire to achieve the "American Dream." However, racial discrimination, financial constraints, and government policy ensured that the exodus was mostly white, leaving the inner core of many American cities inhabited by a growing black population.[62]

Although white flight had been taking place long before the advent of busing, the trend picked up considerably in the 1970s as some whites sought to avoid having their children bused to accomplish school integration. In Richmond, the percentage of white students in the city schools fell from 35 percent to 20 percent between 1970 and 1976 (whites had been approximately 45 percent of the city's population in 1960). And while it would be simplistic to suggest that the transition occurred entirely because of school desegregation or busing, historian Robert Pratt points out that "it seems equally obvious that opposition to busing prompted a good many whites to abandon Richmond in favor of the overwhelmingly white suburbs."[63] The ease with which white parents could commute into the city for work or other reasons also fueled white flight in Richmond—in larger southern cities such as Charlotte and Tampa, a longer commute made moving to surrounding counties logistically more difficult. In Richmond one black student recalled the change in her own neighborhood, located near the Carillon: "When my family first moved into that neighborhood, one of the blocks had ten houses on one side of the street, and there were six white families living in them. Within a year or so, there was only one white family left on that block."[64]

The changing racial demographics in cities across America boded poorly for busing plans and for school integration more broadly. Put simply, an integrated school system was impossible without a biracial population. In Richmond, the dramatic escalation of white flight, which was partly the result of busing, reduced the likelihood of success for the city's court-ordered busing plan within just a few years. As a result, in the summer of 1971 state NAACP attorneys pressed Judge Merhige, in *Bradley v. School Board of the City of Richmond*, to include the counties surrounding Richmond —nearly all-white Chesterfield and Henrico—in the city's busing plan. State conference attorneys, now with support from city officials, argued that the State Department of Education had an obligation to provide a unitary system that was not racially identifiable, and that a merger was the simplest and most effective way to do so.[65]

In January 1972, Judge Merhige agreed. In a 325-page opinion, the judge noted that state education officials in previous years had made countless decisions that led to, and perpetuated, the dual school systems evident in Richmond and the surrounding counties. Because of those choices, Merhige ruled, the state was responsible for creating a unitary school system for the children in all three localities. Interdistrict busing, according to the judge, was the most logical solution.[66]

The Virginia State Board of Education and Henrico and Chesterfield counties quickly appealed Judge Merhige's decision. In hearings before the United States Court of Appeals for the Fourth Circuit that spring, their attorneys argued that Merhige's ruling was without precedent and did not represent a valid interpretation of the Supreme Court's desegregation guidelines. That June, in a 5 to 1 decision, the United States Court of Appeals for the Fourth Circuit agreed, holding that a federal district court judge could not "compel one of the States of the Union to restructure its internal government for the purpose of achieving a racial balance in the assignment of pupils to the public schools."[67]

The U.S. Supreme Court heard the case on appeal the following year. Justice Lewis E. Powell Jr., recently appointed by President Nixon, recused himself from the case because he had served as chairman of the Richmond school board in the 1950s and 1960s. In *School Board of the City of Richmond v. State Board of Education,* handed down in May 1973, the remaining eight justices split evenly on the constitutionality of interdistrict busing. That division allowed the decision of the United States Court of Appeals for the Fourth Circuit—overturning Judge Merhige's interdistrict busing ruling—to stand.[68]

The next year, the Supreme Court heard a similar case dealing with interdistrict busing in Detroit, Michigan. This time the court ruled 5 to 4, with Justices Burger, Blackmun, Powell, and Rehnquist—all Nixon appointees—and Justice Stewart pitted against Justices Marshall, Douglas, Brennan, and White. The decision overturned an interdistrict busing plan and upset many advocates of desegregation. The case, *Milliken v. Bradley,* represented a setback for the NAACP. By prohibiting the use of interdistrict busing to achieve integration, the court reduced the options available to combat segregation in urban areas around the United States. White opposition to busing had already led to increasing rates of white flight from America's cities, and now the court had placed their primary destination—suburban enclaves ringing those urban centers—out of the reach of city busing plans. Thurgood Marshall's dissenting opinion in *Milliken* noted, "After 20 years of small, often difficult steps toward that great end [of equal justice under law], the Court today takes a giant step backwards." The result, as Marshall predicted, was increasingly black urban centers, surrounded by predominantly white counties with separate school systems. As a result, busing within America's urban areas in the 1970s increasingly meant transferring small numbers of white students into overwhelmingly black city schools.[69]

In Virginia, the NAACP's hard-fought campaign to obtain school integration was successful, though not entirely. On the one hand, the South had become the most integrated region of the nation, and school desegregation in Virginia reflected this trend. Many observers recognized the substantial change that had occurred. In 1971, according to HEW estimates, 44 percent of black students attended majority white schools in the South, as opposed to 28 percent who did so in the North and West. By 1974, Secretary of HEW Caspar Weinberger estimated that 90 percent of black children in the eleven-state South attended school with whites.[70] This integration of public schools opened additional avenues for scholastic and economic success for African American students from throughout Virginia, and reduced stereotypes held by both races—improving race relations and promoting better racial understanding.[71]

On the other hand, integration of public education in Virginia's urban areas would not withstand the test of time, and residential segregation in nonurban areas would challenge integration efforts for the foreseeable future. In the cities, court-ordered busing faced great opposition, including judicial headwinds, from the outset, and these challenges grew over time. Within a generation, the same busing plans that had led to significant integration would be overturned by federal courts in Virginia and throughout the nation, as judges determined that localities had eliminated the racial duality of their schools. As a result, the peak of integration was followed by resegregation, meaning rising segregation, especially in urban areas of Virginia and elsewhere. The NAACP's campaign to implement *Brown v. Board of Education* shifted toward preserving the achievements of its hard-fought campaign as the 1970s unfolded.

AFTERWORD

Everything has changed and nothing has changed.
—The Reverend Joseph Lowry on the twenty-fifth
anniversary of the 1963 March on Washington

Questions related to school integration in Virginia, of course, were not resolved in the mid-1970s. Differences of opinion as to the desirability of integration, and questions about how to best accomplish integration (assuming
it is desirable) continued in the 1980s and 1990s, and persist to the present
day. The history of school desegregation since the mid-1950s may provide
some guidance.

In the early 1970s, school integration occurred in localities across Virginia. Guided by the U.S. Supreme Court's recent school desegregation decisions, including *Green v. New Kent County, Virginia*, federal courts agreed
to the requests of NAACP attorneys and ordered school districts to develop
and implement plans to eliminate signs of school segregation. A dramatic
rise in the amount of integration in the state's public schools ensued. On the
twentieth anniversary of *Brown v. Board of Education*, the Legal Defense
Fund reported that Virginia had achieved "full or nearly full" compliance
with the Constitution and that school desegregation conditions in most parts
of the state were "excellent."[1]

One of the keys to successful integration in Virginia was a commitment
to public education. Where white parents transferred their children from
desegregated public schools to private academies, the result was often all- or
largely black public schools. This happened in many sections of the Deep
South, where even today numerous school systems grapple with largely
black public schools and largely white private ones. Virginia experienced
a similar student migration in the early stages of school desegregation, in

part because of the state's policy of tuition grants. However, by the 1970s private school enrollment in Virginia had stagnated, while attendance at the state's public schools continued to grow—in 1974 the State Department of Education reported nearly 1.1 million public school students in Virginia compared to 69,000 pupils enrolled in nonpublic schools.[2] As a result, the vast majority of Virginia's student population attended integrated public schools by the mid-1970s.

The leadership of the Virginia State Conference of the NAACP recognized this accomplishment and in the later 1960s and early 1970s the state NAACP increasingly focused on other aspects of the struggle for racial equality. School integration and issues related to quality education continued to garner attention, but the organization's meetings and directives now concentrated on political participation, housing opportunities, veterans' affairs, and employment. In other words, as court-ordered school desegregation occurred throughout Virginia, the state conference shifted to address issues that continued to challenge the state's African American population.[3]

School integration, however, depended on the federal courts. The NAACP had recognized this fact earlier in the 1900s, and the understanding led to the legal attacks against segregation that resulted in *Brown v. Board of Education* in 1954. In the 1960s, executive branch agencies—specifically the Department of Health, Education, and Welfare (HEW) and the Department of Justice—played a more important role in bringing about school desegregation in the region. However, the federal courts again assumed oversight of the integration process in the late 1960s, and it was federal court orders that overcame the remaining vestiges of segregation in Virginia and throughout the South in subsequent years. Largely as a result of U.S. Supreme Court decisions in the late 1960s and early 1970s, more than 90 percent of southern schools were desegregated by the 1972–73 school year.[4]

At the same time, however, national politics increasingly affected school integration and the extent to which it could be achieved, in Virginia and elsewhere. In 1968 Richard Nixon became the first Republican elected to the White House since Dwight Eisenhower, and President Nixon publicly opposed many of the policies—including busing—that were then used to bring about school integration. Nixon's administration also brought about a shift within key executive agencies, including HEW and the Justice Department, which had previously demonstrated a commitment to bringing about school integration. More broadly, Nixon's election represented the beginning of an ideological shift toward more conservative politics in the United States. As a result, African Americans, who were longtime supporters of the Democratic Party, found themselves with fewer friends in positions of national power. As Benjamin L. Hooks, executive director of the NAACP from 1977 to 1993, explained: "When I took over this organization, I had plans for expanding the mission of the NAACP. I had no idea I would be fighting to retain what I thought we had already won."[5]

President Nixon's appointments to the federal judiciary, and those of his successors, had a profound effect on school integration. Starting in the 1970s and continuing for several decades, the federal courts exhibited less support for school integration, and previously accepted school integration tactics, than before. By the mid-1970s the high court had limited the amount and extent of busing that was considered acceptable, most notably in *Milliken v. Bradley* in 1974, which restricted desegregation plans in urban centers by disallowing plans that involved the surrounding counties. Later, in the 1980s and 1990s, busing plans that had led to integration were abandoned as federal judges ruled that school districts had eliminated the racial identities of their public schools and created unitary systems. This designation removed responsibility for maintaining integrated school districts, and was often accorded even when the resulting changes were likely to bring about resegregation. In the 1990s, the U.S. Supreme Court endorsed this changing milieu in a series of decisions—including *Board of Education of Oklahoma City Public Schools v. Dowell* (1991), *Freeman v. Pitts* (1992), and *Missouri v. Jenkins* (1995)—that encouraged the end of federal judicial oversight of local school policies.[6]

The growing popularity of "color-blind" decision making encouraged the movement away from busing and other student assignment plans that actively promote integration. This approach has been particularly popular among conservative groups and leaders. The "color-blind" ideology is based on the idea that race should no longer be a factor in public policy. Its proponents argue that racial inequities have been overcome and that equality of opportunity now exists—and, therefore, decisions related to schools, and other aspects of life, should be made based on factors excluding the race of those involved.[7] In terms of education policy, this line of thought opposes the use of busing or other attendance policies that utilize race (among other factors) to encourage integration in public education.

As a result of these changes, in recent decades many of the nation's school districts have reverted to neighborhood schools and color-blind pupil assignment policies. Busing has declined. However, the persistence of residential segregation, especially in cities, means that resegregation often occurs when districts shift to neighborhood schools. Whereas busing and other race-based policies helped districts overcome residential segregation and promote integration, geographic-based attendance plans and neighborhood schools generally led to educational facilities that reflect the racial makeup of the communities which surround them. The result has been increased racial segregation in the nation's public school systems.[8]

Not surprisingly, this trend is strongly opposed by many proponents of racial diversity. In 2011, NAACP representatives from throughout the nation gathered in North Carolina to protest the abandonment of diversity-based attendance policies in favor of neighborhood schools in Wake County, which includes the city of Raleigh. The president of the North Carolina State Conference, the Reverend William J. Barber, highlighted the association's concern: "If you've got re-segregation, it's not only going to re-segregate bodies, but also budgets, buildings and every basic building block to high-quality, constitutional, diverse, well-funded public education."[9] Gary Orfield, a professor at the University of Virginia in the late 1960s and currently the codirector of the Civil Rights Project at the University of California, Los Angeles, agrees. In the foreword to one study documenting growing segregation in Virginia's public schools, Orfield explains: "Knowing about the struggles of the past and all the hard work of many educators in making desegregation work, it has been deeply saddening for me to watch policymakers and courts let it erode over time, or simply abandon it through a court decision or inaction."[10]

Virginia's urban school districts have been particularly impacted by the limitations placed on busing and the reversion to neighborhood schools. This is partly because Virginia's cities and counties are separate and distinct units—in the Commonwealth there are no "metropolitan" school districts, where cities and suburbs make up one entity, as there are in many other states. Instead, Virginia's urban school districts serve their residents only, and because of white flight to the suburbs, those residents are largely African American. As a remedy to promote integration, busing across district lines was proposed in the early 1970s, but rejected by the Supreme Court. At the same time, busing within Virginia cities was required by the federal courts but was not particularly effective, particularly as white flight increased in the 1970s. Surrounded by largely white counties, for instance, Richmond found itself busing a largely black public school population. The reversion to neighborhood schools, which certainly offers some advantages to parents and children, has only increased the pace of resegregation in the public schools.[11]

Rural school districts in Virginia have been less affected by these changes, and remain a bright spot in the school desegregation story. In many of Virginia's counties and towns, particularly where residential segregation is negligible, the schools continue to be largely integrated. Neighborhood elementary schools draw children of both races, and one high school often serves the entire system. Integration is particularly established where private academies have failed to attract a large percentage of the white student population, and by and large Virginia's counties continue to support public education. As integration swelled in rural Virginia in the mid-1970s, the State Department of Education reported a county public school population of just over seven hundred thousand and a county private school population of less than thirty thousand.[12] As resegregation challenges urban school districts in Virginia and elsewhere, rural school systems often demonstrate how much has changed since *Brown v. Board of Education.*

In Virginia and throughout the nation, the challenges of racial equality have grown in importance as a result of recent demographic changes. Prior to midcentury, Virginia was populated almost exclusively by black, white, and Native American residents, with the former two groups making up the vast majority of the state's population. Members of other ethnic groups, including those of Asian, Pacific Islander, and Hispanic descent, made up only a small portion of the state's population. In subsequent decades, however, Virginia's population has grown progressively more diverse and this trend is expected to continue. As a result, race and education policy increasingly affects multiethnic communities and shapes the attitudes and interactions of young Virginians in tremendously important ways.[13]

At the same time, studies show that integrated schools offer a variety of benefits for students of all races. For minority students, desegregation helps close the achievement gap, leading to higher test scores, graduation levels, and college-attendance rates. This is most likely the result of better facilities and resources that tend to exist in desegregated schools. For all students, integrated schools offer the opportunity to know and to understand, and to work with, students of different backgrounds. Some surveys suggest that integrated schools promote attitudes and skills related to co-alition building.[14]

During the Jim Crow era, one of the many costs of racial segregation was that blacks and whites rarely comprehended, or truly understood, one another. The two groups interacted largely in public spaces, and their inter-actions were circumscribed by the racial expectations of the day. Countless examples show that the color line prevented true biracial understanding, leading both races to make assumptions about the other, and to adopt and perpetuate stereotypes and prejudices toward one another. Racial integra-tion offered, and offers, the only real possibility of overcoming this legacy of ignorance. As Robert Pratt eloquently explains in his study of school desegregation and resegregation in Richmond, Virginia: "School deseg-regation means much more than black and white children sitting together in the classroom solely for the academic improvement of blacks. Desegre-gation means—or at least it should mean—that black and white children are conditioned at an early age to interact with one another on the basis of equality and mutual respect for the other's cultural heritage." The same should hold true for children of all ethnic and cultural backgrounds.[15]

As the twenty-first century unfolds, questions of race and education re-main controversial and unresolved. By some important measures racial progress has been made in Virginia, there can be no doubt. Legal segrega-tion has been overcome and integrated education is the norm for many of the state's public school students. At the same time, however, the continua-tion of racial disparities and the correlation between race and the American standard of living suggest much remains to be done. As the Reverend Jo-seph Lowry noted on the twenty-fifth anniversary of the March on Wash-ington, "Everything has changed and nothing has changed."[16] With regard to public education, what has changed for the better—and much has—can be attributed at least in part to the NAACP and its efforts to bring about public school desegregation in Virginia in the years following *Brown v. Board of Education*.

NOTES

Introduction

1. Quotation is from James Latimer, "Keep Violence Out of Struggle Over Segregation, Byrd Urges," *Richmond Times-Dispatch*, August 31, 1958, 4.

2. Hershman, "A Rumbling in the Museum," 1.

3. Regarding the lack of scholarship on the NAACP in Virginia, Paul Gaston notes, "Many important aspects of African-American history during the civil rights era in Virginia remain unexplored by scholars, including the activities of state and local branches of the NAACP." Lassiter and Lewis, *Moderates' Dilemma*, 206n27.

4. As historian Robert Pratt, a native Virginian, mused nearly two decades ago: "One of the questions that students ask most often is, 'While civil rights battles were being fought in the streets of Birmingham and Selma, what was going on in Virginia?' Unfortunately, I can never provide an answer that satisfies either them or me." I don't pretend this book can answer that question, but I hope it moves us in the right direction. Robert A. Pratt, "New Directions in Virginia's Civil Rights History," *Virginia Magazine of History and Biography*, vol. 104, no. 1 (Winter 1996): 151.

5. First quotation is from Remarks of Thurgood Marshall at Press Conference, June 30, 1954, in Bracey and Meier, *Papers of the NAACP*, Supplement to Part 1 (1951–55), reel 10; second quotation is from Kluger, *Simple Justice*, 757.

6. Gloster B. Current to W. Lester Banks, July 23, 1974, Part VI, Box C159, Papers of the National Association for the Advancement of Colored People, Library of Congress Manuscript Division, Washington, D.C. (hereafter cited as NAACP Papers).

One | "A Source of Great Consternation"

This chapter's title quotes J. Douglas Smith's *Managing White Supremacy*, in which he writes that the NAACP developed into "a source of great consternation to white Virginians."

1. Quotations are from Kluger, *Simple Justice*, 85. See also Heinemann, *Old Dominion, New Commonwealth*, chapter 12; 1902 Constitution of Virginia.

2. Statistic is from Smith, *Managing White Supremacy*, 135. Quotation is from L. P. Whitten to William Pickens, August 14, 1940, Part II, Box C203, Papers of the National Association for the Advancement of Colored People, Library of Congress Manuscript Division, Washington, D.C. (hereafter cited as NAACP Papers).

3. Special Release, October 31, 1947, by the Press Service of the NAACP, Part II, Box C211, NAACP Papers.

4. "Push Anti-Jim Crow Fight As Va. Legislature Opens," *Atlanta Daily World*, January 22, 1948, in Part II, Box C211, NAACP Papers.

5. For more on equalization and the Virginia NAACP, see Memorandum to Mr. Marshall from Robert L. Carter, Re: State Conference of Branches in Virginia Meeting in Richmond, Virginia, January 16, 1946, Part II, Box C211, NAACP Papers; W. Lester Banks, Oliver W. Hill, and Dr. J. M. Tinsley to NAACP Board of Directors, September 5, 1947, Part II, Box C211, NAACP Papers.

6. Jonas, *Freedom's Sword*, 88, 322; Wilkins with Mathews, *Standing Fast*, 278–84, 338. The board was expanded over time; see, for example, "NAACP expanding board from 48–60," *Richmond Afro-American*, July 21, 1962, 5.

7. Berg, *Ticket to Freedom*, 112–15; Finch, *NAACP*, 121; Lucille Black to Branch Presidents and Campaign Chairmen, April 9, 1945, in Bracey and Meier, *Papers of the NAACP*, Part 26, series A, reel 2; "'Target date' for integration set by NAACP," *Richmond Afro-American*, June 11, 1955, 1.

8. Finch, *NAACP*, 20; Morris, *Origins of the Civil Rights Movement*, 33; Fairclough, *Race and Democracy*, 48; Verney and Sartain, *Long Is the Way and Hard*, xii–xxi.

9. For more on the NAACP Legal Defense and Educational Fund, Inc., see St. James, *NAACP: Triumphs*, 206; August Meier and John H. Bracey Jr., "The NAACP as a Reform Movement, 1909–1965," *Journal of Southern History*, vol. LIX, no. 1 (February 1993): 3–30; Janken, *White*, 73–77. The LDF's records at the Library of Congress, unfortunately, have not yet been opened to scholars.

10. Gloster B. Current to W. Lester Banks, April 27, 1966, Part IV, Box C32, NAACP Papers; Papers of the National Association for the Advancement of Colored People finding aid, Library of Congress, 1041–42, 1212–13, 1277; memorandum from Mr. Current to Mr. Wilkins, October 8, 1946, Part 17, reel 14, in Bracey and Meier, *Papers of the NAACP*; telegram from Roy Wilkins to Franklin Williams, December 19, 1957, and identical telegram the same day from Roy Wilkins to Ruby Hurley, both in Supplement to Part 1 (1956–60), reel 2, in Bracey and Meier, *Papers of the NAACP*; Finch, *NAACP*, 122; St. James, *National Association for the Advancement of Colored People: A Case Study*, 98; Berg, *Ticket to Freedom*, 143.

11. The phrase "State Conference" can also be used to collectively refer to the members of the NAACP in a particular state—e.g., the "Virginia State Conference" was made up of 25,000 members. Generally, however, the term referred to the state office or headquarters in Richmond. See Constitution of the Virginia State Conference, Part IV, Box C32, NAACP Papers; Finch, *NAACP*, 20; Morris, *Origins*

of the Civil Rights Movement, 13; Janken, *White,* 73–77; Muse, *Virginia's Massive Resistance,* 50; Buni, *Negro in Virginia Politics,* 177; Hill, *Big Bang,* 179; St. James, *National Association for the Advancement of Colored People: A Case Study,* 75; "NAACP Memberships Of 386,808 All-Time High, Current Reports," *Richmond Afro-American,* January 14, 1961, 5.

12. John Morsell to Roy Wilkins, February 6, 1961, Part III, Box C160, NAACP Papers; 1961 Freedom Fund Quota from the Virginia State Conference NAACP to Virginia branches, undated [February 1961], Part III, Box C160, NAACP Papers; Wallenstein, *Blue Laws and Black Codes,* chapter 4.

13. For more on Marshall, Hill, and Robinson, see Kluger, *Simple Justice,* 179–97, 253, 324, 471–72; Hill, *Big Bang,* 62, 79–81; Muse, *Virginia's Massive Resistance,* 48; Wallenstein, *Blue Laws and Black Codes,* 86–92.

14. Rick Sauder, "Oliver Hill: A Journey Down the Civil Rights Road," *Richmond News Leader,* January 15, 1992, 1; Oliver W. Hill Sr., interview by author, tape recording, Richmond, Va., April 18, 2000; Hill, *Big Bang,* 123–24, 132–33; Kluger, *Simple Justice,* 215–17; Hershman, "A Rumbling in the Museum," 18.

15. For Banks's hiring and salary, see Executive Board of Directors of the Virginia State Conference to Dear Member, Re: remittances to the National Office, New York, from membership dues, October 5, 1945, in Bracey and Meier, *Papers of the NAACP,* Part 26, series A, reel 23. The Virginia State Conference had sixty-five branches in 1947; see W. Lester Banks to Mrs. William J. Powers, July 22, 1965, Part III, Box C161, NAACP Papers.

16. Quotation is from Hill, *Big Bang,* 179. See also Halifax County membership report, January 3, 1940, Part II, Box C262, NAACP Papers; Robert A. Pratt, "William Lester Banks" in John T. Kneebone et al, *Dictionary of Virginia Biography,* vol. 1 (Richmond: Library of Virginia, 1998), 321–23.

17. Report to the Virginia State Conference Meeting, October 4–6, 1957, Memberships and Freedom Fund Contributions Received by Branches, Part III, Box C158, NAACP Papers; Program, 25th Annual Convention of the Virginia State Conference NAACP, October 7–9, 1960, Part III, Box C159, NAACP Papers; James L. Hicks, "'We're Ready To Move Full Steam Ahead On Schools'—Thurgood Marshall," *Richmond Afro-American,* January 14, 1956, 1.

18. For the preoccupation with memberships, see Lucille Black to Ruby Hurley, January 27, 1954, and Lucille Black to Ruby Hurley, February 11, 1954, in Bracey and Meier, *Papers of the NAACP,* Part 25, series A, reel 4. For NAACP membership policies, see Lucille Black to John Henderson, December 8, 1941, in ibid., Part 26, series A, reel 23.

19. For Virginia NAACP membership figures, see Lucille Black to William Abbot, November 5, 1954, Group II, Box C212, NAACP Papers; Lucille Black to W. Lester Banks, May 12, 1949, Part II, Box C211, NAACP Papers. For Virginia's black population figures, see Roy Wilkins, Draft of Speech to Norfolk, Va., NAACP, December 4, 1955, Part II, Box A571, NAACP Papers. The NAACP's focus

on legal action was periodically questioned; see, for example, Beth T. Bates, "A New Crowd Challenges the Agenda of the Old Guard in the NAACP, 1933–1941," *American Historical Review* 102 (1997): 340–77.

20. On the membership fee and how it was distributed, see Gloster Current to Rev. E. A. Hughes, July 13, 1950, Part II, Box C203, NAACP Papers. NAACP branches elected officers similarly to the Virginia State Conference; see "NAACP Units To Hold Annual Elections," NAACP press release, October 1, 1959, Papers of John Mitchell Brooks, Special Collections and Archives, James Branch Cabell Library, Virginia Commonwealth University.

21. W. Lester Banks to Henry Lee Moon, May 21, 1951, Part II, Box C212, NAACP Papers; Boyle, *Desegregated Heart*, 231; Hill, *Big Bang*, 2, 260; "'Long, Hot Summer Could Be Violent,'" *Richmond Afro-American*, May 30, 1964, 1; "Spingarn retires as NAACP head," *Richmond Afro-American*, January 8, 1966, 1.

22. Two Virginia State Conference officers oversaw the youth councils and college chapters, an elected president and senior adviser. Quotation and information on Virginia's college chapters are from *The Candle*, vol. 1, no. 6, March 1958, Part III, Box C159, NAACP Papers.

23. Address of Dr. J. M. Tinsley, president of the Virginia State Conference, Norfolk, Va., October 23, 1949, Part II, Box C211, NAACP Papers; Program, 25th Annual Convention of the Virginia State Conference NAACP, October 7–9, 1960, Part III, Box C159, NAACP Papers. This growth mirrored that of other southern states.

24. Gates, *Making of Massive Resistance*, chapter 1.

25. Gates, *Making of Massive Resistance*, chapter 1; Smith, *Managing White Supremacy*, 32–33, 306; Muse, *Virginia's Massive Resistance*, 1–2; Beagle and Osborne, *J. Lindsay Almond*, 94–96.

26. Almond quotation is from J. Douglas Smith, "'When Reason Collides With Prejudice': Armistead Lloyd Boothe and the Politics of Moderation," in Lassiter and Lewis, *Moderates' Dilemma*, 22. V. O. Key quotation is from Matthew D. Lassiter and Andrew B. Lewis, "Massive Resistance Revisited: Virginia's White Moderates and the Byrd Organization," in Lassiter and Lewis, *Moderates' Dilemma*, 8.

27. Quotation is from Jonathan Daniels, "Shadowy Oligarchy Rules Over Virginia," in "The Byrd Machine," by Edward T. Folliard, reprinted from *The Washington Post and Times Herald*, undated [1957], located in Harry F. Byrd Sr., Papers, Box 8, Accession 9700-I (Miscellaneous, 1887–1966), Albert and Shirley Small Special Collections Library, University of Virginia.

28. For more on the Byrd Organization, see Wilkinson, *Harry Byrd*; Heinemann, *Harry Byrd of Virginia*.

29. Special Release, October 31, 1947, by the Press Service of the NAACP, Part II, Box C211, NAACP Papers; "Delegates to the Twelfth Annual Convention of State NAACP Branches," *Norfolk Journal and Guide*, November 15, 1947, in Part II, Box C211, NAACP Papers; W. Lester Banks to Clarence Mitchell, February 15, 1962, Part IX, Box 222, NAACP Papers; Larissa M. Smith, "A Civil Rights Vanguard:

Black Attorneys and the NAACP in Virginia," in Lau, *From the Grassroots to the Supreme Court*, 129–53; Smith, *Managing White Supremacy*, 256–58.

30. Benjamin Muse, "Negro Crusaders Should Relax Awhile," Virginia Affairs Column (in the *Washington Post*), June 6, 1954, in Part II, Box A228, NAACP Papers; "Historical Development of Virginia's Public School System, 1870–1970," *Public Education in Virginia*, vol. 5, no. 4 (Winter 1970): 28; Larissa M. Smith, "A Civil Rights Vanguard: Black Attorneys and the NAACP in Virginia," in Lau, *From the Grassroots to the Supreme Court*, 129–53; Smith, *Managing White Supremacy*, 256–58.

31. For the impact of World War II on civil rights in Virginia, see *The Home Front*, February 1944, in Bracey and Meier, *Papers of the NAACP*, Part 26, series A, reel 23; Smith, *Managing White Supremacy*, 63; Hill, *Big Bang*, 194, 219; Buni, *Negro in Virginia Politics*, 151. For equalization in Virginia in the later 1940s, see Sullivan, *Lift Every Voice*, 341; Doxie A. Wilkerson, "The Negro School Movement in Virginia: From 'Equalization' to 'Integration,'" *Journal of Negro Education* 29 (Winter 1960): 17–29.

32. Program, 25th Annual Convention of the Virginia State Conference of the NAACP, October 7–9, 1960, Richmond, VA, Part III, Box C159, NAACP Papers; Kluger, *Simple Justice*, 193; Tushnet, *NAACP's Legal Strategy against Segregated Education*, 103.

33. The NAACP often included a request for equalization too, so that if the courts ruled against its attack on segregation, the NAACP could still win a victory. Tushnet, *Making Civil Rights Law*, 155–56.

34. Greenberg, *Crusaders in the Court*, 123–24.

35. "NAACP Urges End to School Segregation," *Richmond Times-Dispatch*, October 21, 1950, 2; Tushnet, *Making Civil Rights Law*, 155–56; Patterson, "*Brown v. Board of Education*," xxv; Kluger, *Simple Justice*, 471–76.

36. Hill quotation is from Kluger, *Simple Justice*, 291. On Robinson, see Tushnet, *Making Civil Rights Law*, 155–56. See also Wallenstein, *Blue Laws and Black Codes*, 108.

37. Similar strikes occurred elsewhere at this time; see Meier and Rudwick, *Along the Color Line*, 360–62; Patterson, "*Brown v. Board of Education*," 4.

38. Stokes, *Students on Strike*; Kluger, *Simple Justice*, 466–85; Hill, *Big Bang*, 149–51.

39. Smith, *They Closed Their Schools*; Brian E. Lee and Brian J. Daugherity, "Program of Action: The Rev. L. Francis Griffin and the Struggle for Racial Equality in Farmville, 1963," *Virginia Magazine of History and Biography*, vol. 121, no. 3 (Autumn 2013): 250–87.

40. Klarman, *From Jim Crow to Civil Rights*, 291; Kluger, *Simple Justice*, 510, 717. In 1957, Virginia State Conference President Dr. E. B. Henderson termed miscegenation "the great scare"; see Edwin B. Henderson, "Integration in Virginia," *The Virginia Spectator: Jim Crow Issue*, vol. 118, no. 8 (May 1957): 19.

41. Editorial, "Tongue In Cheek," *Farmville Herald,* May 22, 1962, 4. For Virginia's defense of segregation in the *Davis v. Prince Edward County* litigation, see Hershman, "A Rumbling in the Museum," 28; Kluger, *Simple Justice,* 480–507.

42. *Dorothy Davis v. County School Board of Prince Edward County,* 103 F. Supp. 337 (1952). Robinson was also significantly involved in the *Briggs* case, the South Carolina lawsuit; see Kluger, *Simple Justice,* 485, 645. Greenberg, *Crusaders in the Court,* 217; Hill, *Big Bang,* 186.

43. Jack Slater, "1954 Revisited," *Ebony* 29 (May 1974): 126; White, *Earl Warren,* 23; Kluger, *Simple Justice,* 699.

Two | "A New Day Is Being Born"

This chapter's title quotes a 1954 statement on behalf of the Virginia State Conference by Oliver W. Hill, in which he said: "Gentlemen, face the dawn and not the setting sun. A new day is being born."

1. Quotation is from *Brown v. Board of Education,* 347 U.S. 483 (1954).

2. Quotation is from Kluger, *Simple Justice,* x. Wilkins with Mathews, *Standing Fast,* 216; Patterson, *Brown v. Board of Education,* xiv-xvi.

3. Quotations are from "Editorial Excerpts From the Nation's Press on Segregation Ruling," *New York Times,* May 18, 1954, 19.

4. Quotation is from Klarman, *From Jim Crow to Civil Rights,* 345. For Delaware, Missouri, Indiana, Wisconsin, and Nevada, see Daugherity and Bolton, *With All Deliberate Speed,* chapters 8–12.

5. Tushnet, *Making Civil Rights Law,* 218–34; Kluger, *Simple Justice,* 710–20; Wilkins with Mathews, *Standing Fast,* 216.

6. Eastland quotation is from "Mississippi Representative Hopes for Calm, but Eastland Sees Strife," *New York Times,* May 18, 1954, 19. The *Daily News* quotation is from "Editorial Excerpts on School Bias Ruling," *New York Times,* May 19, 1954, 20. For the Talmadge quotation, see "Georgia," *New York Times,* May 18, 1954, 20.

7. Quotations are from "School Segregation Is Unconstitutional," *Richmond Times-Dispatch,* May 18, 1954, 2.

8. Quotation is from Leidholdt, *Standing Before the Shouting Mob,* 66. The Court's ruling surprised many Virginia officials, which may help account for the moderate nature of some initial responses to *Brown;* see Hershman, "A Rumbling in the Museum," 32–39. The fact that Byrd was out of the country may also help explain divergent responses. Stanley's statement was issued two hours after the decision; see Hill, *Big Bang,* 168; "Virginia," *Southern School News,* vol. 1, no. 1, September 1954, 13.

9. Quotation is from "Governor to Call Meeting of State Leaders on School Problem," *Richmond Times-Dispatch,* May 18, 1954, 7; see also Harry F. Byrd Sr., statement on *Brown v. Board of Education,* May 17, 1954, Additional Papers of

Everett R. Combs, Accession 9712-B, J, Box 19, Albert and Shirley Small Special Collections, University of Virginia.

10. Quotation is from Charles McDowell Jr., "Stanley Backs Continued Segregation in Schools," *Richmond Times-Dispatch*, June 26, 1954, 1. A number of historians have suggested that Byrd's opposition to *Brown* was political, in that maintaining segregation in the Commonwealth's schools would solidify the Byrd Organization's political preeminence within the state; see Wilkinson, *Harry Byrd*, chapter 5; Ely, *Crisis of Conservative Virginia*, chapter 3.

11. Many southerners felt racial mixing was unnatural; see Patterson, *Brown v. Board of Education*, xviii–xix, 5–6; Boyle, *Desegregated Heart*, 132–61.

12. Quotation is from Tushnet, *Making Civil Rights Law*, 248.

13. Gates, *Making of Massive Resistance*, 34–36, 43; Kluger, *Simple Justice*, 729–30.

14. Quotation is from "Virginia," *Southern School News*, vol. 1, no. 3, November 1954, 15.

15. Quotation is from John N. Popham, "Bias Ruling Opposed In a 12-State Accord," *New York Times*, June 11, 1954, 1. See also James Latimer, "Southern Governors To Meet Here Today," *Richmond Times-Dispatch*, June 10, 1954, 1.

16. Quotation is from Muse, *Virginia's Massive Resistance*, 159; see also 172. As Sarah Patton Boyle put it, Virginia "was the backbone of the South, which was the backbone of the nation, which was the backbone of the world." Boyle, *Desegregated Heart*, 5.

17. Suggested Program For Southern Branches, 1954–1955, in Bracey and Meier, *Papers of the NAACP*, Supplement to Part 1 (1951–55), reel 11; Thurgood Marshall to Professor C. L. Harper, President, Atlanta branch, February 15, 1954, Part V, Box 2595, Papers of the National Association for the Advancement of Colored People, Library of Congress Manuscript Division, Washington, D.C. (hereafter cited as NAACP Papers); Report of the Executive Secretary for the Month of March, 1954, in Bracey and Meier, *Papers of the NAACP*, Part 16, series B, reel 21; Board of Directors Meeting Minutes, June 30, 1954, in ibid., Supplement to Part 1 (1951–55), reel 1.

18. Motions and/or Recommendations Adopted by the Atlanta Conference, May 22–23, 1954, Part V, Box 2595, NAACP Papers; "Dixie NAACP Leaders Map Plans to Implement Court's Ruling," NAACP press release, May 23, 1954, Part V, Box 2595, NAACP Papers; NAACP press release, May 23, 1954, in Bracey and Meier, *Papers of the NAACP*, Part 3, series C, reel 17. In such gatherings, NAACP representatives voted to adopt or reject resolutions.

19. Quotation is from Address by Thurgood Marshall to 1954 Convention, in Bracey and Meier, *Papers of the NAACP*, Supplement to Part 1 (1951–55), reel 10.

20. Quotation is from Channing Tobias and Walter White to "Dear Branch Officer," May 25, 1954, in Bracey and Meier, *Papers of the NAACP*, Part 3, series C, reel 5.

21. Given Tobias' position, it is unsurprising that the implementation plan was

somewhat conciliatory. Quotation is from "Dixie NAACP Leaders Map Plans to Implement Court's Ruling," NAACP press release, May 23, 1954, Part V, Box V2595, NAACP Papers. See also Wilkins with Mathews, *Standing Fast*, 215.

22. Quotation is from Channing Tobias and Walter White to "Dear Branch Officer," May 25, 1954, Part II, Box A231, NAACP Papers. For a copy of the Atlanta Declaration, see Bracey and Meier, *Papers of the NAACP*, Part 3, series C, reel 13. See also "Dixie NAACP Leaders Map Plans to Implement Court's Ruling," NAACP press release, May 23, 1954, Part V, Box 2595, NAACP Papers.

23. Though NAACP annual conventions offered branch delegates an opportunity to influence national NAACP policy, the conventions generally ratified decisions made by national NAACP staff and the board of directors. For more on the role of the annual convention, see St. James, *National Association for the Advancement of Colored People: A Case Study*, 68, 119; Bracey and Meier, *Papers of the NAACP*, Guide to Supplement to Part 1 (1951–55), xii; Article IX of National NAACP Constitution (Blue Book).

24. Developing Community Action Program To Speed Up Integration, in Bracey and Meier, *Papers of the NAACP*, Part 3, series C, reel 5; Resolutions Adopted [1954 annual convention], Education, in ibid., Supplement to Part 1 (1951–55), reel 10; Robert Carter and Gloster Current to Chairmen, Co-Discussion Leaders, and Consultants, June 21, 1954, Part II, Box A231, NAACP Papers.

25. Quotation is from Resolutions Adopted [1954 annual convention], Education, in Bracey and Meier, *Papers of the NAACP*, Supplement to Part 1 (1951–55), reel 10. See also "Neither Threat Nor Supplication," Address to North Carolina State Conference by Walter White, June 13, 1954, Part II, Box A231, NAACP Papers; Developing Community Action Program to Speed Up Integration, undated [1954], Part II, Box A231, NAACP Papers.

26. Quotation is from Kluger, *Simple Justice*, 639; see also Tushnet, *Making Civil Rights Law*, 197–99.

27. On Thurgood Marshall, see "Supreme Court ends school segregation," *Richmond Afro-American*, May 22, 1954, 8; "N.A.A.C.P. Sets Advanced Goals," *New York Times*, May 18, 1954, 16; Luther A. Huston, "1896 Ruling Upset," *New York Times*, May 18, 1954, 1. Roy Wilkins later wrote, "At first, Thurgood hoped to have desegregation well underway by September 1955. I believe it was Ralph Bunche who said around this time that the country's prejudice against black people was 'more veneer than deep grain'; that 'it could be peeled off with little damage or pain.' Well, we were all wrong." Wilkins with Mathews, *Standing Fast*, 216.

28. Quotation is from Hill, *Big Bang*, 73.

29. Quotation is from Remarks of Thurgood Marshall at Press Conference, June 30, 1954, in Bracey and Meier, *Papers of the NAACP*, Supplement to Part 1 (1951–55), reel 10. See also Thurgood Marshall to State Conference Presidents, September 17, 1954, Part II, Box A231, NAACP Papers; Developing Community Action Program To Speed Up Integration, in Bracey and Meier, *Papers of the NAACP*, Part 3, series C, reel 5.

30. Quotation is from "Spottswood tells legal colleagues he'll see spots," *Richmond Afro-American*, May 22, 1954, 8.

31. Virginia Since May 17, 1954, Part V, Box 2836, NAACP Papers; "NAACP branches to act immediately," *Richmond Afro-American*, May 29, 1954, 6.

32. Follow-Up RE Atlanta Conference, undated [May or June 1954], Part V, Box 2595, NAACP Papers, lays out a recommended course of action for southern State Conferences, allowing one to see similarities between national policy and Virginia State Conference actions in 1954. See also Suggested Program for Southern Branches, 1954–1955, Part II, Box A231, NAACP Papers.

33. Banks quotation is from Hershman, "A Rumbling in the Museum," 41. For more on the gathering, see Report of the Committee on Offenses Against the Administration of Justice, Appendix 11, 1957, in Bracey and Meier, *Papers of the NAACP*, Part 20, reel 12; Virginia State Conference press release, on the June 6 meeting in Richmond, June 7, 1954, Part II, Box A228, NAACP Papers; Newsletter; Arlington Branch, NAACP, vol. 1, no. 5, May-June 1954, Part II, Box C203, NAACP Papers; "NAACP endorses Atlanta decision," *Richmond Afro-American*, June 12, 1954, 22; Report of the Albemarle Branch on Desegregation Activities, August 27, 1954, Part II, Box A228, NAACP Papers.

34. Quotation is from Hershman, "A Rumbling in the Museum," 42. See also Hill, *Big Bang*, 170; Gates, *Making of Massive Resistance*, 29–30; "South's Governors Meet Here June 10," *Richmond Times-Dispatch*, May 25, 1954, 1; James Latimer, "Schools Advised to Continue Segregation," *Richmond Times-Dispatch*, May 28, 1954, 1.

35. Quotation is from James Latimer, "Schools Advised to Continue Segregation," *Richmond Times-Dispatch*, May 28, 1954, 11. See also "NAACP endorses Atlanta decision," *Richmond Afro-American*, June 12, 1954, 22.

36. Quotation is from "Good government is key to integration," *Richmond Afro-American*, October 23, 1954, 18. "Thurgood Marshall here on Sunday," *Richmond Afro-American*, June 19, 1954, 14.

37. Quotation is from Oliver W. Hill, Statement on Behalf of the Virginia State Conference, NAACP Branches, at Public Hearing Before the Commission to Study Public Education At the Mosque on November 15, 1954, Part II, Box A228, NAACP Papers; "Urge NAACP officials to give views on integration," *Richmond Afro-American*, October 23, 1954, 18; "Back Supreme Court," *Richmond Afro-American*, November 13, 1954, 1.

38. "Virginia," *Southern School News*, vol. 1, no. 3, November 1954, 15; "Court Roundup," *Southern School News*, vol. 2, no. 4, October 1955, 6.

39. "Virginia," *Southern School News*, vol. 2, no. 5, November 1955, 13; Sweeney, *Race, Reason, and Massive Resistance*, 29; Beagle and Osborne, *J. Lindsay Almond*, 96; Hershman, "A Rumbling in the Museum," 48–49; Gates, *Making of Massive Resistance*, 36–38, 161–62.

40. The most prominent segregationist organization in the South, the White Citizens' Councils, did not enjoy much influence in Virginia, and the Ku Klux Klan

had long been repudiated by the state's political leaders. Both will be discussed in subsequent chapters. F. W. Burnham, "Virginia Tense on Color Issue," *Christian Century,* August 3, 1955, reported that a May 1955 poll conducted by Richmond Newspapers, Inc., showed that 92 percent of white adults in Richmond favored segregation in public schools.

41. Benjamin Muse, "Negro Crusaders Should Relax Awhile," Virginia Affairs Column (in the *Washington Post*), June 6, 1954, and Roy Wilkins to Dr. E. B. Henderson, December 9, 1954, both in Part II, Box A228, NAACP Papers; Pamphlet produced by the Virginia Council on Human Relations, in Bracey and Meier, *Papers of the NAACP,* Part 20, reel 13; Hershman, "A Rumbling in the Museum," 25, 49, 65; Gates, *Making of Massive Resistance,* 50–52; Muse, *Virginia's Massive Resistance,* 35–39.

42. I use phrases such as liberals, moderates, and massive resisters with some trepidation; the lines separating these groups were blurry and subject to change. See chapter 4 for a discussion of the conflict between massive resisters and moderates during Virginia's school closing crisis in 1958. Both moderates and massive resisters angrily opposed the NAACP; see Hershman, "A Rumbling in the Museum," 95–96; Muse, *Virginia's Massive Resistance,* 48–49.

43. "Virginia," *Southern School News,* vol. 1, no. 2, October 1954, 14; "Virginia," *Southern School News,* vol. 1, no. 3, November 1954, 15.

44. "Board Passes on Segregation At Mixed-Up Meeting," August 6, 1954, unnamed newspaper, in Part II, Box A228, NAACP Papers.

45. "Smooth transition expected in Virginia," *Richmond Afro-American,* May 29, 1954, 7; "Fact sheet on integration issued by Arlington board," *Richmond Afro-American,* November 20, 1954, 9.

46. "Va. officials, citizens, weighing deseg," *Richmond Afro-American,* October 9, 1954, 9; "Charlottesville may welcome integration," *Richmond Afro-American,* November 13, 1954, 12.

47. Quotations are from "Virginia Opposes Integration Now," *New York Times,* April 10, 1955, 36; Kluger, *Simple Justice,* 724. See also Kluger, *Simple Justice,* 723–36.

48. Quotation is from "Leaders denounce school study body," *Richmond Afro-American,* September 4, 1954, 1. Madison Jones, "The Impact and Consequences of the U.S. Supreme Court Decision of May 17, 1954," in Bracey and Meier, *Papers of the NAACP,* Part 3, series C, reel 17; NAACP press release, July 4, 1954, in ibid., Supplement to Part 1 (1951–55), reel 10. On Hill, see Oliver W. Hill, Statement on Behalf of the Virginia State Conference, NAACP Branches, at Public Hearing Before the Commission to Study Public Education At the Mosque on November 15, 1954, Part II, Box A228, NAACP Papers.

49. Smith quotation is from *Managing White Supremacy,* 243. See also 54, 259; Sweeney, *Race, Reason, and Massive Resistance,* 29.

50. Quotations are from "Almond assailed for remarks on NAACP," *Richmond*

Afro-American, August 28, 1954, 1. See also "Virginia," *Southern School News,* vol. 1, no. 2, October 1954, 14.

51. "School activity around the country," *Richmond Afro-American,* September 18, 1954, 20.

52. Quotation is from "Good government is key to integration," *Richmond Afro-American,* October 23, 1954, 18. See also W. Lester Banks, "Va. NAACP readies for '54 convention," *Richmond Afro-American,* September 14, 1954, 18; "NAACP convention set at Martinsville Friday," *Richmond Afro-American,* October 9, 1954, 9; "Convention to study deseg issue," *Richmond Afro-American,* October 9, 1954, 9; "Good govt is key to integration," *Richmond Afro-American,* October 23, 1954, 18. The national NAACP also noted that Virginia was "seeking methods to evade or circumvent the Supreme Court ruling." Status of School Desegregation report, October 1954, Part II, Box A231, NAACP Papers.

53. Quotation is from *Brown v. Board of Education, Topeka, Kansas,* 349 U.S. 294 (1955).

54. Murphy and Marshall were close friends. The conversation is reported in Kluger, *Simple Justice,* 746–47.

55. Quotation is from Directive to the Branches Adopted at Regional Emergency Conference, Atlanta, Ga., June 4, 1955, Part V, Box V2595, NAACP Papers. See also Directive to Branches, proposed draft, subject to action of Regional Emergency Conference, Atlanta, June 4, 1955, Part II, Box A231, NAACP Papers; Robert Carter and Thurgood Marshall, "The Meaning and Significance of the Supreme Court Decree," *Journal of Negro Education* (Washington D.C.: School of Education, Howard University), vol. 24, no. 3 (Summer 1955): 400–403.

56. Quotation is from Present Status of Integration in the Schools, prepared by Thurgood Marshall and Legal Defense Fund staff, February 15, 1955, Part II, Box A231, NAACP Papers.

57. Quotation is from Roy Wilkins, "The Role of the NAACP in the Desegregation Process," *Social Problems* (New York: Johnson Reprint Corp.), vol. 2, no. 4 (April 1955): 201.

58. Italics added by author. Quotation is from Memorandum to Emergency Regional Conference, from Roy Wilkins and Thurgood Marshall, June 4, 1955, in Bracey and Mcier, *Papers of the NAACP,* Part 3, series C, reel 14; see also Resolutions, in ibid., Supplement to Part 1 (1951–55), reel 12.

59. NAACP press release, June 26, 1955, in Bracey and Meier, *Papers of the NAACP,* Part 3, series C, reel 12.

60. Quotation is from Directive to the Branches Adopted at Regional Emergency Conference, Atlanta, Ga., June 4, 1955, Part V, Box V2595, NAACP Papers.

61. Roy Wilkins to W. Lester Banks, June 9, 1955, Part II, Box C212, NAACP Papers; Report of the Committee on Offenses Against the Administration of Justice, Appendix 12, 1957, in Bracey and Meier, *Papers of the NAACP,* Part 20, reel 12.

62. Confidential memorandum from Gloster Current, June 9, 1955, Part II, Box

A231, NAACP Papers; L. M. Wright Jr., "State NAACP to Sue In Some Areas Soon," *Richmond Times-Dispatch*, October 10, 1955, 1.

63. Confidential Directive, June 30, 1955, to Member Branches of the Virginia State Conference NAACP, Re: Petitions, Part II, Box A228, NAACP Papers; Roy Wilkins to W. Lester Banks, June 9, 1955, Part II, Box C212, NAACP Papers.

64. "NAACP Asks Integration At Norfolk," *Richmond Times-Dispatch*, July 14, 1955, 14; "Norfolk NAACP Plans Suit Soon," *Richmond Times-Dispatch*, July 19, 1955, 2.

65. School desegregation petition, Princess Anne County, Virginia, Part II, Box A231, NAACP Papers; Virginia Since May 17, 1954, Part II, Box B147, NAACP Papers; "NAACP to sue to desegregate Virginia schools," *Richmond Afro-American*, "This is Virginia" edition, October 15, 1955, 1; Report of the Commission on Law Reform and Racial Activities, in Bracey and Meier, *Papers of the NAACP*, Part 20, reel 12; L. M. Wright Jr., "State NAACP to Sue In Some Areas Soon," *Richmond Times-Dispatch*, October 10, 1955, 1. Several localities asserted that they could not desegregate their schools had they wanted to; state law preempted their actions.

66. Quotation is from Muse, *Virginia's Massive Resistance*, 49.

67. Quotation is from L. M. Wright Jr., "Prince Edward Can Keep Separate Schools Till '56," *Richmond Times-Dispatch*, July 19, 1955, 2.

68. Memorandum from Roy Wilkins to the NAACP board of directors, September 12, 1955, in Bracey and Meier, *Papers of the NAACP*, Part 16, series B, reel 21.

69. "'Tricky' Contracts Sent Va. Teachers," *Richmond Afro-American*, May 7, 1955, 5; Hershman, "A Rumbling in the Museum," 103–11.

70. Public Education, Report of the [Gray] Commission to the Governor of Virginia, 1955, Part IX, Box 222, NAACP Papers; Sweeney, *Race, Reason, and Massive Resistance*, 76–77; Gates, *Making of Massive Resistance*, 63–69.

71. Sweeney, *Race, Reason, and Massive Resistance*, chapter 3; Gates, *Making of Massive Resistance*, 63–72; Muse, *Virginia's Massive Resistance*, 9–10.

72. Buni, *Negro in Virginia Politics*, 178; Gates, *Making of Massive Resistance*, 64–73.

73. "Third Of Citizens Oppose Defiance Of Supreme Court," *Richmond Afro-American*, December 10, 1955, 19. For more on the NAACP's opposition, see Virginia State Conference press release, November 13, 1955, Part II, Box C212, NAACP Papers; NAACP in Virginia Opposes Private School Proposal, December 1, 1955, Part II, Box A228, NAACP Papers; Hill, *Big Bang*, 171–74.

74. Quotations are from Henry L. Marsh III, interview by Virginia Civil Rights Video Initiative Project, M 312, Special Collections and Archives, James Branch Cabell Library, Virginia Commonwealth University; Hill, *Big Bang*, 171–74.

75. Quotation is from Klarman, *From Jim Crow to Civil Rights*, 367. See also Hustwit, *James J. Kilpatrick*, chapter 2.

76. Burk, *Dwight D. Eisenhower*, 159–60; Ambrose, *Eisenhower*, 414–20; Fairclough, *Race and Democracy*, 187; Patterson, *Brown v. Board of Education*, 80–82; Kluger, *Simple Justice*, 650, 754.

77. Quotation is from Wilkins with Mathews, *Standing Fast,* 222. See also Report of the Executive Secretary for the Month of April, 1956, in Bracey and Meier, *Papers of the NAACP,* Supplement to Part 1 (1956–60), reel 1. For Oliver Hill's perspective, see *Big Bang,* 247.

78. Quotation is from L. M. Wright Jr., "Prince Edward Can Keep Separate Schools Till '56," *Richmond Times-Dispatch,* July 19, 1955, 1. See also L. M. Wright Jr., "Meaning of Court Ruling Will Be Argued Here," *Richmond Times-Dispatch,* July 3, 1955, 3; L. M. Wright Jr., "Prince Edward Plan Rejected by NAACP," *Richmond Times-Dispatch,* July 17, 1955, 1.

79. Quotation is from Robert Carter and Thurgood Marshall, "The Meaning and Significance of the Supreme Court Decree," *Journal of Negro Education,* vol. 24, no. 3 (Summer 1955): 400–401.

80. "Hearing on Segregation Will Open Here Today," *Richmond Times-Dispatch,* July 18, 1955, 1.

81. Quotation is from NAACP press release, July 22, 1955, in Bracey and Meier, *Papers of the NAACP,* Part 3, series C, reel 17.

82. Ruby Hurley to Gloster Current, September 10, 1954, in Bracey and Meier, *Papers of the NAACP,* Part 25, series A, reel 4; Speech of Roy Wilkins to the Charlottesville NAACP, October 7, 1955, Part II, Box A571, NAACP Papers.

83. Quotation is from Board of Directors Meeting Minutes, October 10, 1955, in Bracey and Meier, *Papers of the NAACP,* Supplement to Part 1 (1956–60), reel 1. See also Robert Carter and Thurgood Marshall, "The Meaning and Significance of the Supreme Court Decree," *Journal of Negro Education,* vol. 24, no. 3 (Summer 1955): 402. Considering the cost of litigation, 1955 was the also the best year financially in the NAACP's history; see NAACP press release, January 3, 1956, in Bracey and Meier, *Papers of the NAACP,* Supplement to Part 1 (1956–60), reel 2.

84. Quotations are from Edith T. Burton, "Record of Restraint," Letter to the Editor, *Washington Post,* December 21, 1957, in Part IX, Box 222, NAACP Papers, and Roy Wilkins to Dr. E. B. Henderson, October 25, 1955, Part II, Box A228, NAACP Papers. See also Speech of Roy Wilkins to the Charlottesville, Va., NAACP, October 7, 1955, Part II, Box A571, NAACP Papers.

85. Quotation is from L. M. Wright Jr., "State NAACP to Sue in Some Areas Soon," *Richmond Times-Dispatch,* October 10, 1955, 1. See also Memorandum on Annual State Conference, Part II, Box C212, NAACP Papers; "NAACP to sue to desegregate Virginia schools: Unit agrees upon court action at 3-day state meet," *Richmond Afro-American,* "This is Virginia" edition, October 15, 1955, 1; L. M. Wright Jr., "NAACP Chief Assails Foes Of Integration," *Richmond Times-Dispatch,* October 8, 1955, 1; Report of the Commission on Law Reform and Racial Activities, in Bracey and Meier, *Papers of the NAACP,* Part 20, reel 12; "Virginia Columnist Says NAACP is Powerful Because on Side of Law," NAACP press release, October 27, 1955, Part II, Box A228, NAACP Papers.

Three | "Those Who Were on the Other Side"

This chapter's title quotes historian James H. Hershman Jr.'s doctoral dissertation, "A Rumbling in the Museum," in which he writes: "Most studies of this turbulent and crucial era have focused on those who formulated and sought to carry out the massive resistance program. No one has yet told the story of those who were on the other side."

1. Quotation is from NAACP press release, January 3, 1956, in Bracey and Meier, *Papers of the NAACP*, Supplement to Part 1 (1956–60), reel 2. For more, see "Special Report to the *New York Times*," February 20, 1956, in ibid., Part 3, series D, reel 3; L. M. Wright Jr., "State NAACP to Sue In Some Areas Soon," *Richmond Times-Dispatch*, October 10, 1955, 1; Robert Carter and Thurgood Marshall, "The Meaning and Significance of the Supreme Court Decree," *Journal of Negro Education*, vol. 24, no. 3 (Summer 1955): 401.

2. Report of the Executive Secretary to the Board of Directors, February 14, 1956, in Bracey and Meier, *Papers of the NAACP*, Supplement to Part 1 (1956–60), reel 1. For the conference, Marshall had asked the State Conference representatives to prepare an "up-to-date picture of what has been done in your state since decisions of Supreme Court. A. What has been done by Governors and other state executive officers. B. What has been done by the legislature of your state. C. What has been done by the state board of education. D. What action has been taken by local school boards. [And also an] up to date picture of action by you and your branches since May 31. A. Petitions filed and replies. B. Where suits are contemplated. C. Are your lawyers ready for legal action in certain areas. D. Do your branches want legal action." Thurgood Marshall to State Conference Presidents, January 20, 1956, Part V, Box 2595, Papers of the National Association for the Advancement of Colored People, Library of Congress Manuscript Division, Washington, D.C. (hereafter cited as NAACP Papers).

3. The other states were Alabama, Florida, Georgia, Louisiana, Mississippi, North Carolina, and South Carolina. "Special Report to the *New York Times*," February 20, 1956, in Bracey and Meier, *Papers of the NAACP*, Part 3, series D, reel 3; Report of the Atlanta Conference, February 18–19, 1956, Part V, Box 2595, NAACP Papers.

4. Report of the Executive Secretary for the Month of February, 1956, in Bracey and Meier, *Papers of the NAACP*, Supplement to Part 1 (1956–60), reel 1; Keynote Address by Thurgood Marshall to 47th Annual NAACP Convention, in ibid., Supplement to Part 1 (1956–60), reel 4; Board of Directors Meeting Minutes, May 14, 1956, in ibid., Part 20, reel 12; Board of Directors Meeting Minutes, June 11, 1956, in ibid., Part 20, reel 12; "New NAACP School Suits Planned in State by June," *Richmond Times-Dispatch*, February 20, 1956, 1. For more on NAACP's litigation protocol at this time, see untitled memorandum from Thurgood Marshall, August 15, 1955, in Bracey and Meier, *Papers of the NAACP*, Part 3, series C, reel 4. The

NAACP's determination to treat the southern states individually is one of the reasons for the state-focused approach of this book.

5. Quotation is from "Special Report to the *New York Times*," February 20, 1956, in Bracey and Meier, *Papers of the NAACP*, Part 3, series D, reel 3. See also Resolutions Adopted, 1956 Annual Convention, in ibid., Supplement to Part 1 (1956–60), reel 4.

6. Quotation is from Resolutions Adopted, 1956 Annual Convention, in Bracey and Meier, *Papers of the NAACP*, Supplement to Part 1 (1956–60), reel 4. For some southern State Conferences, this meant less legal support if they initiated litigation on their own.

7. Henderson quotation is from Report of the Atlanta Conference, February 18–19, 1956, Part V, Box 2595, NAACP Papers. See also NAACP press release, January 12, 1956, in Bracey and Meier, *Papers of the NAACP*, Part 3, series D, reel 9; "New NAACP School Suits Planned in State by June," *Richmond Times-Dispatch*, February 20, 1956, 1. After 20 years as president of the Virginia State Conference, Dr. J. M. Tinsley chose not to stand for election in October 1955.

8. Dr. J. M. Tinsley to Ella J. Baker, October 16, 1944, Part II, Box C211, NAACP Papers; Notes of the Business Session, 20th Annual State Convention, October 9, 1955, Part II, Box C212, Virginia State Conference, 1955, NAACP Papers; W. Lester Banks to Jackie Robinson, June 2, 1958, Part III, Box C159, NAACP Papers.

9. Joseph F. Simmons, Report of Political Action Director, Virginia State Conference NAACP, June 1 to June 15, 1956, Part III, Box A271, NAACP Papers; "NAACP Awarded Ten Spots on Two Richmond Radio Stations," undated [just before January 9, 1956], Part III, Box A106, NAACP Papers.

10. Ross Allen Weston to Dr. E. B. Henderson, January 12, 1956, Part V, Box 2582, NAACP Papers; Gates, *Making of Massive Resistance*, 136–66.

11. Hershman, "A Rumbling in the Museum," 142; Gates, *Making of Massive Resistance*, 88–95; Buni, *Negro in Virginia Politics*, 180–83.

12. Quotation is from NAACP press release, January 12, 1956, in Bracey and Meier, *Papers of the NAACP*, Part 3, series D, reel 9.

13. Gates, *Making of Massive Resistance*, 122–23; Hershman, "A Rumbling in the Museum," 169–71; Beagle and Osborne, *J. Lindsay Almond*, 100.

14. Sweeney, *Race, Reason, and Massive Resistance*, 78–79; Beagle and Osborne, *J. Lindsay Almond*, 98–101; Gates, *Making of Massive Resistance*, 76–82.

15. "Arlington School Board Adopts Integration Plan," *Washington Post and Times Herald*, January 15, 1956, in Bracey and Meier, *Papers of the NAACP*, Part 3, series D, reel 9; Paul Bradley, "My parents told me to go, and I went," *Richmond Times-Dispatch*, February 16, 1996, 1; Hershman, "A Rumbling in the Museum," 158–60. For more on Arlington and *Brown v. Board of Education*, see chapter 2.

16. Quotation is from Muse, *Virginia's Massive Resistance*, 33.

17. Sweeney, *Race, Reason, and Massive Resistance*, 127–40; Gates, *Making of Massive Resistance*, 23–28.

18. Senate Joint Resolution No. 3, Commonwealth of Virginia, General Assembly, Part IX, Box 222, NAACP Papers; Gates, *Making of Massive Resistance*, 100–105, 114; Beagle and Osborne, *J. Lindsay Almond*, 100; Hershman, "A Rumbling in the Museum," 160–65.

19. Describing the Southern Manifesto, Senator Byrd said the document was part of "the plan of massive resistance we've been working on." Byrd quotation here is from Beagle and Osborne, *J. Lindsay Almond*, 101. For more on the Southern Manifesto, and Senator Byrd's role, see Matthew D. Lassiter and Andrew B. Lewis, "Massive Resistance Revisited: Virginia's White Moderates and the Byrd Organization," in Lassiter and Lewis, *Moderates' Dilemma*, 7; Peltason, *Fifty-Eight Lonely Men*, 41, 138; Beagle and Osborne, *J. Lindsay Almond*, 93–101.

20. Kilpatrick quotation is from Joseph J. Thorndike, "'The Sometimes Sordid Level of Race and Segregation': James J. Kilpatrick and the Virginia Campaign against *Brown*," in Lassiter and Lewis, *Moderates' Dilemma*, 54. For more on the resolution of interposition, see Interposition Resolution (Senate Joint Resolution No. 3), in Bracey and Meier, *Papers of the NAACP*, Part 3, series D, reel 13; Gates, *Making Massive Resistance*, 110–15; Tushnet, *Making Civil Rights Law*, 240–41.

21. Quotation is from "Delegates Get Move to Keep Schools Same," *Richmond Times-Dispatch*, February 21, 1956, 1. See also "New NAACP School Suits Planned in State by June," *Richmond Times-Dispatch*, February 20, 1956, 1; "North Carolina Planning Action Against NAACP," *Richmond Times-Dispatch*, February 18, 1956, 9;

22. Quotation is from L. M. Wright Jr., "Court Move By NAACP Is Planned," *Richmond Times-Dispatch*, April 22, 1956, 1. See also "Desegregate with no delay, NAACP urges," *Richmond Afro-American*, June 25, 1955, 1; "NAACP to sue to desegregate Virginia schools," *Richmond Afro-American*, "This is Virginia" edition, October 15, 1955, 1.

23. NAACP Legal Defense Fund Summer Report, June-July-August 1956, Part III, Box A237, NAACP Papers; Minutes of the Board of Directors Meeting, May 14, 1956, Report of the Special Counsel, and Minutes of the Board of Directors Meeting, June 11, 1956, Report of the Special Counsel, both in in Bracey and Meier, *Papers of the NAACP*, Part 20, reel 12.

24. (Confidential) Cities for Concentration in Filing Petitions RE Desegregation, undated [1955], Part II, Box A231, NAACP Papers; Membership data from the national office to the Virginia State Conference (untitled), Part III, Box C160, NAACP Papers; Report to the Virginia State Conference Meeting, Suffolk, Va., October 4–6, 1957, Memberships and Freedom Fund Contributions Received From Branches, Part III, Box C158, NAACP Papers. On the petitions, see L. M. Wright Jr., "Desegregation Suits Due To Be Filed Within Month," *Richmond Times-Dispatch*, April 15, 1956, D1; "Virginia Holds Decree Allows Year of Segregated Schooling," *Southern School News*, vol. 2, no. 2, August 1955, 10; "Doubt Cast on Special Assembly Session in Virginia," *Southern School News*, vol. 2, no. 5, November 1955, 12.

25. *The Candle*, vol. 1, no. 5, December 1957, Part III, Box C158, NAACP Papers; Virginia State Conference, Branch Roster, Part III, Box C160, NAACP Papers.

26. Quotation is from J. M. Nabrit Jr., "Desegregation and Reason," *Phylon*, 3rd quarter 1956: 289.

27. Quotation is from Edith T. Burton, "Record of Restraint," Letter to the Editor, *Washington Post*, December 21, 1957, in Part III, Box C158, NAACP Papers. See also "NAACP Planning 10 More State Suits," *Richmond Times-Dispatch*, July 19, 1956, 2. On Newport News, see "Integration in September Asked in Prince Edward," *Richmond Times-Dispatch*, April 24, 1956, 1. Prince Edward County, all along, was considered a poor choice for legal action, even by the NAACP; see Hill, *Big Bang*, 160.

28. Spottswood Robinson, Techniques in the Handling of School Facilities Cases at the Elementary and High School Levels, June 23–25, 1949, Part V, Box 2836, NAACP Papers; untitled memorandum from Thurgood Marshall, August 15, 1955, in Bracey and Meier, *Papers of the NAACP*, Part 3, series C, reel 4; "NAACP reaffirms policy, procedures," *Richmond Afro-American*, November 24, 1956, 5; Oliver W. Hill Sr., interview by author, tape recording, Richmond, Va., April 18, 2000.

29. See Hill, *Big Bang*, 186; St. James, *National Association for the Advancement of Colored People: A Case Study*, 119–20; Finch, *NAACP*, 59; Minutes of the Board of Directors Meeting, May 14, 1956, Report of the Special Counsel, and Minutes of the Board of Directors Meeting, June 11, 1956, Report of the Special Counsel, both in Bracey and Meier, *Papers of the NAACP*, Part 20, reel 12.

30. Quotations are from "NAACP Planning 10 More State Suits," *Richmond Times-Dispatch*, July 19, 1956, 2. See also "NAACP in Virginia Plans New School Suits Before June," *Richmond Times-Dispatch*, February 20, 1956, 1.

31. Quotation is from Muse, *Virginia's Massive Resistance*, 48. See also Brooks, *Walls Come Tumbling Down*, 128; Muse, *Virginia's Massive Resistance*, 31–32. For white moderates and liberals and the NAACP suits, see Hershman, "A Rumbling in the Museum," 215–17.

32. Quotation is from Rick Sauder, "Oliver Hill: A Journey Down the Civil Rights Road," *Richmond News Leader*, January 15, 1992, 7. See also Hill, *Big Bang*, 180, 287–88; NAACP flyer on the Hundley Fund meeting, and attached letter, September 17, 1958, Part IX, Box 222, NAACP Papers; NAACP press release, June 7, 1956, in Bracey and Meier, *Papers of the NAACP*, Part 3, series D, reel 9; Cabell Phillips, "Norfolk Schools Aim To Avoid Little Rock," *New York Times*, February 1, 1959, E6; "Warren Threatened," *Richmond Afro-American*, July 21, 1956, 1.

33. Quotation is from Paul Bradley, "My parents told me to go, and I went," *Richmond Times-Dispatch*, February 16, 1996, 1.

34. Under new state laws, the NAACP could not operate in the affected localities without turning over this information. Fairclough, *Race and Democracy*, 205–12.

35. See also Board of Directors Meeting Minutes, April 9, 1956, in Bracey and

Meier, *Papers of the NAACP*, Supplement to Part 1 (1956–60), reel 1; NAACP, *1956 NAACP Annual Report*, 34.

36. Quotation is from Brooks, *Walls Come Tumbling Down*, 129. See also Minutes of the Board of Directors Meeting, September 10, 1956, in Bracey and Meier, *Papers of the NAACP*, Supplement to Part 1 (1956–60), reel 1.

37. Quotation is from L. M. Wright Jr., "Almond Asks Stanley Call Special Session in July," *Richmond Times-Dispatch*, June 1, 1956, 1. See also "Another Suit By NAACP Is Expected," *Richmond Times-Dispatch*, May 7, 1956, 1. For the July meeting, see James Latimer, "Anti-Integration Move Launched by Governor," *Richmond Times-Dispatch*, July 24, 1956, 1; Muse, *Virginia's Massive Resistance*, 28; Heinemann, *Harry Byrd of Virginia*, 336; Sweeney, *Race, Reason, and Massive Resistance*, 140.

38. Quotations are from L. M. Wright Jr., "Almond Asks Stanley Call Special Session in July," *Richmond Times-Dispatch*, June 1, 1956, 1, and James Latimer, "Speaker Moore Scores Almond Assembly Call: Attorney General 'Shocked' At 'Unwarranted' Attack," *Richmond Times-Dispatch*, June 4, 1956, 1.

39. Paul quotation is from L. M. Wright Jr., "Judge Rules Charlottesville Must Prepare to Integrate," *Richmond Times-Dispatch*, July 13, 1956, 8. *Clarissa Thompson v. County School Board of Arlington County*, 144 F. Supp. 239 (1956); *School Board of the City of Charlottesville v. Doris Allen*, 240 F. 2d 59 (4th Cir. 1956); Rufus Wells, "'Have I Made Myself Clear?,'" *Richmond Afro-American*, July 21, 1956, 1; Wilhoit, *Politics of Massive Resistance*, 303.

40. Quotation is from Buni, *Negro in Virginia Politics*, 185.

41. Acts of the Special Session of the General Assembly of Virginia, August–September, 1956, Part IX, Box 222, NAACP Papers. For more on the special session, see Gates, *Making of Massive Resistance*, 167–90; Ely, *Crisis of Conservative Virginia*, 43–50; Wilkinson, *Harry Byrd*, 130–33.

42. For more on pupil placement, see "Students to Be Assigned By Local School Boards," *Richmond Times-Dispatch*, December 29, 1956, 1, which lists assignment factors and explains the appeals process; Peltason, *Fifty-Eight Lonely Men*, 78–82.

43. For more on the school closing legislation, see Reed Sarratt, A Statistical Summary, State by State, of Segregation-Desegregation Activity Affecting Southern Schools from 1954 to Present, 49–53, in Box 7, M 68, Papers of Edward H. Peeples Jr., Special Collections and Archives, James Branch Cabell Library, Virginia Commonwealth University; Muse, *Virginia's Massive Resistance*, 29–33.

44. Quotations are from "Byrd Bids State Fight Integration," *Richmond Times-Dispatch*, August 26, 1956, 10.

45. Quotation is from Sweeney, *Race, Reason, and Massive Resistance*, 158. See also "Assembly Probe Sought On School Pressures," *Richmond Times-Dispatch*, September 7, 1956, 8.

46. Acts of Special Session of General Assembly of Virginia (Passed September 29, 1956), anti-NAACP legislation, in Bracey and Meier, *Papers of the NAACP*, Part 20, reel 12.

47. Quotation is from Larry Weekley, "Racial Group Bills Ready for House," *Richmond Times-Dispatch*, September 19, 1956, 2. Activist and historian Paul Gaston adds, "the principal partisan of the integration cause—the NAACP—would be, so far as possible, hounded into silence and impotence." Paul Gaston, "Foreword by Way of Memoir," in Lassiter and Lewis, *Moderates' Dilemma*, x

48. Quotation is from Wilkins with Mathews, *Standing Fast*, 241.

49. Quotation is from Virginia State Conference press release, July 23, 1956, in Bracey and Meier, *Papers of the NAACP*, Part 3, series D, reel 9.

50. NAACP press release, October 11, 1956, in Bracey and Meier, *Papers of the NAACP*, Part 3, series D, reel 9; S. J. Ackerman, "The Trials of S. W. Tucker," *Washington Post Magazine*, June 11, 2000, 14.

51. Muse, *Virginia's Massive Resistance*, 31–33.

52. Rufus Wells, "Va. beaten to punch," *Richmond Afro-American*, December 8, 1956, 1. This litigation will be discussed in subsequent chapters.

53. Report of the Committee on Law Reform and Racial Activities, 1957, and Report of the Committee on Offenses Against the Administration of Justice, 1957, both in Bracey and Meier, *Papers of the NAACP*, Part 20, reel 12; W. Lester Banks to Roy Wilkins, December 31, 1959, Re: Report of the Committee on Offenses Against the Administration of Justice, Part III, Box C159, NAACP Papers.

54. NAACP Legal Defense Fund, Fall report and case inventory, November 14, 1957, Part III, Box A237, NAACP Papers; Reed Sarratt, A Statistical Summary, State by State, of Segregation-Desegregation Activity Affecting Southern Schools from 1954 to Present, 49–53, in Box 7, M 68, Papers of Edward H. Peeples Jr., Special Collections and Archives, James Branch Cabell Library, Virginia Commonwealth University.

55. Michael Klarman, in *From Jim Crow to Civil Rights*, 383, estimates that 250 southern branches were closed and approximately 50,000 members lost between 1955 and 1957.

56. The impact of the anti-NAACP laws in Virginia will be discussed in more detail in chapter 4. Memorandum from Lucille Black to State Conference Officers, November 21, 1961, Part III, Box C160, NAACP Papers; Annual Report of Branch Activities, Covington, 1957, Part III, Box C194, NAACP Papers; Muse, *Virginia's Massive Resistance*, 49; Hershman, "A Rumbling in the Museum," 214; Hill, *Big Bang*, 180.

57. On the public stance, see Buni, *Negro in Virginia Politics*, 187.

58. Quotation is from Dr. E. B. Henderson to Dear ____, February 28, 1957, in Bracey and Meier, *Papers of the NAACP*, Part 20, reel 12.

59. Quotation is from W. Lester Banks to Dear Co-Worker (confidential), misdated February 14, 1956 [actual date is 1957], in Bracey and Meier, *Papers of the NAACP*, Part 20, reel 12. See also W. Lester Banks to Roy Wilkins, March 14, 1957, in ibid., Part 20, reel 12; W. Lester Banks to Clarence Mitchell, October 15, 1956, Part IX, Box 222, NAACP Papers.

60. *School Board of the City of Charlottesville v. Doris Allen*, 240 F. 2d 59 (4th

Cir. 1956); NAACP press release, November 29, 1956, in Bracey and Meier, *Papers of the NAACP*, Part 3, series D, reel 9; "Appeal on 2 school cases aired," *Richmond Afro-American*, December 1, 1956, 1.

61. This litigation will be discussed in chapter 4. See Report of the Legal Staff, *The Candle*, vol. 1, no. 5, December 1957, Part III, Box C158, NAACP Papers.

62. L. M. Wright Jr., "Court Move By NAACP Is Planned," *Richmond Times-Dispatch*, April 22, 1956, 5.

63. Quotation is from Wilkins with Mathews, *Standing Fast*, 242.

Four | "Keep On Keeping On"

This chapter's title quotes a 1957 memo by W. Lester Banks, in which he urged NAACP members to "keep on keeping on" until the organization's objectives had been achieved.

1. For more on the two committees, see Hill, *Big Bang*, 178–80; Hershman, "A Rumbling in the Museum," 210–15, 249, 271; Sweeney, *Race, Reason, and Massive Resistance*, 176.

2. Roy Wilkins to John Boatwright, February 13, 1957, Part III, Box A272, Papers of the National Association for the Advancement of Colored People, Library of Congress Manuscript Division, Washington, D.C. (hereafter cited as NAACP Papers); *The Candle*, vol. 1, no. 4, August, 1957, Part III, C158, NAACP Papers.

3. Rufus Wells, "Va. beaten to punch," *Richmond Afro-American*, December 8, 1956, 1; Hill, *Big Bang*, 179–80.

4. W. Lester Banks to Roy Wilkins, December 31, 1959, Re: Report of the Committee on Offenses Against the Administration of Justice, Part III, Box C159, NAACP Papers; Report of the Committee on Law Reform and Racial Activities, 1957, and Report of the Committee on Offenses Against the Administration of Justice, 1957, both in Bracey and Meier, *Papers of the NAACP*, Part 20, reel 12.

5. Quotation is from Minutes of the Meeting of the Board of Directors, April 8, 1957, Part VI, Box A14, NAACP Papers. See also Minutes of the Inc. Fund annual meeting, February 6, 1957, and Minutes of the Meeting of the Board of Directors, December 10, 1956, both in Bracey and Meier, *Papers of the NAACP*, Part 20, reel 12; W. Lester Banks to Lucille Black, August 29, 1957, Part III, Box C158, NAACP Papers. Three NAACP documents from December 1959 titled Exhibit A, Exhibit B, and Exhibit C, in the author's possession, show legal expenses paid by the Virginia State Conference to its legal staff.

6. Quotation is from W. Lester Banks to Roy Wilkins, December 31, 1959, Re: Report of the Committee on Offenses Against the Administration of Justice, Part III, Box C159, NAACP Papers. Banks's letter was accompanied by the entire 1959 COAAJ report.

7. W. Lester Banks to Roy Wilkins, December 31, 1959, Re: Report of the Committee on Offenses Against the Administration of Justice, Part III, Box C159,

NAACP Papers; "Can't Stop NAACP, Legislator Admits: Committee report ask more laws," *Richmond Afro-American*, November 23, 1957, 1.

8. Quotation is from Speech by Harry F. Byrd Sr., undated [Autumn, 1958], Harry F. Byrd Sr., Papers, Accession #9700-F, Box 8, Albert and Shirley Small Special Collections Library, University of Virginia. See also John Boatwright in *Southern School News*, vol. 2, no. 9, March 1956, 1; Muse, *Virginia's Massive Resistance*, 48–49.

9. Quotation is from Speech by Harry F. Byrd Sr., undated [Autumn, 1958], Harry F. Byrd Sr., Papers, Accession #9700-F, Box 8, Albert and Shirley Small Special Collections Library, University of Virginia.

10. Oliver W. Hill Sr., interview by author, tape recording, Richmond, Va., December 4, 1999; Tomiko Brown-Nagin, "The Impact of Lawyer-Client Disengagement on the NAACP's Campaign to Implement *Brown v. Board of Education* in Atlanta," in Lau, *From the Grassroots to the Supreme Court*, 236.

11. Gilbert Ware, "The NAACP-Inc. Fund Alliance: Its Strategy, Power, and Destruction," *Journal of Negro Education*, vol. 63, issue 3 (Summer 1994): 323–35.

12. Quotation is from Oliver Hill Sr., interview for "The Ground Beneath Our Feet," episode 4, 2000, transcript in the author's possession. See also Hill, *Big Bang*, 180.

13. Jonas, *Freedom's Sword*, 74–79, 413.

14. Quotation is from Gates, *Making of Massive Resistance*, 166. See also Sweeney, *Race, Reason, and Massive Resistance*, 29, 41–50, 74–84, 118, 247.

15. Quotation is from V. C. Daniels, Mecklenburg County Unit, Defenders of State Sovereignty and Individual Liberties, to Members, their Wives, Ministers and Lawyers, October 22, 1954, Part II, Box C212, NAACP Papers.

16. Speech by Dr. E. B. Henderson, president of the Virginia State Conference, NAACP, at Bluefield, West Virginia, June 1957, Part III, Box C158, NAACP Papers; June Shagaloff, Summary of Local Developments, Charlottesville, Virginia, September-October, 1958, Part V, Box 2836, NAACP Papers.

17. *The Candle*, vol. 1, no. 6, March 1958, and vol. 1, no. 4, August 1957, both in Part III, Box C159, NAACP Papers. See also *The Citizens' Council*, vol. 3, no. 10, July 1958, Citizens' Council Collection, control number 95-20, Box 3, folder 2, location C-9, Special Collections, J. D. Williams Library, University of Mississippi Archives and Manuscripts.

18. Report of Executive Secretary to the Executive Board, Virginia State Conference, January 29, 1955, Part II, Box C212, NAACP Papers; Total Memberships and Freedom Fund Contributions Received from Virginia Branches, Part III, Box C158, NAACP Papers; Report to the Virginia State Conference Meeting, October 4–6, 1957, Memberships and Freedom Fund Contributions Received by Branches, Part III, Box C158, NAACP Papers.

19. Virginia State Conference, 1962 Membership Campaign, Part III, Box C160, NAACP Papers. Benjamin Muse claimed the Virginia State Conference had a

membership of twenty-seven thousand in 1958, a figure which appears to be incorrect; *Virginia's Massive Resistance*, 47. For the correct figures, see Memberships of Virginia Branches, by Branch, Part III, Box C159, NAACP Papers.

20. *The Candle*, vol. 1, no. 6, March 1958, Part III, Box C159, NAACP Papers.

21. The Virginia State Conference supplemented its income with additional fundraising to counteract the decline. NAACP Income Received from Branches in the State of Virginia, Jan. 1, thru Aug. 31, for 1955, 1956, 1957, in Bracey and Meier, *Papers of the NAACP*, Part 20, reel 12; Memorandum from Gloster Current to Roy Wilkins, May 23, 1957, Part III, Box A106, NAACP Papers; W. Lester Banks to the Thalheimers Awards Committee, Attn: Gloster B. Current, May 31, 1960, Part III, Box C159, NAACP Papers; Princene Hutcherson to W. Lester Banks, August 8, 1961, Part V, Box 2582, NAACP Papers.

22. Quotation is from W. Lester Banks to Roy Wilkins, March 14, 1957, and W. Lester Banks to Roy Wilkins, June 18, 1957, both in Bracey and Meier, *Papers of the NAACP*, Part 20, reel 12. See also Minutes of the Board of Directors Meeting, December 14, 1959, Part VI, Box A14, NAACP Papers.

23. Quotation is from Annual Report of Branch Activities, Covington, 1957, Part III, Box C194, NAACP Papers.

24. Quotation is from *The Candle*, vol. 1, no. 6, March 1958, Part III, Box C159, NAACP Papers. See also Program, 25th Annual Convention of the Virginia State Conference of the NAACP, October 7–9, 1960, Richmond, Virginia, Part III, Box C159, NAACP Papers.

25. Quotation is from W. Lester Banks to the Thalheimers Awards Committee, Attn: Gloster B. Current, May 31, 1960, Part III, Box C159, NAACP Papers.

26. See for example, Klarman, *From Jim Crow to Civil Rights*, 377–84.

27. Minutes of the Board of Directors Meeting, February 14, 1956, and Minutes of the Board of Directors Meeting, April 8, 1956, both in Bracey and Meier, *Papers of the NAACP*, Supplement to Part 1 (1956–60), reel 1. For information on NAACP economic boycotts, see, for example, Barbara Hollis to Ruby Hurley, March 23, 1944, Part II, Box C207, NAACP Papers.

28. Wilkins with Mathews, *Standing Fast*, 238–39.

29. Quotation is from Branch, *Parting the Waters*, 187.

30. Quotation is from "NAACP Keynoter Gives Plan To Make Integration Reality," *Richmond Times-Dispatch*, October 6, 1956, 4.

31. Quotation is from Branch, *Parting the Waters*, 231; see generally 221–35. See also Fairclough, *Race and Democracy*, xvi, 207–16; Klarman, *From Jim Crow to Civil Rights*, 382.

32. Board of Directors Meeting Minutes, December 10, 1956, in Bracey and Meier, *Papers of the NAACP*, Part 20, reel 12; NAACP press release, November 29, 1956, in ibid., Part 3, series D, reel 9.

33. Quotation is from "Newport News Ordered To Desegregate Schools," *Richmond Times-Dispatch*, February 12, 1957, 4. See also *Adkins v. School Board of the City of Newport News*, 148 F. Supp. 430 (1957). Klarman, *From Jim Crow to*

Civil Rights, 356, notes that Senator Byrd "accused Judge Hoffman of 'arrogance,' 'prejudice,' and partisanship in his desegregation rulings."

34. "Prince Edward too," *Richmond Afro-American,* August 11, 1956, 1; "Va. County Must Mix Its Schools: U.S. Circuit Court lays down 'law'," *Richmond Afro-American,* November 16, 1957, 1; Rufus Wells, "NAACP to appeal Virginia decision," *Richmond Afro-American,* August 9, 1958, 1; "Va. schools to open by court order," *Richmond Afro-American,* May 16, 1959, 13; "1965 plan judge set to retire," *Richmond Afro-American,* August 8, 1959, 13.

35. Brian J. Daugherity, "'With All Deliberate Speed': The NAACP and the Implementation of *Brown v. Board of Education* at the Local Level, Little Rock, Arkansas" (M.A. thesis, University of Montana, 1997).

36. Muse, *Virginia's Massive Resistance,* 43.

37. Quotation is from Klarman, *From Jim Crow to Civil Rights,* 398. See also 366–67, 417–24. For more on post-*Brown* southern politics, see Bartley, *Rise of Massive Resistance;* Black, *Southern Governors and Civil Rights.*

38. "Text of Civil Rights Bill as Passed by Congress and Sent to President," *New York Times,* August 31, 1957, 6.

39. "Va. pupil placement laws void," *Richmond Afro-American,* January 19, 1957, 1; "Judge Parker Raps Va.'s School Laws," *Richmond Afro-American,* June 22, 1957, 4; "Placement act falls, Va. appeals," *Richmond Afro-American,* July 20, 1957, 1; "Byrd Plan Doomed," *Richmond Afro-American,* October 26, 1957, 1; "Efficiency is not word for new bill," *Richmond Afro-American,* February 22, 1958, 1; Reed Sarratt, A Statistical Summary, State by State, of Segregation-Desegregation Activity Affecting Southern Schools from 1954 to Present, 49–53, in Box 7, M 68, Papers of Edward H. Peeples Jr., Special Collections and Archives, James Branch Cabell Library, Virginia Commonwealth University.

40. Quotation is from "Assembly record—10 laws a day," *Richmond Afro-American,* March 15, 1958, 1. See also *The Candle,* vol. 1, no. 6, March 1958, Part III, Box C159, NAACP Papers; "Twice as much or half as much trouble as two?" *Richmond Afro-American,* February 22, 1958, 3; Reed Sarratt, A Statistical Summary, State by State, of Segregation-Desegregation Activity Affecting Southern Schools from 1954 to Present, 49–53, in Box 7, M 68, Papers of Edward H. Peeples Jr., Special Collections and Archives, James Branch Cabell Library, Virginia Commonwealth University; Hershman, "A Rumbling in the Museum," 271–73.

41. Quotation is from *Cooper v. Aaron,* 358 U.S. 1 (1958); Tushnet, *Making Civil Rights Law,* 263 [briefs and arguments are on preceding pages]. The Alabama case was *Shuttlesworth v. Birmingham Board of Education* (1958); see United States Commission on Civil Rights, *1961 U.S. Commission on Civil Rights Report,* 8–9.

42. Chester M. Hampton, "Judge Calls Bluff: Va. school must mix in Sept.," *Richmond Afro-American,* May 17, 1958, 1; "Norfolk may get Sept. deadline," *Richmond Afro-American,* May 17, 1958, 1; Hershman, "A Rumbling in the Museum," 227–31.

43. Fisher, *Wit, Will, & Walls,* 75–82; "NAACP promises action in Warren Co.

dispute," *Richmond Afro-American*, August 2, 1958, 2; Chester M. Hampton, "Va. school war in critical stage," *Richmond Afro-American*, August 23, 1958, 13; untitled transcript of an interview, undated [likely 1959], Part III, Box A106, NAACP Papers; "Almond Hints End of a High School," Special to the *New York Times*, September 10, 1958, 20.

44. Quotation is from Minutes of the Board of Directors Meeting, June 9, 1958, Part VI, Box A14, NAACP Papers. See also Memorandum RE Conference on Virginia Schools, June 17, 1958, Part V, Box 2814, NAACP Papers; Minutes of the Board of Directors Meeting, July 9, 1958, Part VI, Box A14, NAACP Papers.

45. Quotation is from James Latimer, "Keep Violence Out of Struggle Over Segregation, Byrd Urges," *Richmond Times-Dispatch*, August 31, 1958, 4. Byrd expressed similar sentiments in another speech that year; see Speech by Harry F. Byrd Sr., undated [Autumn, 1958], Harry F. Byrd Sr., Papers, Accession #9700-F, Box 8, Albert and Shirley Small Special Collections Library, University of Virginia.

46. See "12,700 students locked out of Virginia schools," *Richmond Afro-American*, October 4, 1958, 1; Wilkinson, *Harry Byrd*, 83.

47. Quotation is from Relman Morin, "Virginia At Crossroads," *Richmond Times-Dispatch*, January 4, 1959, 17. See also "Marshall flies to 'resistance' capital," *Richmond Afro-American*, September 20, 1958, 1.

48. James J. Kilpatrick, "Target: Virginia," in *The Citizens' Council*, vol. 3, no. 12, September 1958, Citizens' Council Collection, control number 95–20, Box 3, folder 2, location C-9, Special Collections, J. D. Williams Library, University of Mississippi Archives and Manuscripts.

49. "Suit asks reopening of schools," *Richmond Afro-American*, October 11, 1958, 20; "Resistance nears end, says Thurgood," *Richmond Afro-American*, October 18, 1958, 1; "Norfolk parents sue Governor," *Richmond Afro-American*, November 1, 1958, 1.

50. Hill quotation is from "Legal Maneuver Staves Off Showdown In Virginia, All Areas Segregated," *Southern School News*, vol. 4, no. 4, October 1957, 7. On white moderates, see Hershman, "A Rumbling in the Museum," 70, 114–15; Matthew D. Lassiter, "A 'Fighting Moderate': Benjamin Muse's Search for the Submerged South," in Lassiter and Lewis, *Moderates' Dilemma*, 169.

51. Quotation is from Allan Jones, "Defenders Again Urge Policy Of No Integration in Schools," *Richmond Times-Dispatch*, December 4, 1958, 1. See also Muse, *Virginia's Massive Resistance*, 92–98.

52. In the meantime, the tuition grant program was not implemented. See "Virginia Testing Own School Law," *New York Times*, November 25, 1958, 21; "Norfolk parents sue Governor," *Richmond Afro-American*, November 1, 1958, 1; Muse, *Virginia's Massive Resistance*, 104–6.

53. King was stabbed at a book signing in Harlem by Izola Curry, who had been mentally unstable for several years. For more on the incident, see "King Near Death," *Richmond Afro-American*, September 27, 1958, 1.

54. Quotation is from Dr. Martin Luther King Jr., to "Brother in Christ," Decem-

ber 3, 1958, Clayborne Carson, Susan Carson, Adrienne Clay, Virginia Shadron, and Kieran Taylor, editors, *The Papers of Martin Luther King, Jr., Volume IV: Symbol of the Movement, January 1957-December 1958* (Berkeley: University of California Press, 2000), 589. See also A. P. Randolph to Clarence Mitchell, April 13, 1959, Part IX, Box 222, NAACP Papers; "King backs Va. march," *Richmond Afro-American*, December 20, 1958, 3; Meier and Rudwick, *CORE*, 86–87; James H. Hershman Jr., "Massive Resistance Meets Its Match: The Emergency of a Pro-Public School Majority," in Lassiter and Lewis, *Moderates' Dilemma*, 113–14.

55. A. P. Randolph to Mr. Clarence Mitchell, April 13, 1959, Part IX, Box 222, NAACP Papers; Meier and Rudwick, *Along the Color Line*, 370.

56. In 1960, Reverend Walker led direct action protests against segregated businesses and public facilities in Petersburg, Hopewell, and other locales. A Pilgrimage of Prayer for Public Schools, December 21, 1959, Part III, Box A107, NAACP Papers; Program of Second Annual Pilgrimage of Prayer For Public Schools, Richmond, Virginia, January 1, 1960, Part III, Box C159, NAACP Papers; Program of NAACP 50th Anniversary Freedom Rally in Prince Edward County, September 7, 1959, Part III, Box C159, NAACP Papers; 51st NAACP Convention Hailed By Nation's Top Leaders, Part III, Box C159, NAACP Papers; "Hopewell Negroes Threaten to Picket," *Richmond Times-Dispatch*, April 19, 1960, 3; "King asks support for sit-downers," *Richmond Afro-American*, May 21, 1960, 15.

57. Quotation is from "Excerpts From Federal Court Decision on Closing of Virginia Schools," *New York Times*, January 20, 1959, 29. See also "State School Closing Law Ruled Out by U.S. Court," *Richmond Times-Dispatch*, January 20, 1959, 1.

58. "Key School Segregation Laws Killed by State's High Court," *Richmond Times-Dispatch*, January 20, 1959, 1; "Court Orders Weaken Barriers to Integration," *Richmond Times-Dispatch*, January 24, 1959, 1; "Virginia High Court Voids School Segregation Laws," *New York Times*, January 20, 1959, 1; Chester M. Hampton, "Interpret Almond as inciting violence," *Richmond Afro-American*, January 31, 1959, 1.

59. Southern Regional Council special report, Sanctuaries for Tradition: Virginia's New Private Schools, February 8, 1961, in Bracey and Meier, *Papers of the NAACP*, Part 3, series D, reel 13; United States Commission on Civil Rights, *1961 U.S. Commission on Civil Rights Report*, 88–92; Allan Jones, "House Group Votes Two Tuition Bills," *Richmond Times-Dispatch*, January 30, 1959, 1; Homer Bigart, "Norfolk Will Admit 17 at Institutions Closed by Almond in Fall," *New York Times*, February 2, 1959, 1; "Alexandria Schools Mix," *Richmond Afro-American*, February 14, 1959, 1.

60. Quotation is from "New Day Beginning To Dawn In Old Dominion," *Norfolk Journal and Guide*, February 7, 1959, 8.

61. Quotation is from "No trouble at all in Norfolk," *Richmond Afro-American*, February 7, 1959, 1.

62. Quotation is from "Advent of Integration Condemned," *Richmond Times-Dispatch*, February 3, 1959, 5.

63. Quotation is from Hershman, "A Rumbling in the Museum," 348; see also Muse, *Virginia's Massive Resistance*, 160.

64. Quotation is from Larry Weekley, "Assailant Fires Shot at Governor," *Richmond Times-Dispatch*, April 12, 1959, 1.

65. Oliver W. Hill Sr., interview by author, tape recording, Richmond, Va., December 4, 1999; Muse, *Virginia's Massive Resistance*, 131–43, 162–68; James H. Hershman Jr., "Massive Resistance Meets Its Match: The Emergency of a Pro-Public School Majority," in Lassiter and Lewis, *Moderates' Dilemma*, 115–33; Beagle and Osborne, *J. Lindsay Almond*, 10, 115–16, 129, 143, 162–67.

66. For a discussion of freedom of choice, see chapter 6. Leon Dure, "State Pupil Authority Called Utterly Futile," *Richmond Times-Dispatch*, September 7, 1959, 12; James Latimer, "Sky Brighter For Almond On 2 Issues," *Richmond Times-Dispatch*, August 2, 1959, 1; Allan Jones, "3 School Areas to Test 'Freedom of Choice' Plan," *Richmond Times-Dispatch*, September 6, 1959, D1.

67. United States Commission on Civil Rights, *1961 U.S. Commission on Civil Rights Report*, 62; "Almond, Pupil Board Confer On Court Order; Won't Talk," *Richmond Times-Dispatch*, August 22, 1959, 2; NAACP press release, September 15, 1961, in Bracey and Meier, *Papers of the NAACP*, Part 3, series D, reel 13.

68. Southern Regional Council special report, Sanctuaries for Tradition: Virginia's New Private Schools, February 8, 1961, in Bracey and Meier, *Papers of the NAACP*, Part 3, series D, reel 13; "House Group Votes Two Tuition Bills," *Richmond Times-Dispatch*, January 30, 1959, 1; "Integrated Schools Open In Two Virginia Cities Monday," *Farmville Herald*, February 3, 1959, 1.

69. Quotation is from *Ulysses Allen v. County School Board of Prince Edward County*, 266 F. 2d 507 (4th Cir. 1959).

70. *Griffin v. County School Board of Prince Edward County*, 377 U.S. 218 (1964); Edward H. Peeples, "A Perspective on the Prince Edward County School Issue" (M.A. thesis, University of Pennsylvania, 1963), Manuscripts Reading Room, Virginia Historical Society; Reed Sarratt, A Statistical Summary, State by State, of Segregation-Desegregation Activity Affecting Southern Schools from 1954 to Present, 49–53, in Box 7, M 68, Papers of Edward H. Peeples Jr., Special Collections and Archives, James Branch Cabell Library, Virginia Commonwealth University.

71. NAACP press release, September 15, 1961, in Bracey and Meier, *Papers of the NAACP*, Part 3, series D, reel 13; three untitled documents dated December 1959 and titled Exhibit A, Exhibit B, and Exhibit C, in the author's possession, all related to expenses paid by the Virginia State Conference to its legal staff; Exhibit C lists the location of school desegregation lawsuits and the local attorney helping with the litigation.

72. Quotation is from Klarman, *From Jim Crow to Civil Rights*, 360; see also 324–32. For more, see Statement of Thurgood Marshall, Director-Counsel, Legal Defense Fund, April 29, 1959, Part III, Box A237, NAACP Papers; Tushnet, *Making Civil Rights Law*, 269–70.

73. These 128 districts included both black and white students. United States Commission on Civil Rights, *1961 U.S. Commission on Civil Rights Report,* 236–38; "Virginia School Desegregation," *Southern School News,* vol. 8, no. 3, September 1961, 11; Muse, *Virginia's Massive Resistance,* 159.

Five | Battling Tokenism

1. Quotation is from *The Candle,* vol. 1, no. 5, December, 1957, Part III, Box C158, Papers of the National Association for the Advancement of Colored People, Library of Congress Manuscript Division, Washington, D.C. (hereafter cited as NAACP Papers). See also Program, 25th Annual Convention of the Virginia State Conference, October 7–9, 1960, Richmond, Virginia, Part III, Box C159, NAACP Papers; Wilkins with Mathews, *Standing Fast,* 259. For more on the wade-in, see Bolton, *The Hardest Deal of All,* 97.

2. Meier and Rudwick, *CORE,* 101; Fairclough, *Race and Democracy,* 266–67; Sitkoff, *Struggle for Black Equality,* chapter 3; Carson, *In Struggle,* 9–12.

3. Smith, *Managing White Supremacy,* 257, mentions an NAACP demonstration in Virginia against the firing of a black teacher in the 1930s. In the 1940s, branches in Virginia organized economic boycotts to improve employment opportunities; see, for example, Barbara Hollis to Ruby Hurley, March 23, 1944, Part II, Box C207, NAACP Papers. Arrests at NAACP protests were not unheard of—long before he became executive secretary, Roy Wilkins was arrested at an NAACP protest in Washington, D.C.; see Wilkins with Mathews, *Standing Fast,* 132–35.

4. Program, 25th Annual Convention of the Virginia State Conference, October 7–9, 1960, Richmond, Virginia, Part III, Box C159, NAACP Papers; Wilkins with Mathews, *Standing Fast,* 267; Carson, *In Struggle,* 14; Klarman, *From Jim Crow to Civil Rights,* 378.

5. Quotation is from Tushnet, *Making Civil Rights Law,* 309–10.

6. For more on the NAACP's position on the sit-ins, see "Next for the South?" *Newsweek,* March 28, 1960, 26; "Along the N.A.A.C.P. Battlefront," *The Crisis,* April 1960, 250–51. See also Wilkins with Mathews, *Standing Fast,* 267–68; Meier and Rudwick, *CORE,* 110. For the NAACP Legal Defense Fund, see Tushnet, *Making Civil Rights Law,* 309–10.

7. Hill quotation is from "Hill blasts Va. State Legislature," *Richmond Afro-American,* March 5, 1960, 2. On Robertson, see Al Coates, "NAACP Branch Leaders Stand In for Pickets," *Richmond Times-Dispatch,* February 28, 1960, 4. See also Program of Action by / for the Virginia State Conference Education Committee, One Day Planning Conference, January 30, 1960, Part III, Box C159, NAACP Papers; Program, 25th Annual Convention of the Virginia State Conference, October 7–9, 1960, Part III, Box C159, NAACP Papers; "Students Here Advised by NAACP," *Richmond Times-Dispatch,* April 4, 1960, 4; "Sit-ins Defended By NAACP Unit," *Richmond Times-Dispatch,* May 6, 1960, 20.

8. Program, 25th Annual Convention of the Virginia State Conference, October 7–9, 1960, Richmond, Virginia, Part III, Box C159, NAACP Papers; Hill, *Big Bang*, 183, 285; "Four Fined $20 Apiece In Sitdowns," *Richmond Times-Dispatch*, March 5, 1960, 1; "Negro Woman Fined $10 In Demonstration Case," *Richmond Times-Dispatch*, March 10, 1960, 14. A photograph of Ruth Tinsley's arrest appeared in *Life* magazine on March 7, 1960.

9. Littlejohn and Ford, *Elusive Equality*, 119; Flyer for Sit-in Workshop, October 8, 1960, Part III, Box C159, NAACP Papers.

10. W. T. Johnson, president of the Lynchburg branch, to the editor of the *Lynchburg News*, Local NAACP President Denies Connection to Sit-ins, January 10, 1961, and related correspondence with W. Lester Banks, all in Part III, Box A107, NAACP Papers.

11. Quotation is from W. Lester Banks and Robert Robertson to Roy Wilkins, September 29, 1960, Part III, Box C159, NAACP Papers. See also Gloster Current to W. Lester Banks, March 3, 1960, Part III, Box C159, NAACP Papers; Report of the Executive Secretary, May 21, 1960, Part III, Box C159, NAACP Papers.

12. Program, 25th Annual Convention of the Virginia State Conference, October 7–9, 1960, Richmond, Virginia, Part III, Box C159, NAACP Papers; Carson, *In Struggle*, 46; Forman, *Making of Black Revolutionaries*, 326–27; Dena Sloan, "Civil-rights legend stands tall," *Richmond Times-Dispatch*, October 10, 2005, 1.

13. Meier and Rudwick, *CORE*, 101–10; Wilkins with Mathews, *Standing Fast*, 269–71; Klarman, *From Jim Crow to Civil Rights*, 378–80.

14. Quotation is from Julian Bond, "Introduction," in Wilkins with Mathews, *Standing Fast*, ix–x.

15. For more on Lawson, see Carson, *In Struggle*, 23. For more on Lawson's critique of the NAACP, see Forman, *Making of Black Revolutionaries*, 216. For more on Wilkins's response, see Wilkins with Mathews, *Standing Fast*, 269. For the relationship over time, see Miller, *Roy Wilkins*, 159–60; Forman, *Making of Black Revolutionaries*, 106, 132, 361–66; Branch, *Parting the Waters*, 557; Herbert H. Haines, "Black Radicalization and the Funding of Civil Rights: 1957–1970," *Social Problems* 32 (1984): 31–43.

16. Quotation is from Meier and Rudwick, *CORE*, 105.

17. Quotation is from Klarman, *From Jim Crow to Civil Rights*, 379. See also Forman, *Making of Black Revolutionaries*, 363–64.

18. Quotation is from Wilkins with Mathews, *Standing Fast*, 285.

19. Meier and Rudwick, *CORE*, 103.

20. Meier and Rudwick, *CORE*, 36, 86, 131–37, 172, 261; Arsenault, *Freedom Riders*, 112–18; Gloster Current to W. Lester Banks, September 11, 1959, and James Farmer to W. Lester Banks, September 22, 1959, both in Part III, Box C159, NAACP Papers; Branch, *Parting the Waters*, 413. For more on *Boynton*, see Tushnet, *Making Civil Rights Law*, 308–9.

21. SNCC's first full-time field secretary was Charles Sherrod, a leader of the Richmond, Virginia, sit-ins who became a well-known civil rights leader in South

Carolina and Georgia; see Carson, *In Struggle*, 14, 40, 67, 231. Charles's brother Roland also worked for SNCC and remembered there was not much SNCC activity in Virginia; Roland Sherrod, conversation with Brian Daugherity, Richmond, Virginia, January 9, 2008.

22. Claude Sitton, "Racial Movement Spreads in South," *Richmond Times-Dispatch*, February 9, 1961, 37; "Arrests Probed," *Richmond Times-Dispatch*, July 19, 1963, 4; T. N. Burton, "Woman charges police brutality," *Richmond Afro-American*, July 6, 1963, 17; Meier and Rudwick, *CORE*, 119.

23. Brian E. Lee and Brian J. Daugherity, "Program of Action: The Rev. L. Francis Griffin and the Struggle for Racial Equality in Farmville, 1963," *Virginia Magazine of History and Biography*, vol. 121, no. 3 (Autumn 2013): 250–87; Buni, *Negro in Virginia Politics*, 215–16.

24. Simon Hall, *Peace and Freedom*, 48–54; Carson, *In Struggle*, 67, 138–40, 231; Virginia Students' Civil Rights Committee, 1960–August 1965, n.d., Subgroup A, Atlanta Office, 1959–1972, Series VIII, Research Department, 1959–1969, reels 20, 23, SNCC Papers microfilm.

25. "Hopewell Negroes Threaten to Picket," *Richmond Times-Dispatch*, April 19, 1960, 3; "Civil Rights Lag Is Seen By Minister," *Richmond Times-Dispatch*, February 19, 1962, 2; Julian Bond, "Introduction," in Wilkins with Mathews, *Standing Fast*, xii; Michael Paul Williams, "'Living the Dream' Is Week's Theme," *Richmond Times-Dispatch*, January 7, 1997, 4; Sande Fulk, "Many Blacks Fought Civil Rights Battles Locally," *Richmond Times-Dispatch*, June 23, 1999, S13.

26. Quotation is from Virginia State Unit SCLC to Martin Luther King, December 17, 1962, Part II, series 5, reel 15, John Bracey and August Meier, editorial advisors, *Records of SCLC microfilm, 1954–1970* (Bethesda MD: University Publications of America). See also Richard Wilson, "Massive Resistance Ending, VTA Is Told," *Richmond Times-Dispatch*, November 5, 1960, 1; "1,200 rally to the cause to open Prince Edward schools," *Richmond Afro-American*, January 7, 1961, 1; "60-day sitdown sentences for Rev. Wood, other appealed," *Richmond Afro-American*, March 18, 1961, 1; "Dr. King to speak at Norfolk rally," *Richmond Afro-American*, July 1, 1961, 3; "200 Clerics March," *Richmond Afro-American*, January 20, 1962, 1; "Banquet honors Rev. Griffin, PEC leader," *Richmond Afro-American*, October 13, 1962, 7; "125 Negroes Demonstrate In Danville," *Richmond Times-Dispatch*, June 5, 1963, 1; "800 to 900 Go to Rally At Danville," *Richmond Times-Dispatch*, July 4, 1963, 1; Lea Setegn, "Black History Profiles: Curtis Harris," *Richmond Times-Dispatch*, February 13, 2006, E1.

27. Quotation is from Policy Action Resolutions adopted by the 25th Convention, October 7–9, 1960, Part III, Box C159, NAACP Papers. See also Report of the Executive Secretary, May 21, 1960, Part III, Box C159, NAACP Papers; Gloster Current to W. Lester Banks, March 3, 1960, Part III, Box C159, NAACP Papers; Program of Action by / for the Virginia State Conference Education Committee, One Day Planning Conference, January 30, 1960, Part III, Box C159, NAACP Papers.

28. Correspondence between the Lynchburg branch and the national office con-

cerning its rivalry with SCLC can be found in Part III, Box C155, NAACP Papers; see also R. Walter Johnson to W. Lester Banks, August 23, 1963, Part III, Box C160, NAACP Papers. On Danville, see "Statement of Position on Continuation of the Danville Movement," Danville NAACP press release, November 6, 1963, W. Lester Banks to John Morsell, November 7, 1963, and W. Lester Banks to John Morsell, December 5, 1963, all in Part III, Box C160, NAACP Papers. On Prince Edward County, see W. Lester Banks to Milton A. Reid, February 24, 1961, L. Francis Griffin to Milton A. Reid, February 24, 1961, and Milton A. Reid to W. Lester Banks, February 27, 1961, all in Part III, Box A107, NAACP Papers.

29. Quotation is from Samuel Hoskins, "Race Relations A Many-Sided Thing: In Virginia Protest Is The Vogue, Picket Signs Are Badges Of Status," *Richmond Afro-American*, January 6, 1962, 8.

30. On Prince Edward County, see L. Francis Griffin to W. Lester Banks, March 22, 1961, W. Lester Banks to W. W. Vaughan, Chairman, Board of Supervisors, Prince Edward County, April 27, 1961, and Program, May 17, Celebration, May 20, 1961, all in Part III, Box A107, NAACP Papers. On New Kent County, see Application for NAACP branch charter, Charles City–New Kent County, Virginia, Part VI, Box C8, NAACP Papers; W. Lester Banks to Lucille Blacks, January 24, 1961, Part VI, Box C159, NAACP Papers. For more on Calvin Green and *Green v. New Kent County*, see chapter 7.

31. Robert Carter to W. Lester Banks, November 17, 1961, W. Lester Banks to Robert Carter, October 26, 1961, and Statement Made By W. Lester Banks to the Interstate Commerce Commission, October 25, 1961, all in Part V, Box 2582, NAACP Papers; *Commonwealth v. Banks*, 1961, Part V, Box 2393, NAACP Papers.

32. Brian E. Lee and Brian J. Daugherity, "Program of Action: The Rev. L. Francis Griffin and the Struggle for Racial Equality in Farmville, 1963," *Virginia Magazine of History and Biography*, vol. 121, no. 3 (Autumn, 2013): 250–87.

33. Writing about Charlottesville in 1974, Anna Holden, in *The Bus Stops Here*, 14, explains: "Even with the addition of newer organizations, the NAACP was still the major civil rights organization when this study was done. More militant groups such as . . . SNCC . . . and . . . CORE . . . never got a foothold in Charlottesville in the 1960s." Hershman, "A Rumbling in the Museum," 337–39, draws similar conclusions.

34. United States Commission on Civil Rights, *1961 U.S. Commission on Civil Rights Report*, 22. Littlejohn and Ford, *Elusive Equality*, 122–23.

35. Southern Regional Council special report, Sanctuaries for Tradition: Virginia's New Private Schools, February 8, 1961, in Bracey and Meier, *Papers of the NAACP*, Part 3, series D, reel 13; United States Commission on Civil Rights, *1961 U.S. Commission on Civil Rights Report*, 62; United States Commission on Civil Rights, *1964 Staff Report*, 234–71.

36. Reed Sarratt, A Statistical Summary, State by State, of Segregation-Desegregation Activity Affecting Southern Schools from 1954 to Present, 49–53,

in Box 7, M 68, Papers of Edward H. Peeples Jr., Special Collections and Archives, James Branch Cabell Library, Virginia Commonwealth University.

37. Tom Flake, "Tuition Grants Under Test In Two Courts," *Southern School News*, vol. 8, no. 2, August 1961, 1; United States Commission on Civil Rights, *1961 U.S. Commission on Civil Rights Report*, 88–89; Southern Regional Council special report, Sanctuaries for Tradition: Virginia's New Private Schools, February 8, 1961, in Bracey and Meier, *Papers of the NAACP*, Part 3, series D, reel 13; Muse, *Virginia's Massive Resistance*, 158–59.

38. Quotation is from Virginia State Conference press release, January 29, 1962, Part III, Box C160, NAACP Papers. For more, see Hamilton Crockford, "Emporia Attorney Given Reprimand," *Richmond Times-Dispatch*, January 25, 1962, 2; S. J. Ackerman, "The Trials of S. W. Tucker," *Washington Post Magazine*, June 11, 2000, 14.

39. Louis Lautier, "Thurgood takes aim at Va. laws," *Richmond Afro-American*, April 4, 1959, 1; "Va. gets its anti-NAACP laws back," *Richmond Afro-American*, June 13, 1959, 2; Louis Lautier, "Delay death blow to Va. NAACP laws," *Richmond Afro-American*, June 13, 1959, 8.

40. See *NAACP v. Button*, 371 U.S. 415 (1963); *NAACP v. Patty*, 159 F. Supp. 503 (1958); *Harrison v. NAACP*, 360 U.S. 167 (1959); *NAACP v. Harrison, Race Relations Law Reporter* 5 (Winter 1960): 1152; W. Lester Banks to Dear Co-worker, June 12, 1959, Part IX, Box 222, NAACP Papers.

41. Quotation is from Hill, *Big Bang*, 180.

42. Wilkins quotation is from "Supreme Court knocks out Va. anti-NAACP law," *Richmond Afro-American*, January 19, 1963, 1. *New York Times* quotation is from Anthony Lewis, "Curb by Virginia on N.A.A.C.P. Is Nullified by Supreme Court," *New York Times*, January 15, 1963, 1. See also *NAACP v. Button*, 371 U.S. 415 (1963).

43. Director FBI, to SACS Richmond, Washington Field, Chicago, December 28, 1960, and related files regarding Oliver White Hill, Record / Information Dissemination Section, Records Management Division, Federal Bureau of Investigation, Washington, D.C., in the author's possession; "Oliver Hill named to key housing post," *Richmond Afro-American*, May 20, 1961, 1; Hill, *Big Bang*, 183–84. Robinson was appointed to the United States Commission on Civil Rights by President Kennedy and served on it until he resigned in 1963; Director FBI, to SACS New York, Richmond, Chicago, Washington Field, June 25, 1963, and related files regarding Spottswood William Robinson III, Record / Information Dissemination Section, Records Management Division, Federal Bureau of Investigation, Washington, D.C., in the author's possession; L. Douglas Wilder, "Spottswood Robinson Qualifies as Exemplary Role Model," *Richmond Times-Dispatch*, September 7, 1997, F3.

44. On the Virginia State Conference legal staff, see Martin A. Martin to Robert D. Robertson, November 20, 1961, Part III, Box C160, NAACP Papers;

S. W. Tucker to Members of Legal Staff, January 21, 1963, Part III, Box C160, NAACP Papers. On Tucker, see "NAACP May Reopen Suit On Greensville Schools," *Richmond Times-Dispatch*, September 5, 1979, B4; S. J. Ackerman, "Samuel Wilbert Tucker," *Journal of Blacks in Higher Education*, no. 28 (Summer 2000): 98–103; Wallenstein, *Blue Laws and Black Codes*, 86.

45. "Va. NAACP wants U.S. To Reopen P.E. Schools," *Richmond Afro-American*, October 28, 1961, 18, which includes an image of Virginia State Conference legal staff; "Atty. Martin eulogized as an 'illustrious son'," *Richmond Afro-American*, May 11, 1963, 9; "Va. NAACP tackles education problem," *Richmond Afro-American*, November 13, 1965, 18; "Ruth Harvey elected in Va.," *Richmond Afro-American*, August 20, 1966, 7; "Va. NAACP Officers," *Richmond Afro-American*, November 4, 1967, 11.

46. Quotation is from S. J. Ackerman, "The Trials of S. W. Tucker," *Washington Post Magazine*, June 11, 2000, 14. See also "25 Years After *Brown*," *Richmond Times-Dispatch*, May 13, 1979, G1; Hill, *Big Bang*, 183; Henry L. Marsh III, interview by Jody Allen and author, tape recording, Richmond, Va., November 25, 2002.

47. "Thurgood to be U.S. judge," *Richmond Afro-American*, September 23, 1961, 1; Cliff Sessions, "Thurgood's New Role," *Richmond Afro-American*, September 11, 1965, 1; "LBJ Picks Thurgood: 'Mr. Civil Rights' Named To Supreme Court," *Richmond Afro-American*, June 17, 1967, 1.

48. Quotation is from Roy Wilkins to Carl Murphy, June 2, 1961, and Carl Murphy to Roy Wilkins, June 1, 1961, both in Part III, Box A237, NAACP Papers.

49. Memorandum from Roy Wilkins to Presidents of Branches, State Conferences, and Youth Groups, November 28, 1962, Re: Procedure in Legal Cases, Part V, Box 2719, NAACP Papers.

50. Memorandum from Robert Carter to Liaison Committee, November 14, 1961, and Robert Carter to Dr. Joseph J. Klein, September 16, 1963, both in Part V, Box 2719, NAACP Papers; NAACP Legal Defense Fund Docket Report, August 1963, Part III, Box J9, NAACP Papers; "NAACP donor list declared 'off-limits' to Virginia aides," *Richmond Afro-American*, December 14, 1963, 6; Hill, *Big Bang*, 179–80.

51. Memorandum from Robert Carter to Liaison Committee, November 14, 1961, and Robert Carter to Dr. Joseph J. Klein, September 16, 1963, both in Part V, Box 2719, NAACP Papers; NAACP Legal Defense Fund Docket Report, August 1963, Part III, Box J9, NAACP Papers; Hill, *Big Bang*, 179–80; Jonas, *Freedom's Sword*, 73–79; "Wilder To Seek Reynold's Seat," *Richmond Afro-American*, August 30, 1969, 1.

52. Wilkins quotation is from Wilkins with Mathews, *Standing Fast*, 272, see also 273–77; Hill, *Big Bang*, 183–84, 258–65; Michael J. Klarman, "How *Brown* Changed Race Relations: The Backlash Thesis," *Journal of American History* 81 (1994): 110–11.

53. Quotation is from Wilkins with Mathews, *Standing Fast*, 272; see also 279–86.

54. United States Department of Justice press release, April 26, 1961, Part III, Box A107, NAACP Papers; "U.S. Asks to Intervene In Prince Edward Case," *Richmond Times-Dispatch*, April 27, 1961, 1; Brian E. Lee, "We Will Move: The Kennedy Administration and Prince Edward County, Virginia, 1961," independent study paper in the author's possession, produced fall 2008.

55. Kennedy was guided by the advice of state leaders and bar associations in his federal court appointments; see "Judgeship Views Given By Kennedy," *Richmond Times-Dispatch*, November 6, 1960, 1. On Cox, see Wilkins with Mathews, *Standing Fast*, 283–84.

56. Memorandum from Clarence Mitchell, Re: Justice Department Suit on School Desegregation, Part V, Box 2836, NAACP Papers; *U.S.A. v. Prince George County*, September 17, 1962, and related correspondence, Part IX, Box 222, NAACP Papers.

57. W. Lester Banks and Robert Robertson to Roy Wilkins, September 29, 1960, Part III, Box C159, NAACP Papers; Reed Sarratt, A Statistical Summary, State by State, of Segregation-Desegregation Activity Affecting Southern Schools from 1954 to Present, 49–53, in Box 7, M 68, Papers of Edward H. Peeples Jr., Special Collections and Archives, James Branch Cabell Library, Virginia Commonwealth University.

58. Quotation is from Hill, *Big Bang*, 176. See also Peltason, *Fifty-Eight Lonely Men*, 57–58.

59. Quotation is from "Newport News Ordered To Desegregate Schools," *Richmond Times-Dispatch*, February 12, 1957, 4. See also Klarman, *From Jim Crow to Civil Rights*, 321–40; Wilkinson, *From "Brown" to "Bakke,"* 80–86; Mark Tushnet, "Commentary," in Eagles, *The Civil Rights Movement in America*, 122.

60. Quotation is from United States Commission on Civil Rights, *1963 Staff Report*, 50. See also United States Commission on Civil Rights, *1964 Staff Report*, 234–71; Carl Tobias, "Public School Desegregation in Virginia During the Post-Brown Decade," *William & Mary Law Review*, vol. 37, issue 4 (1996): 1261–1306; Statement by G. W. Foster Jr., in Support of the Nomination of Judge Clement F. Haynsworth Jr., to the Supreme Court of the United States, Hearings before the U.S. Senate Committee on the Judiciary, 91st Congress, 1st Session, September 1969 (Washington, DC: U.S. Government Printing Office, 1969), 602–11.

61. Quotations are from *Watson v. City of Memphis*, 373 U.S. 526 (1963).

62. *Goss v. Board of Education of Knoxville*, 373 U.S. 683 (1963); "High Court Warns States On Schools: Says Desegregation Delay Must Come to End Soon," *Richmond Times-Dispatch*, May 28, 1963, 1; United States Commission on Civil Rights, *1963 Staff Report*, 50–51.

63. United States Commission on Civil Rights, *1963 Staff Report*, 7. Such figures vary slightly from source to source.

64. Statistic is from United States Commission on Civil Rights, *1963 Staff Report*, 137. See also Charles C. Bolton, "The Last Holdout: Mississippi and the *Brown* Decision," in Daugherity and Bolton, *With All Deliberate Speed*, 123–38; United States Commission on Civil Rights, *1964 Staff Report*, 2.

65. Quotation is from Annual Report of the Virginia State Conference Education Committee, October 7, 1960, in Bracey and Meier, *Papers of the NAACP*, Part 3, series D, reel 13; W. Lester Banks to Dr. R. C. Wesley, Education Committee chairman, Lynchburg, Va., branch, February 14, 1962, Part III, Box A106, NAACP Papers.

66. Quotation is from Policy Action Resolutions adopted by the 25th Convention, Virginia State Conference, October 7–9, 1960, Part III, Box C159, NAACP Papers.

67. At this time, it was unlikely that white students, or their parents, would request admission into formerly all-black schools. Virginia State Conference NAACP, Education Committee Program, January 21, 1961, Part III, Box A289, NAACP Papers; Allan Jones, "1,200 Negroes Hope to Enter White Schools," *Richmond Times-Dispatch*, May 3, 1963, 1.

68. Quotation is from "NAACP Extending Its Va. School Integration Push," NAACP press release, September 22, 1962, Part III, Box A106, NAACP Papers. See also Reed Sarratt, A Statistical Summary, State by State, of Segregation-Desegregation Activity Affecting Southern Schools from 1954 to Present, 49–53, in Box 7, M 68, Papers of Edward H. Peeples Jr., Special Collections and Archives, James Branch Cabell Library, Virginia Commonwealth University; "2 Desegregation Suits Filed in Federal Court," *Richmond Times-Dispatch*, May 3, 1963, 2.

69. Quotation is from "Virginia NAACP In New School Action," NAACP press release, September 21, 1962, Part III, Box A106, NAACP Papers.

70. Construction plans were particularly important in urban areas because of widespread residential segregation. "NAACP Seeks More Desegregation in Arlington County," NAACP press release, January 6, 1962, Part III, Box A106, NAACP Papers; "NAACP Again Attacks Pupil Placement," NAACP press release, October 6, 1961, Part III, Box A106, NAACP Papers; "NAACP Sues To Stop Building Of Jim Crow Virginia School," NAACP press release, May 3, 1963, Part III, Box A106, NAACP Papers; Herman Ford to W. Lester Banks, April 20, 1963, Part III, Box A106, NAACP Papers.

71. In the late 1950s, NAACP leaders including Thurgood Marshall and Roy Wilkins offered qualified support for gradual desegregation plans. See Roy Wilkins to City Editor, *New York Times*, August 5, 1958, Part III, Box A107, NAACP Papers; Kluger, *Simple Justice*, 291.

72. Quotation is from "Grade-A-Year Plan Approved By Board," *The (Lynchburg, Va.) News*, February 14, 1962, in Part III, Box A106, NAACP Papers. The city adopted a grade-a-year plan instead. See also Robert Carter to W. Lester Banks, March 15, 1962, Part III, Box A106, NAACP Papers.

73. Quotation is from Report of the Executive Secretary, May 21, 1960, Part III, Box C159, NAACP Papers.

74. Quotation is from Untitled article, *Richmond Afro-American*, May 26, 1962, in Part III, Box A106, NAACP Papers.

75. Virginia State Conference press release, January 18, 1963, Part III, Box C160,

NAACP Papers; June Shagaloff, Summary of Local Developments, Charlottesville, Virginia, September-October, 1958, Part V, Box 2836, NAACP Papers.

76. Quotation is from 1963 brochure titled *1,117 Viginia Negro Youth To Enjoy Educational Constitutional Rights in Virginia for the 1962–63 School Term*, Part III, Box C160, NAACP Papers.

77. United States Commission on Civil Rights, *1961 U.S. Commission on Civil Rights Report*, 62; Reed Sarratt, A Statistical Summary, State by State, of Segregation-Desegregation Activity Affecting Southern Schools from 1954 to Present, 49–53, in Box 7, M 68, Papers of Edward H. Peeples Jr., Special Collections and Archives, James Branch Cabell Library, Virginia Commonwealth University.

78. "Is This Assumption Correct?" *Richmond Afro-American*, August 4, 1962, in Part III, Box C160, NAACP Papers; Allan Jones, "1,200 Negroes Hope to Enter White Schools," *Richmond Times-Dispatch*, May 3, 1963, 1; "New door to school desegregation," *Richmond Afro-American*, July 25, 1962, in Part IX, Box 222, NAACP Papers. Oglesby was a strong proponent of segregation and a supporter of the Defenders; see "To Build Or Not To Build Schools?—Va.," *Richmond Afro-American*, April 27, 1957, 17; "Appeals Court Again Tells Ole Miss To Desegregate," *Richmond Afro-American*, August 4, 1962, 17; Sweeney, *Race, Reason, and Massive Resistance*, 117–19; Pratt, *Color of Their Skin*, 40.

79. United States Commission on Civil Rights, *1963 Staff Report*, 42; United States Commission on Civil Rights, *1964 Staff Report*, 231–38; "Almost Twice As Many Negroes Reported in Biracial Schools," *Southern School News*, vol. 9, no. 3, September 1962, 3.

80. W. Lester Banks and Robert D. Robertson to Roy Wilkins, September 29, 1960, Part III, Box C159, NAACP Papers.

81. Quotation is from *Dodson v. School Board of City of Charlottesville*, 289 F. 2d 439 (4th Cir. 1961).

82. Memorandum from Jim Nabrit RE Lynchburg School Segregation Case, March 17, 1962, Part III, Box C160, NAACP Papers; *Cynthia D. Green v. School Board of the City of Roanoke*, 4th Circuit Court of Appeals ruling, May 22, 1962, Part V, Box 2400, NAACP Papers.

83. Quotation is from "Full Integration Seen For Norfolk Schools," *Richmond Times-Dispatch*, August 24, 1961, 2.

84. Quotations are from "Negro Lawyer Calls for Speed In Integration," *Richmond Times-Dispatch*, June 1, 1963, 1.

85. United States Commission on Civil Rights, *1964 Staff Report*, 242–43; Lon Savage, "City School Board Abolishes System of 'Feeder Schools,'" *Richmond Times-Dispatch*, March 19, 1963, 1; "Judge Gives Provisions Of Expected Court Order," *Richmond Times-Dispatch*, June 1, 1963, 2; "High Court Strikes Down Minority Transfer Plans," *Richmond Times-Dispatch*, June 4, 1963, 2; "Court favors injunction to spur school deseg," *Richmond Afro-American*, May 18, 1963, 1; "President Attacks School Segregation," *Richmond Afro-American*, June 15, 1963, 16.

86. United States Commission on Civil Rights, *1961 U.S. Commission on Civil Rights Report,* 55–57, 62, 236–38; United States Commission on Civil Rights, *1964 Staff Report,* Appendix Table 1a and Appendix Table 2; Eugene Piedmont, "Changing Racial Attitudes at a Southern University: 1947–1964," *Journal of Negro Education,* vol. 36, issue 1 (Winter 1967): 33–34; "Table Shows Virginia School Integration for the 1962–1963 Year," *Richmond News Leader,* August 21, 1962, Part III, Box C160, NAACP Papers; "Almost Twice As Many Negroes Reported in Biracial Schools," *Southern School News,* vol. 9, no. 3, September 1962, 3; "Ability, Distance Dropped As Qualifications," *Southern School News,* vol. 9, no. 12, June 1963, 19; "State Board Assigns 1,200 Negroes to Biracial Classes," *Southern School News,* vol. 10, no. 1, July 1963, 12.

87. United States Commission on Civil Rights, *1963 Staff Report,* 40; "52 Schools to Start Pupil Desegregation," *Richmond Times-Dispatch,* August 22, 1962, 3; Muse, *Virginia's Massive Resistance,* 155.

88. Quotation is from Muse, *Virginia's Massive Resistance,* 156. See also "Six Districts to Desegregate For First Time," *Southern School News,* vol. 8, no. 2, August 1961, 5; Reed Sarratt, A Statistical Summary, State by State, of Segregation-Desegregation Activity Affecting Southern Schools from 1954 to Present, 49–53, in Box 7, M 68, Papers of Edward H. Peeples Jr., Special Collections and Archives, James Branch Cabell Library, Virginia Commonwealth University.

89. Quotation is from W. Lester Banks to Gloster B. Current, September 11, 1959, Part III, Box C159, NAACP Papers. See also "Lawsuits Keep Up The Pressure," *Richmond Afro-American,* May 2, 1959, 3; "Mixing in all Va. school districts, official claims," *Richmond Afro-American,* September 11, 1965, 5; Reed Sarratt, A Statistical Summary, State by State, of Segregation-Desegregation Activity Affecting Southern Schools from 1954 to Present, 49–53, in Box 7, M 68, Papers of Edward H. Peeples Jr., Special Collections and Archives, James Branch Cabell Library, Virginia Commonwealth University; Muse, *Virginia's Massive Resistance,* 59–62.

90. "Table Shows Virginia School Integration for the 1962–1963 Year," *Richmond News Leader,* August 21, 1962, in Part III, Box C160, NAACP Papers; Reed Sarratt, A Statistical Summary, State by State, of Segregation-Desegregation Activity Affecting Southern Schools from 1954 to Present, 49–53, in Box 7, M 68, Papers of Edward H. Peeples Jr., Special Collections and Archives, James Branch Cabell Library, Virginia Commonwealth University.

91. United States Commission on Civil Rights, *1963 Staff Report,* 40; Reed Sarratt, A Statistical Summary, State by State, of Segregation-Desegregation Activity Affecting Southern Schools from 1954 to Present, 49–53, in Box 7, M 68, Papers of Edward H. Peeples Jr., Special Collections and Archives, James Branch Cabell Library, Virginia Commonwealth University.

92. They lived closer to a black school. United States Commission on Civil Rights, *1964 Staff Report, Public Education,* 237–38.

93. Jody L. Allen and Brian J. Daugherity, "Recovering a 'Lost' Story Using Oral History: The United States Supreme Court's Historic *Green v. New Kent County, Virginia,* Decision," *Oral History Review,* vol. 3, issue 2 (June 2006): 25–45; Leonard Colvin, "Norfolk in 1959: When 17 brave students stood tall," *Norfolk Journal and Guide,* July 7, 1999, 1; Cynthia Gaines, interview by Jody L. Allen and author, tape recording, New Kent County, Va., July 24, 2002.

94. Quotation is from Williams, *My Soul Looks Back in Wonder,* 67. See chapter 10 generally.

95. "School mixing halts dances in Virginia town," *Richmond Afro-American,* November 4, 1961, 18; "Va. School Board Adds Medic," *Richmond Afro-American,* July 21, 1962, 16; William Lakeman, "Pupils Asked to Avoid Programs," *The Free Lance-Star,* August 6, 1962, 1; "Negroes Protest Plea On Extracurriculars," *The Free Lance-Star,* August 18, 1962, 1; "Supervisors to Oppose Mixed School Activities," *The Free Lance-Star,* September 13, 1962, 1; William Lakeman, "Stafford Board Orders Cut In Some Extracurriculars," *The Free Lance-Star,* October 9, 1962, 1. West Point, Virginia, also suspended all social functions at its high school in 1961; see "Official Says HEW Requires Publicity For Localities Approval School Plans," *Richmond Times-Dispatch,* August 6, 1965, 6.

96. Klarman, *From Jim Crow to Civil Rights,* 434–36; Wilkins with Mathews, *Standing Fast,* 286–89.

97. Klarman, *From Jim Crow to Civil Rights,* 374.

98. Paul Gaston, *Sitting In In The Sixties: A Historian's Memoir,* 1997, pamphlet in the author's possession; Brian E. Lee and Brian J. Daugherity, "Program of Action: The Rev. L. Francis Griffin and the Struggle for Racial Equality in Farmville, 1963," *Virginia Magazine of History and Biography,* vol. 121, no. 3 (Autumn 2013): 250–87; "NAACP Spurs Letters To Congressmen: To rile Congress up with letters," *Richmond Afro-American,* August 3, 1963, 1; "Rights leader is jailed in bathrobe," *Richmond Afro-American,* August 3, 1963, 1; "Jailing is costly mistake," *Richmond Afro-American,* July 20, 1963, 1.

99. Quotation is from Virginia Center for Digital History, University of Virginia, http://www2.vcdh.virginia.edu/civilrightstv/wdbj/segments/WDBJ04_25.html, accessed June 18, 2015. See also W. Lester Banks to Dr. John A. Morsell, November 7, 1963, Part III, Box C160, NAACP Papers; W. Lester Banks to Dr. John A. Morsell, December 5, 1963, Part III, Box C160, NAACP Papers; Newsletter, Southern Christian Leadership Conference, November 5, 1963, *Records of SCLC, 1954–1970,* John H. Bracey Jr., and August Meier, editorial advisors (Bethesda MD: University Publications of America); Field Reports, Virginia, January 30, 1964, reel 17, SNCC Papers microfilm, 1959–1972; Lewis, *King,* 211–14.

100. Quotation is from W. Lester Banks to Dear NAACP Officers, July 18, 1963, Part III, Box C160, NAACP Papers.

101. Evers was shot and killed the following month because of his leadership role in the civil rights struggle in Mississippi. Quotation is from Sitkoff, *Struggle for*

Black Equality, 135. See also "Wilkins Arrested in Jackson, 3 of Negroes' Demands Met," *Richmond Times-Dispatch*, June 2, 1963, 1. Fairclough, *Race and Democracy*, 282–83, covers Wilkins's move toward more militant action.

102. On the Virginia State Conference, see Action Program for the State of Virginia, Virginia State Conference NAACP, Summer 1963, Part III, Box C160, NAACP Papers; Annual Report memorandum from W. Lester Banks to Gloster Current, December 6, 1963, Part III, Box C160, NAACP Papers. Banks was assaulted during the incident; "Arrest White For Attack on NAACP VA Executive," NAACP press release, August 3, 1963, Part III, Box C160, NAACP Papers; "W. Lester Banks assaulted at diner," *Richmond Afro-American*, July 27, 1963, 1.

103. On the march, see W. Lester Banks to Dear NAACP Officers, September 9, 1963, Part III, Box C160, NAACP Papers; Allan Jones, "Virginia Group Totals 2,500," *Richmond Times-Dispatch*, August 29, 1963, 1; Kirsten B. Mitchell, "Time For A Wake-Up Call: The Atmosphere Was So Awesome," *Richmond Times-Dispatch*, August 24, 2003, 1; Clayborne Carson, "Martin Luther King Jr.: Charismatic Leadership in a Mass Struggle," *Journal of American History* 74 (1987): 448–54.

104. Quotation is from NAACP press release, June 19, 1963, Part III, Box C160, NAACP Papers.

105. Klarman, *From Jim Crow to Civil Rights*, 432–36; Wilkins with Mathews, *Standing Fast*, 284–85.

106. Hamilton Crockford, "Why Did Racial Test Occur in Danville? Nobody Agrees," *Richmond Times-Dispatch*, September 9, 1963, 2; Field Reports, Virginia, January 30, 1964, reel 17, SNCC Papers microfilm, 1959–1972.

Six | A New "Holy Prerogative"

This chapter's title quotes J. Harvie Wiklinson III's *From "Brown" to "Bakke,"* in which he writes, "What was unthinkable five or six years ago suddenly assumed, in light of more threatening alternatives, the status of holy prerogative."

1. Statistics are from United States Commission on Civil Rights, *Southern School Desegregation, 1966–1967*, 5, 104.

2. Quotation is from Wilkins with Mathews, *Standing Fast*, 276. See also 295–98.

3. Quotation is from Roy Wilkins speech to the 25th annual Virginia State Convention, NAACP, October 9, 1960, Part III, Box C159, Papers of the National Association for the Advancement of Colored People, Library of Congress Manuscript Division, Washington, D.C. (hereafter cited as NAACP Papers).

4. Wilkins with Mathews, *Standing Fast*, 299–302; Klarman, *From Jim Crow to Civil Rights*, 436; Wilkinson, *From "Brown" to "Bakke,"* 103–4.

5. Quotation is from Wilkins with Mathews, *Standing Fast*, 297. See Hall, *Peace and Freedom*, 86–91.

6. United States Commission on Civil Rights, *Southern School Desegregation, 1966–1967*, 42; *Southern Education Report*, vol. 1, no. 1, July-August 1965, 32.

7. Quotation and statistic are from United States Commission on Civil Rights, *Southern School Desegregation, 1966–1967*, 2.

8. Title VI of the Civil Rights Act of 1964 and subsequent guidelines by the Department of Health, Education, and Welfare [78 Stat. 246, 42 U.S.C. 2000c-d, 45 CFR 80.1–80.13, 181.1–181.76 (1967)]; "Integrate Or Lose U.S. $$, Dixie Told: Localities get warning of cutoff," *Richmond Afro-American*, January 9, 1965, 1; Wilkinson, *From "Brown" to "Bakke,"* 102–8; Statement by G. W. Foster Jr., in Support of the Nomination of Judge Clement F. Haynsworth Jr., to the Supreme Court of the United States, Hearings before the U.S. Senate Committee on the Judiciary, 91st Congress, 1st Session, September 1969 (Washington, DC: U.S. Government Printing Office, 1969), 602–11.

9. United States Commission on Civil Rights, *Southern School Desegregation, 1966–1967*, 12; "Mixed Schools Are Required by Fall, 1967," *Richmond Times-Dispatch*, April 30, 1965, 1.

10. Statistic is from United States Commission on Civil Rights, *Southern School Desegregation, 1966–1967*, 2.

11. For more, see *Southern Education Report*, vol. 1, no. 1, July-August 1965, 31–33; *Southern Education Report*, vol. 1, no. 3, November-December 1965, 30–32; United States Commission on Civil Rights, *Southern School Desegregation, 1966–1967*, 163.

12. Statement by United States Commissioner of Education Harold Howe II, and Revised Statement of Polices for School Desegregation Plans Under Title VI of the Civil Rights Act of 1964, Part IV, Box A69, NAACP Papers; United States Commission on Civil Rights, *Federal Rights Under School Desegregation Law*, 18–19.

13. Quotation is from Wilkinson, *From "Brown" to "Bakke,"* 104. See also Davison Douglas, "*Brown v. Board of Education* and Its Impact on Black Education in America," in Lau, *From the Grassroots to the Supreme Court*, 365; Michael J. Klarman, "How *Brown* Changed Race Relations: The Backlash Thesis," *Journal of American History* 81 (1994): 83.

14. Quotation is from "Courts Let Agency Set Mixing Pace," *Richmond News Leader*, August 2, 1965, 1; see also "Court Junks Most Dixie Pupil Plans," *Norfolk Journal and Guide*, June 1, 1968, 1.

15. Statistics are from United States Commission on Civil Rights, *Southern School Desegregation, 1966–1967*, 5, 102–4. See also *Southern Education Report*, vol. 1, no. 1, July–August 1965, 29, which reports slightly lower figures.

16. Italics added by author. Quotation is from *United States v. Jefferson County Board of Education*, 380 F. 2d 385 (5th Cir. 1967). See also *United States v. Jefferson County*, 372 F. 2d 836 (5th Cir. 1966); United States Commission on Civil Rights, *Southern School Desegregation, 1966–1967*, 3.

17. "Mixing in all Va. school districts, official claims," *Richmond Afro-American*, September 11, 1965, 5; "78 Pledges On Schools Are Received," *Richmond Times-Dispatch*, March 4, 1965, 1; "Signed Form Not to Assure School Funds," *Richmond Times-Dispatch*, April 22, 1965, 1; "Mixed Schools Are Required by Fall, 1967,"

Richmond Times-Dispatch, April 30, 1965, 1, "Middlesex Plan Is Sent to HEW," *Richmond Times-Dispatch,* June 4, 1965, 4; "Sussex Says Deadline No Factor," *Richmond Times-Dispatch,* June 16, 1965, 11; "NAACP chipping 'Northern-style' school segregation in 24 states," *Richmond Afro-American,* September 25, 1965, 15; United States Commission on Civil Rights, *Survey of School Desegregation in the Southern and Border States,* 42, in Part IV, Box A69, NAACP Papers.

18. Quotation is from United States Commission on Civil Rights, *1964 Staff Report,* 275. See also 237–38; "Williamsburg Area to Obey Rights Law," *Richmond Times-Dispatch,* May 15, 1965, 4.

19. "Henrico Prepares Free-Choice Plan," *Richmond Times-Dispatch,* June 3, 1965, 1; Pratt, *Color of Their Skin,* 40.

20. Quotations are from "Williamsburg Area to Obey Rights Law," *Richmond Times-Dispatch,* May 15, 1965, 4. See also "Frederick Gives Court School Plan," *Richmond Times-Dispatch,* March 30, 1964, 2.

21. Robert Holland, "HEW Guidelines Are Said Unchanged," *Richmond Times-Dispatch,* June 4, 1968, B3; "About 120 Negroes Apply at Nottoway White Schools," *Richmond Times-Dispatch,* May 27, 1965, 4; "Louisa Plans To Desegregate All 12 Grades," *Richmond Times-Dispatch,* June 1, 1965, 8; "Amelia Airs Free-Choice Plan," *Richmond Times-Dispatch,* June 1, 1965, 8; "Board Discusses Hanover Schools Compliance Plan," *Richmond Times-Dispatch,* June 2, 1965, 2; "Henrico Prepares Free-Choice Plan," *Richmond Times-Dispatch,* June 3, 1965, 1; "U.S. Turns Down 3 'Choice' Plans," *Richmond News Leader,* May 27, 1968, 1.

22. Statistics are from United States Commission on Civil Rights, *1964 Staff Report,* 290–91.

23. 1964 statistic is from "Desegregation Is Spreading In State Schools," *Richmond Times-Dispatch,* September 4, 1964, 2. Figures from 1965 are from United States Commission on Civil Rights, *Southern School Desegregation, 1966–1967,* 104.

24. Quotation is from United States Commission on Civil Rights, *Southern School Desegregation, 1966–1967,* 102. The states are in order, from first to third. The statistics are from the same report, 103–4.

25. "Public School Desegregation in Amelia Seen," *Richmond Times-Dispatch,* May 11, 1965, 2; "Amelia Airs Free-Choice Plan," *Richmond Times-Dispatch,* June 1, 1965, 8.

26. "Mecklenburg Schools To Allow Free Choice," *Richmond Times-Dispatch,* June 3, 1965, 6; United States Commission on Civil Rights, *Southern School Desegregation, 1966–1967,* 54–58, 163; *Southern Education Report,* vol. 1, no. 4, January–February 1966, Tables II and III.

27. Quotations are from W. Lester Banks and John M. Brooks to Dear NAACP Leader, September 21, 1966, Part IV, Box C32, NAACP Papers. See also Adopted Resolutions, Virginia State Conference NAACP, 31st Annual Convention, October 1966, Part IV, Box C32, NAACP Papers; David E. Langley [*sic*], "KKK Continues To Spew Hate: Anti-Klan Laws Not Enforced," *Richmond Afro-American,* August 27, 1966, 1.

28. Annual Report of Branch Activities, 1966, Lunenburg County, Part IV, Box C44, NAACP Papers; Annual Report of Branch Activities, 1970, Lunenburg County, Part VI, Box C183, NAACP. The latter report includes a number of news clippings; one claims the Virginia Klan was then the third largest in the nation.

29. Quotation is from "NAACP Official Urges More Desegregation," *Richmond Times-Dispatch*, May 16, 1965, 10B. The association also opposed HEW's 1966 guidelines; see Memorandum from Lewis Steel to Robert Carter, February 21, 1966, Part V, Box 2814, NAACP Papers.

30. Quotations are from Urgent Memorandum from W. Lester Banks and S. W. Tucker to All Virginia NAACP Branch Officers, May 21, 1965, Part V, Box 2836, NAACP Papers. See also Special Memorandum from W. Lester Banks to All Negro parents of the Commonwealth of Virginia, and an Application for Placement of Pupil, Virginia Pupil Placement Board, both in Part V, Box 2836, NAACP Papers; "NAACP Official Urges More Desegregation," *Richmond Times-Dispatch*, May 16, 1965, 10B.

31. "Va. NAACP tackles education problem," *Richmond Afro-American*, November 13, 1965, 18; "Ruth Harvey elected in Va.," *Richmond Afro-American*, August 20, 1966, 7; "Va. NAACP Officers," *Richmond Afro-American*, November 4, 1967, 11; Henry L. Marsh III, interview by Jody Allen and author, tape recording, Richmond, Va., November 25, 2002.

32. *Griffin v. County School Board of Prince Edward County*, 375 U.S. 391 (1964); Robert Holland, "Prince Edward Reopens Schools After Five Years," *Richmond Times-Dispatch*, September 9, 1964, 1; NAACP, "U.S. Court Cites County in Virginia for Contempt," NAACP press release, July 2, 1966, Part IV, Box A71, NAACP Papers; "Prince Edward Board Cleared of Contempt," *Richmond Times-Dispatch*, April 24, 1965, 1; United States Commission on Civil Rights, *1964 Staff Report*, 250–65; Delores P. Aldridge, "Litigation and Education of Blacks: A Look at the U.S. Supreme Court," *Journal of Negro Education*, vol. 47, no. 1 (Winter 1978): 105–6.

33. Allan Jones, "House Group Votes Two Tuition Bills," *Richmond Times-Dispatch*, January 30, 1959, 1; Allan Jones, "Tuition Program Now Law," *Richmond Times-Dispatch*, February 1, 1959, 1.

34. Reed Sarratt, A Statistical Summary, State by State, of Segregation-Desegregation Activity Affecting Southern Schools from 1954 to Present, 49–53, in Box 7, M 68, Papers of Edward H. Peeples Jr., Special Collections and Archives, James Branch Cabell Library, Virginia Commonwealth University; United States Commission on Civil Rights, *1961 U.S. Commission on Civil Rights Report*, 88–92.

35. Quotation and statistic are from *Cochyese Griffin v. State Board of Education*, reply brief, December 1964, Part III, Box A106, NAACP Papers. See also Frank Walin, "Court Hits Tuition Grants," *Richmond Times-Dispatch*, December 3, 1964, 1; "NAACP Wins on Virginia School Tuition Grants," NAACP press release, December 4, 1964, in Bracey and Meier, *Papers of the NAACP*, Part 3, series D, reel 13; "State's Argument On Grants Rebuffed," *Richmond Times-Dispatch*,

December 9, 1964, 1; "Eight Schools May Still Get State Grants," *Richmond Times-Dispatch*, October 7, 1965, 7; Allan Jones, "Grant Decision Opposed," *Richmond Times-Dispatch*, March 15, 1965, 1.

36. *Bradley v. School Board of the City of Richmond*, 382 U.S. 103 (1965); "Williamsburg Area to Obey Rights Law," *Richmond Times-Dispatch*, May 15, 1965, 4; "Negro Teacher Dismissals Are Protested," *Richmond Times-Dispatch*, May 21, 1965, 7; "Negro Teachers' Rehiring Urged," *Richmond Times-Dispatch*, September 28, 1965, 3.

37. Quotation is from Revised Statement of Policies for School Desegregation Plans Under Title VI of the Civil Rights Act of 1964, U.S. Office of Education, March 1966, reprinted in United States Commission on Civil Rights, *Federal Rights Under School Desegregation Law*, 13; "Desegregation Curtailing Activities At Negro High School in Staunton," *Richmond Times-Dispatch*, September 19, 1965, 6B; Cecelski, *Along Freedom Road*, 7–11, 57; United States Commission on Civil Rights, *Federal Rights Under School Desegregation Law*, 1, 4, 9.

38. *Mary Franklin v. County School Board of Giles County*, 360 F. 2d 325 (4th Cir. 1966); "Negro Teachers' Rehiring Urged," *Richmond Times-Dispatch*, September 28, 1965, 3; "Negro Teacher Dismissals Are Protested," *Richmond Times-Dispatch*, May 21, 1965, 7.

39. Tucker quotation is from S. J. Ackerman, "The Trials of S. W. Tucker," *Washington Post Magazine*, June 11, 2000, 14.

40. Quotation is from "Six county school systems hit by desegregation suits," *Richmond Afro-American*, March 20, 1965, 3. See also "NAACP Presses for School Integration in Virginia," NAACP press release, May 29, 1965, Part III, Box A106, NAACP Papers; Allan Jones, "Latest School Suits Seek Voluntary Integration," *Richmond Times-Dispatch*, March 13, 1965, 1; "Two Suits Are Filed On Schools," *Richmond Times-Dispatch*, March 18, 1965, 6; "8 Counties sued on school policy," *Richmond Afro-American*, March 27, 1965, 3. The Virginia State Conference began planning this litigation in early 1964; see List of attendees, Virginia State Conference Planning Conference, February 8, 1964, Part III, Box C161, NAACP Papers.

41. Quotation is from "NAACP Presses for School Integration in Virginia," NAACP press release, May 29, 1965, Part III, Box A106. See also "Fredericksburg Amends School Desegregation Plans," *Richmond Times-Dispatch*, July 7, 1963, 8; "Prince Edward barred from using funds," *Richmond Afro-American*, October 12, 1963, 19; "Goochland Now Facing School Integration Suit," *Richmond Times-Dispatch*, May 21, 1965, 7; Allan Jones, "Grant Decision Opposed," *Richmond Times-Dispatch*, March 15, 1965, 1.

42. "NAACP Official Urges More Desegregation," *Richmond Times-Dispatch*, May 16, 1965, 10B; "Goochland Now Facing School Integration Suit," *Richmond Times-Dispatch*, May 21, 1965, 7; "About 120 Negroes Apply at Nottoway White Schools," *Richmond Times-Dispatch*, May 27, 1965, 4; "Appeals Court to Hear Norfolk Schools Case," *Richmond Times-Dispatch*, May 31, 1965, 4; "Maintains

Segregation, Lawyer Says," *Richmond Times-Dispatch*, June 1, 1965, 6; "Nottoway School Board Defends Free-Choice Desegregation Plan," *Richmond Times-Dispatch*, June 2, 1965, 7; "NAACP Appeals Two School Cases," *Richmond Times-Dispatch*, August 4, 1965, 3.

43. Quotation is from Kluger, *Simple Justice*, 572. See also Tushnet, *Making Civil Rights Law*, 177.

44. Quotation is from "Pupil Placing Attacked Anew," *Richmond Times-Dispatch*, July 26, 1965, 2.

45. Quotation is from "School Desegregation Plan Approved in Norfolk, Va.," NAACP Legal Defense Fund press release, March 22, 1966, Part IV, Box A71, NAACP Papers; "Norfolk School Attendance Setup Hit," *Richmond Times-Dispatch*, March 24, 1965, 6; Littlejohn and Ford, *Elusive Equality*, 141–42.

46. NAACP press release, February 2, 1967, Part IV, Box C32, NAACP Papers; List of Current NAACP Cases, November 8, 1965, Part V, Box 2586, NAACP Papers; Monthly Report of the General Counsel, April-May 1966, Part IV, Box A53, NAACP Papers; Monthly Report of the General Counsel, September 1967, Part IV, Box A53, NAACP Papers.

47. NAACP Legal Defense Fund Docket Report, November 1966, and related reports, Part V, Box 2588, NAACP Papers; "Rights Lawyers List 1966 Legal Emphasis," NAACP Legal Defense Fund press release, January 5, 1966, Part IV, Box A57, NAACP Papers. It is important to note that conflict over finances and litigation greatly strained the relationship between the national office of the NAACP and the Legal Defense Fund during the mid-1960s. See Part III, Box A237, NAACP Papers; Part V, Box 2719, NAACP Papers; Part VI, Box A14, NAACP Papers; Part VI, Box A18 NAACP Papers; Part VIII, Box 350, NAACP Papers.

48. Jody L. Allen and Brian J. Daugherty, "Recovering a 'Lost' Story Using Oral History: The United States Supreme Court's Historic *Green v. New Kent County, Virginia*, Decision," *Oral History Review*, vol. 3, issue 2 (June 2006): 25–45; NAACP Legal Defense Fund Docket Reports, November 1966 and June 1967, both in Part V, Box 2588, NAACP Papers; W. Lester Banks to Lucille Black, January 24, 1961, Part VI, Box C159, NAACP Papers; Allan Jones, "Latest School Suits Seek Voluntary Integration," *Richmond Times-Dispatch*, March 13, 1965, 1; Allan Jones, "Grant Decision Opposed," *Richmond Times-Dispatch*, March 15, 1965, 1.

49. Dr. Calvin C. Green, interview by Jody Allen and author, tape recording, New Kent County, Va., November 2, 2001; Cynthia Gaines, interview by Jody Allen and author, tape recording, New Kent County, Va., November 13, 2001.

50. Quotation is from Dr. Calvin C. Green, interview by Jody Allen and author and Sarah Trembanis, tape recording, New Kent County, Va., October 9, 2001. See also, "New Kent Issue," *Richmond Times-Dispatch*, July 16, 1965, 4.

51. *Charles C. Green v. County School Board of New Kent County, Virginia*, 391 U.S. 430 (1968); "Schools Are Desegregated in Appomattox and Bedford," *Richmond Times-Dispatch*, August 17, 1965, 3; Wilkinson, *From "Brown" to "Bakke*," 115.

52. Quotation is from Cynthia Gaines, interview by Jody Allen and author, tape recording, New Kent County, Va., November 13, 2001.

53. Quotation is from "Pioneers Recall Pain of Being Sacrificial Lambs," *Richmond Times-Dispatch,* April 12, 1993, B1. Cynthia Gaines, interview by Jody Allen and author, tape recording, New Kent County, Va., November 13, 2001. On Franklin, see E. D. Harrell to Roy Wilkins, October 2, 1965, Part IV, Box C32, NAACP Papers. I have corrected a misspelling in the Harrell quotation.

54. NAACP Legal Defense Fund Docket Reports, November 1966 and June 1967, both in Part V, Box 2588, NAACP Papers; *Charles Green v. County School Board of New Kent County,* 382 F. 2d 338 (4th Cir. 1967); Hill, *Big Bang,* 184. Hill resumed work with the Hill, Tucker, and Marsh law firm in Richmond.

55. Michie quotation is from "Federal Court Upholds Frederick School Plan," *Richmond Times-Dispatch,* September 16, 1965, 4. See also Wilkinson, *From "Brown" to "Bakke,"* 108.

56. Quotations are from *Bradley v. School Board of City of Richmond,* 345 F. 2d 310 (4th Cir. 1965), and *United States v. Jefferson County Board of Education,* 372 F. 2d 836 (5th Cir. 1966). See also Delores P. Aldridge, "Litigation and Education of Blacks: A Look at the U.S. Supreme Court," *Journal of Negro Education,* vol. 47, no. 1 (Winter 1978): 105–6; Statement by G. W. Foster Jr., in Support of the Nomination of Judge Clement F. Haynsworth Jr., to the Supreme Court of the United States, Hearings before the U.S. Senate Committee on the Judiciary, 91st Congress, 1st Session, September 1969 (Washington, DC: U.S. Government Printing Office, 1969), 602–11.

57. *Charles Green v. County School Board of New Kent County,* 382 F. 2d 338 (4th Cir. 1967); *Bowman v. County School Board of Charles City County,* 382 F. 2d 326 (4th Cir. 1967); "LDF Attorneys Argue 11 Cases in 10 Days," NAACP Legal Defense Fund press release, Part IV, Box A5, NAACP Papers; "Federal Court Upholds Frederick School Plan," *Richmond Times-Dispatch,* September 16, 1965, 4; "NAACP Appeals Two School Cases," *Richmond Times-Dispatch,* August 4, 1965, 3.

58. Quotation is from Henry L. Marsh III, interview by Jody Allen and author, tape recording, Richmond, Va., November 25, 2002. See also Excerpts from Legal Brief of Supreme Court of the United States, No. 695, *Charles C. Green, et al, v. County School Board of New Kent County, Virginia, et al;* S. J. Ackerman, "The Trials of S. W. Tucker," *Washington Post Magazine,* June 11, 2000, 14.

Seven | The *Green* Light

1. Charles McDowell Jr., "State Rated Second In School Mixing," *Richmond Times-Dispatch,* May 28, 1968, 2; "Court Junks Most Dixie Pupil Plans," *Norfolk Journal and Guide,* June 1, 1968, 1.

2. Statistic in text and quotation here are from Charles McDowell Jr., "State

Rated Second In School Mixing," *Richmond Times-Dispatch*, May 28, 1968, 2. McDowell noted, "Although these statistics . . . were calculated on a slightly different basis from those of past years, and precise comparisons are not possible, the general trend is up."

3. Robert Holland, "New Guidelines for Schools Take on Firmer Overtones," *Richmond Times-Dispatch*, March 25, 1968, B1; "New Guidelines Set To Foster Equality In Northern Schools," *New York Times*, March 19, 1968, 1; "King William Plan Due By Sept. 30," *Richmond Times-Dispatch*, August 29, 1968, C2.

4. Both quotations are from Hamilton Crockford, "'Mature Mood' in Virginia Noted During Past 15 Years," *Richmond Times-Dispatch*, May 18, 1969, F4. See also United States Commission on Civil Rights, *Reviewing a Decade of School Desegregation, 1966–1975*, 14–19; Wilkinson, *From "Brown" to "Bakke,"* 61, 118.

5. For more information on *Green*, see chapter 6.

6. Quotations are from *Charles C. Green v. County School Board of New Kent County, Virginia*, 391 U.S. 430 (1968). See also Martin, Ruiz, Salvatore, Sullivan, and Sitkoff, *Racial Desegregation in Public Education in the U.S. Theme Study*, 91.

7. Italics added by author. Quotations are from *Charles C. Green v. County School Board of New Kent County, Virginia*, 391 U.S. 430 (1968). See also Jody L. Allen and Brian J. Daugherity, "Recovering a 'Lost' Story Using Oral History: The United States Supreme Court's Historic *Green v. New Kent County, Virginia*, Decision," *Oral History Review*, vol. 3, issue 2 (June 2006): 25–45.

8. Quotation is from *Charles C. Green v. County School Board of New Kent County, Virginia*, 391 U.S. 430 (1968). See also Jody Allen, Brian Daugherity, and Sarah Trembanis, "New Kent School and the George W. Watkins School: From Freedom of Choice to Integration," in Menkart, Murray, and View, *Putting the Movement Back into Civil Rights Teaching*, 270–73.

9. Quotation is from *Charles C. Green v. County School Board of New Kent County, Virginia*, 391 U.S. 430 (1968). See also Hamilton Crockford, "Two Questions Stood Out In Court's School Cases," *Richmond Times-Dispatch*, April 7, 1968, B1; "New Kent Schools Defended by Brown," *Richmond Times-Dispatch*, April 7, 1968, B1; Hamilton Crockford, "New Kent School Plan Is Nullified," *Richmond Times-Dispatch*, May 28, 1968, 1.

10. Quotation is from Rufus Wells, "Court Orders Mixed Schools In Prince Edward Co.," *Richmond Afro-American*, July 23, 1955, 2.

11. Quotation is from "Supreme Court's School Decisions Contradictory," *Los Angeles Times*, November 18, 1969, 7.

12. Quotation is from *Keyes v. School District No. 1, Denver, Colorado*, 413 U.S. 189 (1972).

13. "Court Junks Most Dixie Pupil Plans: Limit On 'Freedom of Choice' Ruling Could Affect 90% Of Southern School Districts," *Norfolk Journal and Guide*, June 1, 1968, 1.

14. Quotation is from Wilkinson, *From "Brown" to "Bakke,"* 108; see also 104.

15. Quotation is from James J. Kilpatrick, "The Supreme Court vs. Human Nature," *Los Angeles Times*, June 4, 1968, 5.

16. Dr. Calvin C. Green, interview by Jody Allen and author, tape recording, New Kent County, Va., December 17, 2002.

17. Judge Merhige visited other localities when hearing their desegregation cases as well. Judge Robert R. Merhige Jr., interview by Jody Allen and author, tape recording, Richmond, Va., November 6, 2002; "Judge Plans Petersburg School Visit," *Richmond Times-Dispatch*, March 4, 1969, B5. See also Robert Holland, "New Kent Proposes School Mixing Plan," *Richmond Times-Dispatch*, June 13, 1968, 1; "Merhige Plans to Visit New Kent Tomorrow," *Richmond Times-Dispatch*, August 15, 1968, D1; Editorial, "For Orderly Desegregation," *Richmond Times-Dispatch*, August 21, 1968, 12.

18. Robert Holland, "New Kent Proposes School Mixing Plan," *Richmond Times-Dispatch*, June 13, 1968, 1.

19. Dorine Bethea, "An Honor Restored In New Kent," *Richmond Times-Dispatch*, June 15, 1998, B1. On Prince Edward County, see John Clement, "School Names Changes Voted," *Richmond Times-Dispatch*, November 11, 1969, B1; John Clement, "New Mood Between Races Noted in Prince Edward," *Richmond Times-Dispatch*, November 16, 1969, B4. On Bedford, see Annual Report of Branch Activities, Bedford County, 1970, Part VI, Box C183, Papers of the National Association for the Advancement of Colored People, Library of Congress Manuscript Division, Washington, D.C. (hereafter cited as NAACP Papers).

20. Quotation is from United States Commission on Civil Rights, *Your child and busing*, 14. See also United States Commission on Civil Rights, *Schools Can Be Desegregated*, 6. For Lynchburg, see "Black Power Button Case Under Advisement," *Richmond Times-Dispatch*, November 21, 1970, B3. For school closings in Virginia, see "Martinsville to Close Two All-Negro Schools," *Richmond Times-Dispatch*, April 10, 1968, B5; Web DeHoff, "Four Negro Principals Reassigned," *Richmond Times-Dispatch*, April 19, 1969, B1.

21. Statistic is from United States Commission on Civil Rights, *Title IV and School Desegregation*, 17. Quotation is from Kristin Davis, "Local teachers part of evolution," *The Free Lance-Star*, May 16, 2004, A8; on Fredericksburg, see Davis. See also "Desegregation Curtailing Activities At Negro High School in Staunton," *Richmond Times-Dispatch*, September 19, 1965, B6; "Negro Teacher Job Survey Begun in State," *Richmond Times-Dispatch*, September 28, 1965, 3; "Negro Teachers' Rehiring Urged," *Richmond Times-Dispatch*, September 28, 1965, 3.

22. Quotation is from "Spotsylvania NAACP fights school problems," *Richmond Afro-American*, January 25, 1969, 3.

23. Annual Report of Branch Activities, Greensville County, 1970, Part VI, Box C183, NAACP Papers; Annual Report of Branch Activities, Hanover County, 1970, Part VI, Box C183, NAACP Papers; NAACP Legal Defense Fund, 20th Anniversary of *Brown v. Board of Education*, A Report to the American People (advance copy), May 17, 1974, Part VIII, Box 350, NAACP Papers.

24. Quotation is from Preston M. Yancy, "The Situation At Va. State," *Richmond Afro-American*, January 17, 1970, 5. For the NAACP's point of view, see "'Complete Integration Our Goal In Multi-Racial Society' —Wilkins," *Richmond Afro-American*, January 27, 1968, 8.

25. Quotation is from Hamilton Crockford, "New Kent School Plan Is Nullified," *Richmond Times-Dispatch*, May 28, 1968, 1. See also, Buell G. Gallagher, "Integrated Schools in the Black Cities?" *Journal of Negro Education*, vol. 42, no. 3 (Summer 1973): 336–50.

26. Frank Walin, "NAACP Again Attacks 'Freedom of Choice,'" *Richmond Times-Dispatch*, June 22, 1968, 1; "Gloucester to Seek Suit Dismissal," *Richmond Times-Dispatch*, July 4, 1968, C1; "NAACP Files 6 Suits On Schools," *Richmond Times-Dispatch*, August 29, 1968, C1; "Tucker keeps word: files 3 more suits," *Richmond Afro-American*, August 31, 1968, 1; Littlejohn and Ford, *Elusive Equality*, 147–48.

27. Quotation is from Hamilton Crockford, "New Kent School Plan Is Nullified," *Richmond Times-Dispatch*, May 28, 1968, 2. Shortly after the decision, the NAACP's national legal staff underwent a period of prolonged turmoil. General Counsel Robert Carter and the remainder of the legal team resigned after the firing of one of their own for an article, titled "Nine Men In Black Who Think White" published in *The New York Times Magazine*. See "NAACP's Entire Legal Staff Quits," *Richmond Afro-American*, November 2, 1968, 1.

28. Quotation in text and quotation here are from Martin, Ruiz, Salvatore, Sullivan, and Sitkoff, *Racial Desegregation in Public Education in the U.S. Theme Study*, 91, 90. The study refers to *Green* as the "most important decision regarding school desegregation since *Brown.*" See also Bradley and Fishkin, *Encyclopedia of Civil Rights in America*, 411.

29. Quotation is from Davison Douglas, "*Brown v. Board of Education* and Its Impact on Black Education in America," in Lau, *From the Grassroots to the Supreme Court*, 365. J. Harvie Wilkinson III adds: "*Green* marked the end of gradualism and the dawn of something quite new: an attempt at massive integration only dreamed of at the time of *Brown.*" Wilkinson, *From "Brown" to "Bakke,"* 126.

30. Quotation is from Henry L. Marsh III, interview by Jody Allen and author, tape recording, Richmond, Va., November 25, 2002.

31. Charles Cox, "School Opening Is Smooth In Richmond, Area Counties," *Richmond Times-Dispatch*, September 3, 1969, 1; "Third of Negro Pupils in South To Be in Mixed Classes in Fall," *Richmond Times-Dispatch*, August 20, 1969, 19; Cynthia Kay Bechter, "How the Goochland County Public Schools Desegregated," *Goochland County Historical Society Magazine*, vol. 27 (1995): 38–41.

32. Quotation is from *Cochyese Griffin v. State Board of Education*, 296 F. Supp. 1178 (1969). See also "Tuition Grants Attacked Anew By NAACP," *Richmond Times-Dispatch*, July 31, 1968, 1; Frank Walin, "Grants Law Assailed, Defended," *Richmond Times-Dispatch*, January 24, 1969, B1; Frank Walin, "U.S. Court Knocks Out State Tuition Grants," *Richmond Times-Dispatch*, February 12, 1969, 1; "Vir-

ginia Program Voided," *New York Times*, February 12, 1969, 24; "Court knocks out state tuition grants," *Richmond Afro-American*, February 22, 1969, 3; Allan Jones, "Grant Decision Opposed," *Richmond Times-Dispatch*, March 15, 1965, 1; "Eight Schools May Still Get State Grants," *Richmond Times-Dispatch*, October 7, 1965, 7; *Cochyese Griffin v. State Board of Education*, 239 F. Supp. 560 (1965); "NAACP Wins on Virginia School Tuition Grants," NAACP press release, December 4, 1964, in Bracey and Meier, *Papers of the NAACP*, Part 3, series D, reel 13.

33. "U.S. sues two school districts in Virginia," *Richmond Afro-American*, December 7, 1968, 23.

34. Quotation is from James J. Kilpatrick, "Georgia Finding Answers," *The Tuscaloosa News*, November 2, 1969, 4. See also Jim Leeson, "The Matter of Choice," *Southern Education Report*, vol. 4, no. 2, September 1968, 30–31; "State of Georgia Named In U.S. School Bias Suit," *Richmond Times-Dispatch*, August 2, 1969, 1.

35. Charles McDowell Jr., "State Rated Second In School Mixing," *Richmond Times-Dispatch*, May 28, 1968, 2; "Third of Negro Pupils in South To Be in Mixed Classes in Fall," *Richmond Times-Dispatch*, August 20, 1969, 19; "Freedom-of-Choice—Going," *The Virginian-Pilot*, September 3, 1968, 10; "Court Junks Most Dixie Pupil Plans," *Norfolk Journal and Guide*, June 1, 1968, 1; "Freedom-of-Choice Restricted," *The Virginian-Pilot*, May 28, 1968, 1.

36. Quotation is from Wilkins with Mathews, *Standing Fast*, 333; see also Kluger, *Simple Justice*, 765.

37. Quotation is from United States Commission on Civil Rights, *Reviewing a Decade of School Desegregation, 1966–1975*, 14.

38. Quotation is from Wilkinson, *From "Brown" to "Bakke,"* 217; see also 119; Kluger, *Simple Justice*, 764–68.

39. Kotlowski, *Nixon's Civil Rights*, 14, 37, 171; Sokol, *There Goes My Everything*, 91–98.

40. Quotation is from Wilkinson, *From "Brown" to "Bakke,"* 121. See also Woodward and Armstrong, *The Brethren*, 36–56; Fairclough, *Race and Democracy*, 441–45.

41. Quotation is from *Alexander v. Holmes County Board of Education*, 396 U.S. 1218 (1969). See also "U.S. Supreme Court rules for immediate desegregation," *Richmond Afro-American*, January 3, 1970, 18.

42. Quotation is from *Nesbit v. Statesville City Board of Education*, 418 F. 2d 1040 (4th Cir. 1969). Virginia Department of Education statistics are from "School Desegregation Up 50 Percent," *Public Education in Virginia: A News Magazine of the State Department of Education*, vol. 6, no. 4 (Winter 1971): 15. See also "U.S. Court Orders Fast Integration," *New York Times*, December 3, 1969, 37.

43. "Agnew Busing Remark Seen as Not Out of Line," *Richmond Times-Dispatch*, September 19, 1969, 21; "Third of Negro Pupils in South To Be in Mixed Classes in Fall," *Richmond Times-Dispatch*, August 20, 1969, 19; Elsie Cuff Walker, "School board rejects HEW plan for Va. desegregation," *Richmond Afro-American*, July 5, 1969, 22.

44. Hamilton Crockford, "'Mature Mood' in Virginia Noted During Past 15 Years," *Richmond Times-Dispatch*, May 18, 1969, F4. See also Shelley Rolfe, "NAACP Relevancy Stressed At Convention Opening Here," *Richmond Times-Dispatch*, October 25, 1969, B4.

45. *Bradley v. School Board of the City of Richmond*, 317 F. Supp. 555 (1970); Pratt, *Color of Their Skin*, 40–54; Pamela Stallsmith, "'The Whole World Changed,'" *Richmond Times-Dispatch*, August 8, 1999, C1.

46. Quotation is from Kluger, *Simple Justice*, 765; see also Wilkins with Mathews, *Standing Fast*, 339.

47. Quotation is from Judge Robert R. Merhige Jr., interview by Jody Allen and author, tape recording, Richmond, Va., November 6, 2002; Henry L. Marsh III, interview by Jody L. Allen and author, tape recording, Richmond, Va., November 25, 2002; "Marshals To Patrol At Merhiges," *Richmond Times-Dispatch*, July 23, 1970, 3.

48. "Delegates urged to fight against racism, separatism," *Richmond Afro-American*, November 8, 1969, 14.

49. Memorandum from Norman J. Chachkin to Attorneys with School Desegregation Cases, July 1, 1970, Part V, Box 2836, NAACP Papers; Wilkinson, *From "Brown" to "Bakke,"* 137.

50. Quotations are from *Brewer v. School Board of the City of Norfolk*, 434 F. 2d 408 (4th Cir. 1970). See also untitled legal document pertaining to *Brewer v. School Board of the City of Norfolk*, Part V, Box 2836, NAACP Papers; Memorandum from Norman J. Chachkin to Attorneys with School Desegregation Cases, July 1, 1970, Part V, Box 2836, NAACP Papers. Hoffman's decision came in *Beckett v. School Board of the City of Norfolk*, 308 F. Supp. 1274 (1969). See also Littlejohn and Ford, *Elusive Equality*, 165–72.

51. Littlejohn and Ford, *Elusive Equality*, 172–75; "Schools Open Quietly, Despite Busing Howl," *Norfolk Journal and Guide*, September 5, 1970, B1; "School Board Requests U.S. Funds For Busing," *Norfolk Journal and Guide*, October 31, 1970, 9.

52. Quotation is from *Cecelia Jackson et al v. School Board of the City of Lynchburg* ruling, April 28, 1970, issued by Judge Robert R. Merhige, Part V, Box 2836, NAACP Papers; Charles Cox, "Merhige's Decision on Mixing Could Be Landmark Ruling," *Richmond Times-Dispatch*, August 13, 1970, C1.

53. Quotation is from Charles Cox, "Inconsistencies Pose Dilemma," *Richmond Times-Dispatch*, August 23, 1970, B1. See also *Cynthia Green v. School Board of the City of Roanoke*, 428 F. 2d 811 (4th Cir. 1970), decided June 17, 1970, in Part V, Box 2836, NAACP Papers; "School Plan Speedup Rejected: Judge Denies NAACP Plan," *Richmond Times-Dispatch*, July 31, 1969, C1; "Virginia Schools: No Incidents," *The Sumter Daily Item*, Sumter, S.C., August 31, 1970, 11.

54. Quotations are from *James Swann v. Charlotte-Mecklenburg Board of Education*, 431 F. 2d 138 (4th Cir. 1970). See also Frank Walin, "U.S. Court to Review Charlotte Busing Issue," *Richmond Times-Dispatch*, April 6, 1970, B3; "Excerpts

From the Supreme Court Ruling Upholding Busing to End Segregation," *New York Times*, April 21, 1971, 28; Wilkinson, *From "Brown" to "Bakke*," 139–49.

55. Quotation is from *Swann v. Charlotte-Mecklenburg Board of Education*, 402 U.S. 1 (1971). See also Davison Douglas, *Reading, Writing and Race*, chapters 7–8.

56. Quotation is from *Swann v. Charlotte-Mecklenburg Board of Education*, 402 U.S. 1 (1971); United States Commission on Civil Rights, *Understanding school desegregation*; Wilkinson, *From "Brown" to "Bakke*," 139–49.

57. Charles Cox, "City Delay on Buses May Be Expensive," *Richmond Times-Dispatch*, May 12, 1971, B1; Pamela Stallsmith, "'The Whole World Changed,'" *Richmond Times-Dispatch*, August 8, 1999, C1; "School Desegregation Up 50 Percent," *Public Education in Virginia: A News Magazine of the State Department of Education*, vol. 6, no. 4 (Winter 1971): 15; *Inequality in Education: Perspectives On Busing* (Center for Law and Education), no. 11, 15, in Part V, Box 2814, NAACP Papers.

58. Quotations are from Kluger, *Simple Justice*, 764–68. See also Wilhoit, *Politics of Massive Resistance*, 278–80. For more on the NAACP's support of busing and its opposition to Nixon's policies, see Part V, Box 2814, NAACP Papers.

59. Wilkins with Mathews, *Standing Fast*, 334; Kluger, *Simple Justice*, 764; "Court Puts A Stone Wall Before the School Bus," *New York Times*, July 28, 1974, 159.

60. Quotation is from Kluger, *Simple Justice*, 768.

61. See, for example, *Keyes v. Denver School District No. 1* (1973); "HEW Offers New Guides For Schools," *Richmond Times-Dispatch*, March 19, 1968, 1; "H.E.W. Finds North Lags In Rate of Pupil Integration," *New York Times*, January 15, 1971, 1; "South Integrates Schools as North Lags," *New York Times*, June 18, 1971, 1; John Herbers, "Antibusing Stance Spreads in North, West," *Richmond Times-Dispatch*, September 5, 1971, F2; "Cross-District Busing Incenses Detroit Area," *Richmond Times-Dispatch*, October 18, 1971, 2.

62. Wolters, *Race and Education, 1954–2007*, 40–42.

63. Quotation is from Pratt, *Color of Their Skin*, 62. For the statistics, see Wilkinson, *From "Brown" to "Bakke*," 151–52. See also "Report Stresses Flight of Whites," *Richmond Times-Dispatch*, January 16, 1972, 1; "Some White Flight to Suburbs Anticipated," *Richmond Times-Dispatch*, February 6, 1972, F5.

64. Quotation is from Pratt, *Color of Their Skin*, 63. See also 93; Wilkinson, *From "Brown" to "Bakke*," 152. The same phenomenon occurred in other Virginia cities. See, for example, "Norfolk Begins to Work On New School Proposal," *Richmond Times-Dispatch*, June 25, 1970, F6.

65. Charles Cox, "78,000 Would Be Bused In Merger, Court Told," *Richmond Times-Dispatch*, August 18, 1971, 1; "Report Stresses Flight of Whites," *Richmond Times-Dispatch*, January 16, 1972, 1.

66. *Carolyn Bradley v. School Board of the City of Richmond*, 338 F. Supp. 67 (1972); Charles Cox, "Merhige Sets July 1 Takeover By Areawide School Board," *Richmond Times-Dispatch*, B1; "Rights Lawyers Hail Richmond Decision," *New York Times*, January 13, 1972, 32.

67. Quotation is from *Carolyn Bradley v. School Board of the City of Richmond*, 462 F. 2d 1058 (4th Cir. 1972).

68. *School Board of the City of Richmond v. State Board of Education*, 412 U.S. 92 (1973); Pamela Stallsmith, "Walls Came Down but State Fought Desegregation for Many Years," *Richmond Times-Dispatch*, January 2, 2000, S4. J. Harvie Wilkinson III, in *From "Brown" to "Bakke,"* 164, notes that Henry Marsh fought Powell's confirmation to the Supreme Court.

69. Quotation is from *Milliken v. Bradley*, 418 U.S. 717 (1974). See also Kluger, *Simple Justice*, 771–73; "Court Puts a Stone Wall before the School Bus," *New York Times*, July 28, 1974, 159.

70. On HEW, see Wilkinson, *From "Brown" to "Bakke,"* 121. On Weinberger, see "Weinberger Defends HEW, Cites Northern Opposition," *Richmond Times-Dispatch*, September 7, 1974, 1; Wilkinson, *From "Brown" to "Bakke,"* 46.

71. "Norfolk School Gaining in Racial Harmony," *New York Times*, October 24, 1971, 68.

Afterword

1. Quotations are from NAACP Legal Defense Fund, 20th Anniversary of *Brown v. Board of Education*, A Report to the American People (advance copy), May 17, 1974, Part VIII, Box 350, Papers of the National Association for the Advancement of Colored People, Library of Congress Manuscript Division, Washington, D.C. (hereafter cited as NAACP Papers).

2. Statistics are from Racial-Ethnic Survey of Public School Students and Professional Staff in Virginia, 1974–1975, Appendix A, State Department of Education Technical Assistance Program, Library of Virginia, Richmond, Virginia.

3. Signs of this shift can be seen in the late 1960s. See, for example, 36th Annual Convention of the Virginia State Conference NAACP, Important Convention News, 1971, Part VI, C159, NAACP Papers.

4. Erwin Chemerinsky, "The Segregation and Resegregation of American Public Education: The Courts' Role," in Boger and Orfield, *School Resegregation*, 32.

5. Quotation is from Bell, *Till Victory Is Won*, 142.

6. Charles J. Russo, J. John Harris, III, and Rosetta F. Sandidge, *"Brown v. Board of Education* at 40: A Legal History of Equal Educational Opportunities in American Public Education," *Journal of Negro Education*, vol. 63, no. 3 (Summer 1994): 297–309; Peter William Moran, "Border State Ebb and Flow: School Desegregation in Missouri, 1954–1999," in Daugherity and Bolton, *With All Deliberate Speed*, 196–98.

7. Littlejohn and Ford, *Elusive Equality*, 174–75.

8. In 2001, according to a Civil Rights Project report from Harvard University, approximately 40 percent of black students in the United States attended schools whose minority student enrollment topped 90 percent; see Michael Fletcher, "Inherently Unequal," *The Crisis*, vol. 111, no. 3 (May/June 2004): 24–31. See also

Byron Lutz, "The End of Court-Ordered Desegregation," *Economic Policy* 3 (May 2011): 130–68.

9. Quotation is from Lori Wiggins, "NAACP Looks at Resegregation of American Schools," *The Crisis*, vol. 118, no. 1 (Winter 2011): 40–41.

10. Quotation is from Genevieve Siegel-Hawley with Jennifer Ayscue, John Kuscera, and Gary Orfield, "Miles to Go: A Report on School Segregation in Virginia, 1989–2010" (Los Angeles: The Civil Rights Project, 2014), iii.

11. Littlejohn and Ford, *Elusive Equality*, chapter 6; Pratt, *Color of Their Skin*, 99–109; Ryan, *Five Miles Away*, chapter 2.

12. Racial-Ethnic Survey of Public School Students and Professional Staff in Virginia, 1974–1975, Appendix A, State Department of Education Technical Assistance Program, Library of Virginia, Richmond, Virginia.

13. Virginia Population Statistics, by Race, 1790–1990, U.S. Census Bureau, https://www.census.gov/population/www/documentation/twps0076/twps0076 .pdf, Table 47, accessed June 18, 2015, copy in the author's possession.

14. Gary Orfield, "The Southern Dilemma: Losing *Brown*, Fearing *Plessy*," in Boger and Orfield, *School Resegregation*, 1–25.

15. Quotation is from Pratt, *Color of Their Skin*, 109; Ryan, *Five Miles Away*, 12.

16. Quotation is from Charles Mohr, "Capital Rally to Recall Dr. King and His Dream," *New York Times*, August 26, 1988, B5.

BIBLIOGRAPHY

Archival Sources

AFRO-American Newspapers Archives and Research Center, Baltimore, MD
Library of Congress Manuscript Division
    Papers of the National Association for the Advancement of Colored People
    Papers of Thurgood Marshall
Library of Virginia
    Virginia Department of Education records
    Virginia newspaper collection
Nashville (Tennessee) Public Library, Civil Rights Reading Room
    Southern School News collection
    Southern Education Report collection
Richmond (Virginia) Public Library, Main Branch
    Newspaper clippings files
Tulane University, Amistad Research Center
    SNCC microfilm collection
    SCLC microfilm collection
    CORE microfilm collection
University of Mississippi, J. D. Williams Library, Special Collections
    Citizens' Council collection
University of Virginia, Albert and Shirley Small Special Collections Library
    Harry Flood Byrd Sr. Papers
    Harry Byrd Jr. Papers
    Everett Combs Papers
Virginia Commonwealth University, Cabell Library Special Collections
    John Mitchell Brooks Papers
    Heslip Lee Papers
    Edward H. Peeples Papers
    S. W. Tucker Papers
Virginia Historical Society
    Newspaper clippings files
    Vertical files
    Edward H. Peeples Papers

Newspapers and Periodicals

Free Lance-Star (Fredericksburg, Va.)
New York Times
Norfolk Journal and Guide
Race Relations Law Reporter
Richmond Afro-American
Richmond News Leader
Richmond Times-Dispatch
Southern Education Report
Southern School News

Court Cases

Alexander v. Holmes County Board of Education, 396 U.S. 1218 (1969)
Allen v. School Board of the City of Charlottesville, 240 F. 2d 59 (4th Cir. 1956)
Alston v. School Board of City of Norfolk, 112 F. 2d 992 (4th Cir. 1940)
Boynton v. Virginia, 364 U.S. 454 (1960)
Bradley v. School Board of City of Richmond, 382 U.S. 103 (1965)
Bradley v. School Board of the City of Richmond, 462 F. 2d 1058 (4th Cir. 1972)
Brewer v. School Board of the City of Norfolk, 434 F. 2d 408 (1970)
Briggs v. Elliott, 132 F. Supp 776 (1955)
Brown v. Board of Education, Topeka, Kansas, 347 U.S. 483 (1954)
Brown v. Board of Education, Topeka, Kansas, 349 U.S. 294 (1955)
Cooper v. Aaron, 358 U.S. 1 (1958)
Davis v. County School Board, Prince Edward County, Virginia, 103 F. Supp. 337 (1952)
Davis v. County School Board, Prince Edward County, Virginia, 142 F. Supp. 616 (1956)
Franklin v. County School Board of Giles County, 360 F. 2d 325 (4th Cir. 1966)
Goss v. Board of Education of Knoxville, 373 U.S. 683 (1963)
Green v. County School Board of New Kent County, 391 U.S. 430 (1968)
Green v. School Board of the City of Roanoke, 304 F. 2d 118 (4th Cir. 1962)
Griffin v. County School Board of Prince Edward County, 377 U.S. 218 (1964)
Griffin v. State Board of Education, 296 F. Supp. 1178 (1969)
Harrison v. Day, 106 S.E. 2nd 636 (1959)
Harrison v. NAACP, 360 U.S. 167 (1959)
Harper v. Virginia State Board of Elections, 383 U.S. 663 (1966)
James v. Almond, 170 F. Supp. 342 (1959)
Milliken v. Bradley, 418 U.S. 717 (1974)
Morgan v. Virginia, 328 U.S. 373 (1946)
NAACP v. Button, 371 U.S. 415 (1963)
NAACP v. Harrison, 202 Va. 142 (1960)

NAACP v. Patty, 159 F. Supp. 503 (1958)

Plessy v. Ferguson, 163 U.S. 537 (1896)

School Board of the City of Richmond v. State Board of Education, 412 U.S. 92 (1973)

Scull v. Virginia, 359 U.S. 344 (1959)

Swann v. Charlotte-Mecklenburg Board of Education, 402 U.S. 1 (1971)

Sweatt v. Painter, 339 U.S. 629 (1950)

Thompson v. County School Board of Arlington County, 144 F. Supp. 239 (1956)

United States v. Jefferson County Board of Education, 372 F. 2d 836 (5th Cir. 1966)

United States v. Jefferson County Board of Education, 380 F. 2d 385 (5th Cir. 1967)

Watson v. City of Memphis, 373 U.S. 526 (1963)

Published Sources

Adams, Sherman. *Firsthand Report: The Story of the Eisenhower Administration*. New York: Harper, 1961.

Ambrose, Stephen E. *Eisenhower: The President*. Vol. 2. New York: Simon & Schuster, 1983.

Arsenault, Raymond. *Freedom Riders: 1961 and the Struggle for Racial Justice*. New York: Oxford University Press, 2007.

Barnes, Catherine A. *Journey from Jim Crow: The Desegregation of Southern Transit*. New York: Columbia University Press, 1983.

Bartley, Numan V. *The New South, 1945–1980*. Baton Rouge: Louisiana State University Press, 1995.

———. *The Rise of Massive Resistance: Race and Politics in the South During the 1950's*. Baton Rouge: Louisiana State University Press, 1969.

Bates, Daisy. *The Long Shadow of Little Rock*. New York: D. McKay, 1962.

Beagle, Ben, and Ozzie Osborne. *J. Lindsay Almond: Virginia's Reluctant Rebel*. Roanoke: Full Court Press, Inc., 1984.

Beals, Melba. *Warriors Don't Cry: A Searing Memoir of the Battle to Integrate Little Rock's Central High*. New York: Pocket Books, 1994.

Bell, Janet Cheatham, ed. *Till Victory Is Won*. New York: Washington Square Press, 2002.

Berg, Manfred. *"The Ticket to Freedom": The NAACP and the Struggle for Black Political Integration*. Gainesville: University Press of Florida, 2005.

Bernstein, Patricia. *The First Waco Horror: The Lynching of Jesse Washington and the Rise of the NAACP*. College Station: Texas A & M University Press, 2006.

Black, Earl. *Southern Governors and Civil Rights*. Cambridge: Harvard University Press, 1976.

Blossom, Virgil T. *It Has Happened Here*. New York: Harper and Brothers, 1959.

Boger, John Charles, and Gary Orfield, eds. *School Resegregation: Must the South Turn Back?* Chapel Hill: University of North Carolina Press, 2005.

Bolton, Charles C. *The Hardest Deal of All: The Battle Over School Integration in Mississippi, 1870–1980.* Jackson: University Press of Mississippi, 2007.

Bonastia, Christopher. *Southern Stalemate: Five Years without Public Education in Prince Edward County, Virginia.* Chicago: University of Chicago Press, 2012.

Borstelmann, Thomas. *The Cold War and the Color Line: American Race Relations in the Global Arena.* Cambridge: Harvard University Press, 2001.

Boyle, Sarah Patton. *The Desegregated Heart: A Virginian's Stand in Time of Transition.* New York: William Morrow and Company, 1962.

Bracey, John H., and August Meier, eds. *Papers of the NAACP* (microfilm). Bethesda: University Publications of America, 1982.

Bradley, David, and Shelley F. Fishkin, eds. *The Encyclopedia of Civil Rights in America.* Armonk, NY: Sharpe Reference, 1998.

Branch, Taylor. *At Canaan's Edge: America in the King Years, 1965–68.* New York: Simon & Schuster, 2006.

———. *Parting the Waters: America in the King Years, 1954–63.* New York: Simon & Schuster, 1988.

———. *Pillar of Fire: America in the King Years, 1963–65.* New York: Simon & Schuster, 1998.

Brooks, Thomas R. *Walls Come Tumbling Down: A History of the Civil Rights Movement.* Englewood Cliffs, NJ: Prentice-Hall, 1974.

Buni, Andrew. *The Negro in Virginia Politics, 1902–1965.* Charlottesville: University Press of Virginia, 1967.

Burk, Robert F. *Dwight D. Eisenhower: Hero and Politician.* Boston: Twayne Publishers, 1986.

———. *The Eisenhower Administration and Black Civil Rights.* Knoxville: University of Tennessee Press, 1984.

Bush, Rod. *We Are Not What We Seem: Black Nationalism and Class Struggle in the American Century.* New York: New York University Press, 1999.

Bynum, Thomas. *NAACP Youth and the Fight for Black Freedom, 1936–1965.* Knoxville: University of Tennessee Press, 2013.

Carmichael, Stokely, and Charles V. Hamilton. *Black Power: The Politics of Liberation in America.* New York: Random House, 1967.

Carmichael, Stokely, and Ekwueme Michael Thelwell. *Ready for Revolution: The Life and Struggles of Stokely Carmichael.* New York: Scribner, 2003.

Carson, Clayborne. *In Struggle: SNCC and the Black Awakening.* Cambridge: Harvard University Press, 1981.

Carson, Clayborne, David Garrow, Gerald Gill, Vincent Harding, and Darlene Clark Hine. *The Eyes on the Prize Reader: Documents, Speeches, and First-hand Accounts from the Black Freedom Struggle.* New York: Penguin Books, 1991.

Carter, Dan T. *The Politics of Rage: George Wallace, the Origins of the New Conservatism, and the Transformation of American Politics.* New York: Simon & Schuster, 1995.

Catsam, Derek. *Freedom's Main Line: The Journey of Reconciliation and the Freedom Rides.* Lexington: University Press of Kentucky, 2011.

Cecelski, David S. *Along Freedom Road: Hyde County, North Carolina, and the Fate of Black Schools in the South.* Chapel Hill: University of North Carolina Press, 1994.

Chafe, William H. *Civilities and Civil Rights: Greensboro, North Carolina, and the Black Struggle for Freedom.* New York: Oxford University Press, 1980.

Colburn, David R., and Elizabeth Jacoway, eds. *Southern Businessmen and Desegregation.* Baton Rouge: Louisiana State University Press, 1982.

D'Angelo, Raymond. *The American Civil Rights Movement: Readings and Interpretations.* New York: McGraw-Hill, 2001.

Dabney, Virginius. *Virginia: The New Dominion.* Garden City, NY: Doubleday, 1971.

Daugherity, Brian J., and Charles C. Bolton, eds. *With All Deliberate Speed: Implementing "Brown v. Board of Education."* Fayetteville: University of Arkansas Press, 2008.

Dittmer, John. *Black Georgia in the Progressive Era, 1900–1920.* Champaign: University of Illinois Press, 1977.

———. *Local People: The Struggle for Civil Rights in Mississippi.* Champaign: University of Illinois Press, 1995.

Douglas, Davison M. *Jim Crow Moves North: The Battle Over Northern School Segregation, 1865–1954.* New York: Cambridge University Press, 2006.

———. *Reading, Writing, and Race: The Desegregation of the Charlotte Schools.* Chapel Hill: University of North Carolina Press, 1995.

Du Bois, W. E. B. *The Souls of Black Folk.* New York: Penguin Books, 1989 reprint.

Dudziak, Mary L. *Cold War Civil Rights: Race and the Image of American Democracy.* Princeton: Princeton University Press, 2000.

Dulles, Foster Rhea. *The Civil Rights Commission: 1957–1965.* East Lansing: Michigan State University Press, 1968.

Eagles, Charles W., ed. *The Civil Rights Movement in America.* Jackson: University Press of Mississippi, 1986.

Egerton, John. *Speak Now against the Day: The Generation before the Civil Rights Movement in the South.* Chapel Hill: University of North Carolina Press, 1994.

Ellison, Ralph. *Invisible Man.* New York: Random House, 1952.

Ely, James. *The Crisis of Conservative Virginia: The Byrd Organization and the Politics of Massive Resistance.* Knoxville: University of Tennessee Press, 1976.

Eskew, Glenn T. *But for Birmingham: The Local and National Movements in the Civil Rights Struggle.* Chapel Hill: University of North Carolina Press, 1998.

Fairclough, Adam. *Martin Luther King, Jr.* Athens: University of Georgia Press, 1995.

———. *Race and Democracy: The Civil Rights Struggle in Louisiana, 1915–1972.* Athens: University of Georgia Press, 1995.

———. *Teaching Equality: Black Schools in the Age of Jim Crow.* Athens: University of Georgia Press, 2001.

Farmer, James. *Lay Bare the Heart: An Autobiography of the Civil Rights Movement.* New York: Arbor House, 1985.

Ferrell, Robert, ed. *The Eisenhower Diaries.* New York: Norton, 1981.

Finch, Minnie. *The NAACP: Its Fight for Justice.* Metchen, NJ: The Scarecrow Press, Inc., 1981.

Fisher, Betty Kilby. *Wit, Will, & Walls.* Euless, TX: Cultural Innovations, 2002.

Foner, Eric. *Reconstruction: America's Unfinished Revolution, 1863–1877.* New York: Harper and Row, 1988.

Forman, James. *The Making of Black Revolutionaries.* Seattle: University of Washington Press, 1972.

Franklin, John Hope, and August Meier, eds. *Black Leaders of the Twentieth Century.* Urbana: University of Illinois Press, 1982.

Frazier, E. Franklin. *Black Bourgeoisie: The Rise of a New Middle Class in the United States.* New York: Collier Books, 1962.

Freyer, Tony Allen. *The Little Rock Crisis: A Constitutional Interpretation.* Westport, CT: Greenwood Press, 1984.

Friddell, Guy. *What Is It About Virginia?* Richmond: Dietz Press, 1966.

Garrow, David. *Bearing the Cross: Martin Luther King, Jr., and the Southern Christian Leadership Conference.* New York: Morrow, 1986.

Gates, Robbins L. *The Making of Massive Resistance: Virginia's Politics of Public School Desegregation, 1954–1956.* Chapel Hill: University of North Carolina Press, 1962.

Gitlin, Todd. *The Sixties: Years of Hope, Days of Rage.* New York: Bantam Books, 1987.

Goings, Kenneth W. *NAACP Comes of Age: The Defeat of Judge John J. Parker.* Bloomington: Indiana University Press, 1990.

Greenberg, Jack. *Crusaders in the Courts: How a Dedicated Band of Lawyers Fought for the Civil Rights Revolution.* New York: Basic Books, 1994.

Greene, John R. *The Limits of Power: The Nixon and Ford Administrations.* Bloomington: Indiana University Press, 1992.

Halberstam, David. *The Fifties.* New York: Random House, 1993.

Hall, Simon. *Peace and Freedom: The Civil Rights and Antiwar Movements in the 1960s.* Philadelphia: University of Pennsylvania Press, 2005.

Hampton, Henry, Steve Fayer, and Sarah Flynn. *Voices of Freedom: An Oral History of the Civil Rights Movement from the 1950s through the 1980s.* New York: Bantam Books, 1990.

Harris, Jacqueline. *History and Achievement of the NAACP.* New York: Franklin Watts, 1992.

Hays, Brooks. *A Southern Moderate Speaks.* Chapel Hill: University of North Carolina Press, 1959.

Heinemann, Ronald L. *Depression and New Deal in Virginia: The Enduring Dominion.* Charlottesville: University Press of Virginia, 1983.

———. *Harry Byrd of Virginia.* Charlottesville: University Press of Virginia, 1996.

———. *Old Dominion, New Commonwealth: The History of Virginia, 1607–2000.* Charlottesville: University of Virginia Press, 2008.

Hershman, James H., Jr. "A Rumbling in the Museum: The Opponents of Virginia's Massive Resistance." Ph.D. diss., University of Virginia, 1978.

Hill, Oliver White, Sr. *The Big Bang: "Brown v. Board of Education" and Beyond; the Autobiography of Oliver W. Hill, Sr.* Edited by Jonathan K. Stubbs. Winter Park, FL: Four-G Publishers, Inc., 2000.

Hoff, Joan. *Nixon Reconsidered.* New York: Basic Books, 1994.

Holden, Anna. *The Bus Stops Here: A Study of Desegregation in Three Cities.* New York: Agathon Press, 1974.

Huckaby, Elizabeth. *Crisis at Central High.* Baton Rouge: Louisiana State University Press, 1980.

Hughes, Langston. *Fight for Freedom: The Story of the NAACP.* New York: Norton, 1962.

Hustwit, William P. *James J. Kilpatrick: Salesman for Segregation.* Chapel Hill: University of North Carolina Press, 2013.

Irons, Peter. *Jim Crow's Children: The Broken Promise of the "Brown" Decision.* New York: Viking, 2002.

Jacoway, Elizabeth, and David R. Colburn, eds. *Southern Businessmen and Desegregation.* Baton Rouge: Louisiana State University Press, 1982.

Janken, Kenneth Robert. *White: The Biography of Walter White, Mr. NAACP.* New York: The New Press, 2003.

Johnson, James W. *Along This Way: The Autobiography of James Weldon Johnson.* Cambridge, MA: Da Capo Press, 2000.

Jonas, Gilbert. *Freedom's Sword: The NAACP and the Struggle against Racism in America, 1909–1969.* New York: Routledge, 2007.

Kelley, Robin D. G. *Hammer and Hoe: Alabama Communists during the Great Depression.* Chapel Hill: University of North Carolina Press, 1990.

Kellogg, Charles Flint. *NAACP, A History of the National Association for the Advancement of Colored People.* Baltimore: Johns Hopkins University Press, 1967.

Key, V. O. *Southern Politics in State and Nation.* Knoxville: University of Tennessee Press, 1984.

Kilpatrick, James Jackson. *The Southern Case for School Segregation.* New York: Cromwell-Collier Press, 1962.

King, Martin Luther, Jr. *Stride Toward Freedom*. New York: Harper and Row, 1958.

———. *Where Do We Go From Here: Chaos or Community?* New York: Harper and Row, 1967.

Klarman, Michael J. *From Jim Crow to Civil Rights: The Supreme Court and the Struggle for Racial Equality*. Oxford: Oxford University Press, 2004.

Kluger, Richard. *Simple Justice: The History of "Brown v. Board of Education" and Black America's Struggle for Equality*. New York: Random House, 1975.

Kneebone, John T. *Southern Liberal Journalists and the Issue of Race, 1920–1944*. Chapel Hill: University of North Carolina Press, 1985.

Kotlowski, Dean J. *Nixon's Civil Rights: Politics, Principle, and Policy*. Cambridge: Harvard University Press, 2001.

Lassiter, Matthew, and Andrew Lewis, eds. *The Moderates' Dilemma: Massive Resistance to School Desegregation in Virginia*. Charlottesville: University Press of Virginia, 1998.

Lau, Peter, ed. *From the Grassroots to the Supreme Court: "Brown v. Board of Education" and American Democracy*. Durham, NC: Duke University Press, 2004.

Lawson, Steven. *Black Ballots: Voting Rights in the South, 1944–1969*. New York: Columbia University Press, 1976.

———. *Running for Freedom: Civil Rights and Black Politics in America since 1941*. Philadelphia: Temple University Press, 1991.

Leidholdt, Alexander. *Standing before the Shouting Mob: Lenoir Chambers and Virginia's Massive Resistance to Public-School Integration*. Tuscaloosa: University of Alabama Press, 1997.

Lewis, Anthony. *Portrait of a Decade: The Second American Revolution*. New York: Random House, 1964.

Lewis, David Levering. *King: A Critical Biography*. Urbana: University of Illinois Press, 1978.

Lewis, Earl. *In Their Own Interests: Race, Class, and Power in Twentieth-Century Norfolk, Virginia*. Berkeley: University of California Press, 1991.

Lewis, John. *Walking with the Wind: A Memoir of the Movement*. New York: Mariner Books, 1999.

Littlejohn, Jeffrey L., and Charles H. Ford. *Elusive Equality: Desegregation and Resegregation in Norfolk's Public Schools*. Charlottesville: University of Virginia Press, 2012.

Lomax, Louis E. *The Negro Revolt*. New York: New American Library, 1962.

Marable, Manning. *Race, Reform, and Rebellion: The Second Reconstruction in Black America, 1945–1990*. Jackson: University Press of Mississippi, 1991.

Martin, Waldo, Vicki Ruiz, Susan Salvatore, Patricia Sullivan, and Harvard Sitkoff, eds. *Racial Desegregation in Public Education in the U.S. Theme Study*. Washington, DC: National Park Service, 2000.

Martin, Waldo E., Jr., ed. *"Brown v. Board of Education": A Brief History with Documents.* Boston: Bedford / St. Martin's, 1998.

McMillen, Neil R. *The Citizens' Council: Organized Resistance to the Second Reconstruction, 1954–1964.* Urbana: University of Illinois Press, 1971.

McNeil, Genna R. *Groundwork: Charles Hamilton Houston and the Struggle for Civil Rights.* Philadelphia: University of Pennsylvania Press, 1983.

McPherson, James M. *The Abolitionist Legacy: From Reconstruction to the NAACP.* Princeton: Princeton University Press, 1975.

Meier, August. *Negro Thought in America, 1880–1915.* Ann Arbor: University of Michigan Press, 1988.

Meier, August, and Elliott Rudwick. *Along the Color Line: Explorations in the Black Experience.* Urbana: University of Illinois Press, 1976.

———. *CORE: A Study in the Civil Rights Movement, 1942–1968.* Champaign: University of Illinois Press, 1973.

———. *From Plantation to Ghetto.* New York: Hill & Wang, 1966.

Menkart, Deborah, Alana D. Murray, and Jenice L. View, eds. *Putting the Movement Back into Civil Rights Teaching.* Washington, DC: Teaching for Change, 2004.

Miller, Calvin Craig. *Roy Wilkins: Leader of the NAACP.* Greensboro, NC: Morgan Reynolds Publishing, 2005.

Miller, Francis Pickens. *Man from the Valley: Memoirs of a Twentieth-Century Virginian.* Chapel Hill: University of North Carolina Press, 1971.

Moody, Ann. *Coming of Age in Mississippi.* New York: Dell Publishing, 1968.

Moon, Henry Lee. *Balance of Power: The Negro Vote.* Westport, CT: Greenwood Press, 1977.

Morris, Aldon. *The Origins of the Civil Rights Movement: Black Communities Organize for Change.* New York: Free Press, 1984.

Muse, Benjamin. *Ten Years of Prelude.* New York: Viking Press, 1964.

———. *Virginia's Massive Resistance.* Bloomington: Indiana University Press, 1961.

Myrdal, Gunnar, et al. *An American Dilemma: The Negro Problem and Modern Democracy.* New York: Harper and Row, 1962.

National Association for the Advancement of Colored People. *The Crisis.* New York: National Association for the Advancement of Colored People.

———. *NAACP Annual Report.* New York: National Association for the Advancement of Colored People.

———. *NAACP: Celebrating a Century, 100 Years in Pictures.* New York: Gibbs Smith, 2009.

———. *NAACP: Thirty Years of Lynching in the United States, 1889–1918.* New York: The Lawbook Exchange, 1919.

Norrell, Robert J. *Reaping the Whirlwind: The Civil Rights Movement in Tuskegee.* New York: Knopf, 1985.

Ogletree, Charles J., Jr. *All Deliberate Speed: Reflections on the First Half Century of "Brown v. Board of Education."* New York: W. W. Norton, 2004.

Ovington, Mary W. *The Walls Came Tumbling Down: The Autobiography of Mary White Ovington.* New York: Schocken, 1970.

Patterson, James T. *"Brown v. Board of Education": A Civil Rights Milestone and Its Troubled Legacy.* New York: Oxford University Press, 2001.

——. *Grand Expectations: The United States, 1945–1974.* New York: Oxford University Press, 1996.

Payne, Charles. *I've Got the Light of Freedom: The Organizing Tradition and the Mississippi Freedom Struggle.* Berkeley: University of California Press, 1995.

——. *Scalawag: A White Southerner's Journey through Segregation to Human Rights Activism.* Charlottesville: University of Virginia Press, 2014.

Peltason, J. W. *Fifty-Eight Lonely Men: Southern Federal Judges and School Desegregation.* New York: Harcourt, Brace & World, Inc., 1961.

Pfeffer, Paula F. *A. Philip Randolph: Pioneer of the Civil Rights Movement.* Baton Rouge: Louisiana State University Press, 1990.

Pitre, Merline. *In Struggle against Jim Crow: Lulu B. White and the NAACP, 1900–1957.* College Station: Texas A & M University Press, 2010.

Powledge, Fred. *Free at Last? The Civil Rights Movement and the People Who Made It.* Boston: Little, Brown, 1991.

Pratt, Robert A. *The Color of Their Skin: Education and Race in Richmond Virginia 1954–89.* Charlottesville: University Press of Virginia, 1992.

Rabinowitz, Howard N. *Race Relations in the Urban South, 1865–1890.* Champaign: University of Illinois Press, 1980.

Raines, Howell. *My Soul Is Rested: The Story of the Civil Rights Movement in the Deep South.* New York: Putnam, 1977.

Ransby, Barbara. *Ella Baker and the Black Freedom Movement: A Radical Democratic Vision.* Chapel Hill: University of North Carolina Press, 2005.

Reed, Christopher Robert. *The Chicago NAACP and the Rise of Black Professional Leadership, 1910–1966.* Bloomington: Indiana University Press, 1997.

Robinson, Armstead L., and Patricia Sullivan. *New Directions in Civil Rights Studies.* Charlottesville: University Press of Virginia, 1991.

Ryan, James E. *Five Miles Away, A World Apart: One City, Two Schools, and the Story of Educational Opportunity in Modern America.* New York: Oxford University Press, 2010.

Ryan, Yvonne. *Roy Wilkins: The Quiet Revolutionary and the NAACP.* Lexington: University Press of Kentucky, 2013.

Sartain, Lee. *Borders of Equality: The NAACP and the Baltimore Civil Rights Struggle, 1914–1970.* Oxford: University Press of Mississippi, 2013.

——. *Invisible Activists: Women of the Louisiana NAACP and the Struggle for Civil Rights, 1915–1945.* Baton Rouge: Louisiana State University Press, 2007.

Savage, David G. *Turning Right: The Making of the Rehnquist Supreme Court.* New York: Wiley and Sons, 1992.

Sitkoff, Harvard. *A New Deal for Blacks: The Emergence of Civil Rights as a National Issue: The Depression Decade.* New York: Oxford University Press, 1978.

———. *The Struggle for Black Equality, 1954–1992.* New York: Hill & Wang, 1993.

Smith, Bob. *They Closed Their Schools, Prince Edward County, Virginia, 1951–1964.* Chapel Hill: University of North Carolina Press, 1965.

Smith, J. Douglas. *Managing White Supremacy: Race, Politics, and Citizenship in Jim Crow Virginia.* Chapel Hill: University of North Carolina Press, 2002.

Smith, Larissa M. "Where the South Begins: Black Politics and Civil Rights Activism in Virginia, 1930–1951." Ph.D. diss., Emory University, 2001.

Sokol, Jason. *There Goes My Everything: White Southerners in the Age of Civil Rights, 1945–1975.* New York: Knopf, 2006.

Sterling, Dorothy. *Tear Down the Walls: A History of the American Civil Rights Movement.* Garden City, NY: Doubleday, 1968.

St. James, Warren. *NAACP, Triumphs of a Pressure Group.* Smithtown, NY: Exposition Press, 1980.

———. *The National Association for the Advancement of Colored People: A Case Study in Pressure Groups.* Smithtown, NY: Exposition Press, 1958.

Stokes, John A. *Students on Strike: Jim Crow, Civil Rights, Brown, and Me.* New York: Scholastic, 2008.

Sugrue, Thomas J. *The Origins of the Urban Crisis: Race and Inequality in Postwar Detroit.* Princeton: Princeton University Press, 1996.

———. *Sweet Land of Liberty: The Forgotten Struggle for Civil Rights in the North.* New York: Random House, 2009.

Sullivan, Patricia. *Days of Hope: Race and Democracy in the New Deal Era.* Chapel Hill: University of North Carolina Press, 1996.

———. *Lift Every Voice: The NAACP and the Making of the Civil Rights Movement.* New York: The New Press, 2009.

Sweeney, James R., ed. *Race, Reason, and Massive Resistance: The Diary of David J. Mays, 1954–1959.* Athens: University of Georgia Press, 2008.

Thompson, David C. *The Negro Leadership Class.* Englewood Cliffs, NJ: Prentice-Hall, 1963.

Titus, Jill Ogline. *Brown's Battleground: Students, Segregationists, and the Struggle for Justice in Prince Edward County, Virginia.* Chapel Hill: University of North Carolina Press, 2012.

Tushnet, Mark. *Making Civil Rights Law: Thurgood Marshall and the Supreme Court, 1936–1961.* New York: Oxford University Press, 1994.

———. *Making Constitutional Law: Thurgood Marshall and the Supreme Court, 1962–1991.* New York: Oxford University Press, 1994.

———. *The NAACP's Legal Strategy against Segregated Education, 1925–1950.* Chapel Hill: University of North Carolina Press, 1987.

Tyson, Timothy B. *Radio Free Dixie: Robert F. Williams and the Roots of Black Power*. Chapel Hill: University of North Carolina Press, 1999.

United States Commission on Civil Rights. *1961 U.S. Commission on Civil Rights Report, Book 2: Education*. Washington, DC: United States Commission on Civil Rights, 1961.

———. *1963 Staff Report, Public Education*. Washington, DC: United States Commission on Civil Rights, 1963.

———. *1964 Staff Report, Public Education*. Washington, DC: United States Commission on Civil Rights, 1964.

———. *Federal Rights Under School Desegregation Law*. Washington, DC: United States Commission on Civil Rights, 1966.

———. *Increasing Pace Of School Desegregation After 1964: Understanding School Desegregation*. Washington, DC: United States Commission on Civil Rights, 1971.

———. *Reviewing a Decade of School Desegregation, 1966–1975: Report of a National Survey of School Superintendents*. Washington, DC: United States Commission on Civil Rights, 1977.

———. *Southern School Desegregation, 1966–1967*. Washington, DC: United States Commission on Civil Rights, 1967.

———. *Title IV and School Desegregation: A Study of a Neglected Federal Program*. Washington, DC: United States Commission on Civil Rights, 1973.

———. *Understanding School Desegregation*. Washington, DC: United States Commission on Civil Rights, 1971.

———. *Your Child and Busing*. Washington, DC: United States Commission on Civil Rights, 1972.

Verney, Kevern, and Lee Sartain. *Long Is the Way and Hard: One Hundred Years of the NAACP*. Fayetteville: University of Arkansas Press, 2009.

Wallenstein, Peter. *Blue Laws and Black Codes: Conflict, Courts, and Change in Twentieth-Century Virginia*. Charlottesville: University of Virginia Press, 2004.

———. *Tell the Court I Love My Wife: Race, Marriage, and Law—An American History*. New York: Palgrave Macmillan, 2004.

Ward, Brian, and Tony Badger, eds. *The Making of Martin Luther King and the Civil Rights Movement*. London: Macmillan, 1996.

Warren, Earl. *The Memoirs of Earl Warren*. Garden City, NY: Doubleday, 1977.

Washington, Booker T. *Up from Slavery: An Autobiography*. New York: Doubleday, 1901.

Washington, James M. *A Testament of Hope: The Essential Writings and Speeches of Martin Luther King, Jr.* San Francisco: HarperCollins, 1991.

Watson, Denton L. *Lion in the Lobby: Clarence Mitchell, Jr.'s Struggle for the Passage of Civil Rights Laws*. New York: Morrow, 1990.

Wedin, Carolyn. *Inheritors of the Spirit: Mary White Ovington and the Founding of the NAACP*. Hoboken: Wiley, 1999.

Weisbrot, Robert. *Freedom Bound: A History of America's Civil Rights Movement*. New York: Norton, 1990.

Weiss, Nancy J. *Farewell to the Party of Lincoln: Blacks Politics in the Age of FDR*. Princeton: Princeton University Press, 1983.

———. *The National Urban League, 1910–1940*. New York: Oxford University Press, 1974.

White, G. Edward. *Earl Warren: A Public Life*. New York: Oxford University Press, 1987.

White, Walter. *A Man Called White: The Autobiography of Walter White*. New York: Viking Press, 1948.

Wilhoit, Francis. *The Politics of Massive Resistance*. New York: Braziller, 1973.

Wilkins, Roy, with Tom Mathews. *Standing Fast: The Autobiography of Roy Wilkins*. New York: Viking, 1982.

Wilkinson, J. Harvie, III. *From "Brown" to "Bakke": The Supreme Court and School Integration: 1954–1978*. Oxford: Oxford University Press, 1979.

———. *Harry Byrd and the Changing Face of Virginia Politics, 1945–1966*. Charlottesville: University Press of Virginia, 1968.

Williams, Juan. *Eyes on the Prize: America's Civil Rights Years, 1954–1965*. New York: Penguin Books, 1987.

———. *My Soul Looks Back in Wonder: Voices of the Civil Rights Experience*. New York: Sterling Publishing Company, 2004.

———. *Thurgood Marshall: American Revolutionary*. New York: Times Books, 1998.

Williams, Robert F. *Negroes with Guns*. New York: Marzani & Munsell, Inc., 1962.

Wilson, Sondra Kathryn. *In Search of Democracy: The NAACP Writings of James Weldon Johnson, Walter White, and Roy Wilkins, 1920–1977*. New York: Oxford University Press, 1999.

Wolters, Raymond. *Negroes and the Great Depression: The Problem of Economic Recovery*. Westport, CT: Greenwood Publishing, 1970.

———. *Race and Education, 1954–2007*. Columbia: University of Missouri Press, 2009.

Woodward, Bob, and Scott Armstrong, *The Brethren: Inside the Supreme Court*. New York: Simon & Schuster, 1979.

Woodward, C. Vann. *The Strange Career of Jim Crow: A Brief Account of Segregation*. New York: Oxford University Press, 1955.

Young, Whitney M. *Beyond Racism: Building an Open Society*. New York: McGraw-Hill, 1969.

Zangrando, Robert L. *The NAACP Crusade against Lynching, 1909–1950*. Philadelphia: Temple University Press, 1980.

Zinn, Howard. *SNCC: The New Abolitionists*. Boston: Beacon Press, 1964.

INDEX

Italicized page numbers refer to illustrations.

massive resistance, 59–60, 74–76; anti-NAACP laws, 54–56, 61, 68–69, 88, 171n47; "Little Rock bills," 68; massive resistance laws, 53–58, 68–69; resolution of interposition, 48, 49; special sessions, 39–40, 52, 53–55, 74–75, 76; support for private schools, 76–77, 87. *See also* massive resistance; *names of individual legislators*

geographic attendance zones. *See under* pupil placement

Georgia, 23, 35, 83, 135, 166n3, 180n21

Giles County, VA, 116, 130

Gloucester County, VA, 117–18

Godwin, Mills E., 48

Goldberg, Arthur, 94

Goochland County, VA, 117–18

Goss v. Board of Education of Knoxville (1963), 94, 98

grade-a-year plans, 77, 96, 97, 98

Gray, Frederick, 88

Gray, Garland, 25, 30, 40, 52

Gray Commission (Commission on Public Education), 30, 31–32, 47, 52, 55; appointment by Governor Stanley, 24; 1955 report (Gray Plan), 39–40, 47. *See also* Gray, Garland

Green, Calvin C., 85, 120–21, 129

Green v. County School Board of New Kent County (1968): history of, 108–9, 120–23, 124–25, 126–27; impact on school integration, 126–27, 129, 132–33, 133, 141, 147, 199n29; implementation in New Kent, 128–29; importance of, 1, 128, 133, 199n28; lower court decisions, 123

Green v. School Board of the City of Roanoke (1970), 140–41

Greenberg, Jack, 90, 91, 119, 122–23, 132

Greene County, VA, 95

Greensboro, NC, 79, 80

Greensville County, VA, 87–88, 117–18, 130

Griffin, L. Francis, Sr., 20, 84, 85, *85*, 96, *114*

Griffin v. County School Board of Prince Edward County (1964), 77, 113

Griffin v. State Board of Education (1969), 113–15, 134

Halifax County, VA, 103, 117–18, 137

Hamm, Dorothy, 52

Hampton, VA, 82, 101

Hampton Institute, 14

Hanover County, VA, 77, 117–18, 130–31

Harris, Curtis, 84

Harrison, Albertis, 72, 74, 88, 103

Harrison v. Day (1959), 72–73, 74

Harrison v. NAACP (1959), 61

Harvey, Ruth, 113

Hastie, William, 90

Hawthorne, Nathaniel Lee, 111–12

Haynsworth, Clement, 142

Henderson, E. B., 40, 46, 57, 157n40

Henderson, John B., 75

Henrico County, VA, 144–45

HEW. *See* Department of Health, Education, and Welfare, U.S.

Hill, Oliver W., Sr., 62–63, *85*, 91; in *Davis v. Prince Edward County*, 19–21, *38*, 169n27; education, 11; equalization work, 11, 12, 19; friendship with Thurgood Marshall, 11; on implementation of *Brown*, 27, 28, 29, 30, 33, 34, 40, 42–43, 49, 51, 57–58, 70–71, 93; harassment of, 51; head of Virginia State Conference legal staff, 10, 46, 77; Kennedy administration position, 88–89, 91, 92; legal career,

education, 2, 40; legal work, 89, 112, *114*, 115, 122–23, 132, 133, 139, 203n68

Marshall, Thurgood, 4, 16, 18, 19, 26, 27, 28, 44–45, 57–58, 61, 63, 163n54, 166n2, 186n71; and *Brown v. Board of Education* (1954), 21, 118, 160n27; on *Brown v. Board of Education* (1955), 35; education, 2, 11; friendship with Oliver Hill, 11; head of NAACP Legal Defense Fund, 9, 62, 91; in Virginia, 11, 29–30, 34, 42; judge/justice, 90, 106, 128, 143, 145; opposition to token school desegregation, 77; on sit-ins, 80–81; U.S. solicitor general, 90

Martin, Martin A., 17, 46, *56*, 89

Martinsville, VA, 30, 34

Maryland, 10, 22, 25, 35

Mason, Vivian Carter, 75

massive resistance: Byrd calls for, 1, 47–48, 168n19; end of, 59–60, 74–75; state laws, 53–56, 57–58, 69

massive resisters, 1, 31–32, 47–48, 53, 162n42; on abandonment of massive resistance, 72, 74–75

Mays, David J., 55

McMillan, James, 141

Mecklenburg County, VA, 63, 67, 111

Merhige, Robert R., Jr., 129, 132, *133*, 138, 140, 144–45, 198n17

Michie, Thomas, 98, 116, 122

Middlesex County, VA, 37, 117–18

Milliken v. Bradley (1974), 145, 149

Ming, Robert, 87, 90

minority transfer provisions. *See* pupil placement

miscegenation, 20, 24, 30, 157n40, 159n11

Mississippi, 23, 52, 79, 80, 83, 92, 94, 103, 105, 136–37, 166n3

Missouri, 23

Missouri v. Jenkins (1995), 149

Montgomery, AL, 48, 65–66, 80, 84

Moore, E. Blackburn, 52–53

Morgan v. Virginia (1946), 33

Murphy, Carl, 35, 90, 163n54

Muse, Benjamin, 25, 38, 51, 173n19

NAACP v. Button (1963), 88, 91; as *NAACP v. Almond*, 60–61

Nabrit, James (Jim), 50, 122–23

Nashville, TN, 77

National Association for the Advancement of Colored People (NAACP) national office, 2, 11, 33, 34, 44, 48, 62, 131; annual conventions, 4, 8, 27, 28, 32, 45–46, 73, 102, 160n23; Atlanta conferences, 26, 27, 28, 35, 36, 45–46, 159n18; attack on constitutionality of segregation, 18–19, 148, 157n33; board of directors, 8, 9, 18, 26, 35, 42, 60, 61, 62, 82, 91, 103, 154n6; direct action, 80–81, 102–3; freedom of choice, 112, 124; growth after World War II, 14, 156n23; hierarchical control over state conferences and branches, 4, 8, 9, 10, 12, 13, 25–26, 28, 36, 60, 161n32; impact of anti-NAACP laws, 52, 55–58, 60, 63, 65–66, 88, 91, 171n55; income, 64, 165n83; and Legal Defense Fund, 89–91, 195n47; legal focus, 13, 65–66, 80, 92–94, 155n19; legal protocol, 26–27, 50–51, 89–91, 166n4; March on Washington, 103; membership drives, 13, 52; membership fee, 13, 14, 64; middle-class nature, 13, 82; opposition to massive resistance, 55; petitions (legal), 26, 36, 37–38, 45, 48; records, 5; regional office system, 10, 52, 66; relations with other civil rights organizations, 65–66, 82–83, 103; response to